Schools under Surveillance

CULTURES OF CONTROL IN PUBLIC EDUCATION

Edited by
TORIN MONAHAN
AND
RODOLFO D. TORRES

RUTGERS UNIVERSITY PRESS
New Brunswick, New Jersey, and London

LIBRARY OF CONGRESS CATALOGING-IN-PUBLICATION DATA

Monahan, Torin.
    Schools under surveillance : cultures of control in public education / Torin
Monahan and Rodolfo D. Torres.
    p. cm.—(Critical issues in crime and society)
    Includes bibliographical references and index.
    ISBN 978-0-8135-4679-7 (hardcover : alk. paper) —
ISBN 978-0-8135-4680-3 (pbk. : alk. paper)
    1. School violence—United States—Prevention. 2. Public schools—Security
measures—United States. 3. Electronic surveillance—United States. I. Torres,
Rodolfo D., 1949–   II. Title.
    LB3013.3.M66 2010
    371.7'82—dc22   2009006045

A British Cataloging-in-Publication record for this book is available
from the British Library.

Visit our Web site: http://rutgerspress.rutgers.edu

Manufactured in the United States of America

CONTENTS

PART III   PREPARING FOR THE WORST

7   *Reading, Writing, and Readiness*   123
     RICHARD A. MATTHEW

8   *Risky Youth and the Psychology of Surveillance:*
     The Crisis of the School Shooter   140
     TYSON LEWIS

ACCOUNTABILITY REGIMES:
TESTS, STANDARDS, AND AUDITS

PART IV   AS SURVEILLANCE

9   *"Politics by Other Means": Education*
     Accountability and the Surveillance State   159
     PAULINE LIPMAN

10   *The Measure of Success: Education,*
     Markets, and an Audit Culture   175
     MICHAEL W. APPLE

11   *Lying, Cheating, and Teaching to the Test: The Politics*
     of Surveillance Under No Child Left Behind   194
     JOHN GILLIOM

EVERYDAY RESISTANCE:

PART V   CONTESTING SYSTEMS OF CONTROL

12   *Scan This: Examining Student*
     Resistance to School Surveillance   213
     JEN WEISS

13   *Seductions of Risk, Social Control,*
     and Resistance to School Surveillance   230
     ANDREW HOPE

     Contributors   247
     Index   253

Schools under Surveillance

Introduction

Torin Monahan and Rodolfo D. Torres

THE IMPERATIVE TO PROTECT CHILDREN is seldom questioned. It would seem degenerate to do so. But one must wonder what it means when armed police officers roam school hallways, when students line up for more than an hour before class just to get past security screening checkpoints, when fingerprinting is required for students to enter schools or use school cafeterias, or when schools look more like prisons, with barbed-wire perimeters, video surveillance, and police cars parked on campus. Sometimes public schools are even located in former prisons.[1]

Public education is one important domain where the perceived need for greater security has given rise to new formations in school discipline, primarily for students but increasingly for teachers and administrators too. Some of the well-known mechanisms of student and teacher discipline include high-stakes standardized testing, zero-tolerance policies for violence, rigid schedules, and architectures of visibility and containment. Less obvious is the host of new institutional arrangements and technologies that augment these existing disciplinary mechanisms: on-site police officers who routinize experiences of crime control and effectively interlink public education and criminal justice systems; advanced surveillance technologies that are used to subject students to constant monitoring and to demand that they engage in ritual performances—such as submitting to metal detectors—to demonstrate their innocence; and new bureaucratic developments in so-called decision-support systems and performance audits, by which students and teachers are evaluated from afar and micro-managed or disciplined accordingly.[2]

Most school surveillance today is of the kind just described, though it must not be forgotten that face-to-face human surveillance in schools is far from extinct. Examples of such surveillance include simple observation, watching, listening, and following; the use of human spies, undercover operatives, and informers; and mandatory drug tests and searches. Some peer-to-peer surveillance occurs when students use cell phones or social networking Web sites to find out about each other's activities, allowing for social bonding but sometimes creating distrust and violence among students.[3] The most intensive authoritarian surveillance regimes have been constructed around not much more than these basic ingredients, usually combined with a strong sense of mistrust and fear of infiltration, persecution, or invasion of privacy. At its root, therefore, surveillance is not simply about monitoring or tracking individuals and their data—it is about the structuring of power relations through human, technical, or hybrid control mechanisms.

Perhaps not surprisingly, racial minorities are disproportionately subjected to contemporary surveillance and policing apparatuses. The emerging governance regimes may be fueled by public fears of crime, but control mechanisms are applied differentially and with different effects. Thus, students in poorer inner-city schools are subjected to more invasive hand searches and metal-detector screenings, while students in more affluent schools tend to be monitored more discreetly with video surveillance cameras. Lower-income minority students, especially males, also get funneled more systematically into the criminal justice system by police officers on school campuses. Similarly, military recruiters enjoy a great deal of access to poorer students—mostly in urban and rural schools—and actively collect intelligence on them in order to further their mission of enlisting soldiers. Given that public education putatively supports the progressive goal of equality, the use of surveillance to target and sort students along lines of race, class, and gender deserves continued scrutiny and critique, especially as the institution of education further aligns itself with the criminal justice system, the military, and private industry.

POLITICAL AND ECONOMIC CONTEXT

To begin to understand the complexity of surveillance and security practices in public education, it may be useful to outline some of the factors contributing to such cultures of control. Certainly fear should not be under-estimated. Tragedies of school shootings become shared media and cultural spectacles, instigating moral panics that overshadow any cold, objective assessment of risk (Monahan 2006c). After all, schools continue to be perhaps *the* safest place for children; far safer than streets, cars, or homes (ACLU 2001; Dinkes et al. 2007; Rand and Catalano 2007). Recent statistics show that in the United States one homicide or suicide occurs while at school for every 3.2 million students—for a total of 14 homicides and 3 suicides between July 1, 2005, and June 30, 2006 (Dinkes et al. 2007).[4] School violence does not appear to be a pressing problem at all compared to the reported 1,530 child fatalities caused by abuse or neglect each year (Child Welfare Information Gateway 2008) or the 3.6 million children reported as possible victims of abuse or neglect each year, which is likely a very conservative figure (Pew Charitable Trusts 2007). Nonetheless, the threat of "another Columbine" (or Virginia Tech, and so on) haunts the social imaginary, leading parents, policy makers, and others to the sober conclusion that any security measure is worth whatever trade-offs are involved in order to ensure safety.[5] Never mind the fact that an armed guard and a video surveillance system were present at Columbine, which is why many people have such vivid memories of the attack. Now, instead of being apprehensive about being targets of surveillance, many people—students included—may be afraid that they are *not* being watched, or, more importantly, not being *watched over* by some authority figure (Lewis, chapter 8 of this volume).

The socio-legal landscape has shifted dramatically over the past few decades too. We have come to understand crime as that which causes fear, rather than as acts of deviance; crime is less about breaches in social acceptability than perceptions of individual vulnerability (Lianos forthcoming). This helps explain the furor over school violence in suburban and rural communities: crime in "good" neighborhoods elicits more moral outrage than crime in "bad" ones because it is apparently worse if people think that they are safe and then discover that they are not. At the same time, policing practices have shifted since the 1970s to stress crime containment, risk management, and outsourcing of policing responsibilities. As David Garland explains: "In the past, official criminology has usually viewed crime *retrospectively* and *individually*, in order to itemise individual wrongdoing and allocate punishment or treatment. The new criminologies tend to view crime *prospectively* and in *aggregate* terms, for the purpose of calculating risks and shaping preventative measures" (Garland 2001, 128; emphasis in original). Fortification and securitization epitomize such "preventative measures," whether in gated communities, malls, airports, or schools. And a host of scaled-up punitive interventions has accompanied these developments so that any instance of crime is severely punished, transforming what scholars have described as "the welfare state," predicated on ideals of rehabilitation and inclusion, into "the penal state," enforcing maximum punishments and exclusion (Garland 2001; Simon 2007).

In public education settings, these socio-legal changes manifest in zero-tolerance policies for the possession of weapons or drugs, for any acts of violence, and even for verbal threats. The presence of police officers on school grounds ensures that violators will be charged with crimes for infractions, such as school fights or thefts, that previously might have resulted in softer forms of punishment, such as detention, expulsion, or conferences between parents (or guardians), students, and school officials (Kupchik and Bracy, chapter 1 of this volume). Concentrations of "school resource officers" (SROs), who are trained police officers, are greatest in urban areas of highest poverty (Devine 1996; Gootman 2004), and their numbers have skyrocketed in recent years so that now 68 percent of all high schools and middle schools in the United States have SROs (Kupchik and Bracy, chapter 1 of this volume). One inimical result of this phenomenon is the augmentation of a "school-to-prison pipeline," disproportionately escorting low-income, minority students into prisons and contributing to astronomical levels of incarceration in the United States (Kupchik and Monahan 2006; Wald and Losen 2003). Current estimates put the total number of U.S. inmates at 2.3 million, or a rate of 1 in 100 for the entire adult population and 1 in 9 for African American males between the ages of twenty and thirty-four (Gonnerman 2008).

Rather than surmise that the present articulation of school discipline emerged organically, one can identify specific laws, policies, and reports that catalyzed the norms and forms of school discipline today. Notably, the Safe Schools Act of 1994 provided funds for public schools if they could demonstrate an existing crime problem, which compelled schools to implement data-collection systems and categorize crimes as broadly as possible (Simon 2007, 214–220). Various grants from government agencies further supported school-police partnerships, as did an amendment to the 1968 Omnibus Crime Control and Safe Streets Act in 1998 (Kupchik and Bracy, chapter 1 of this volume). Zero-tolerance policies for drug use were solidified in 2002, when the U.S. Supreme Court upheld the legality of mandatory drug tests for students absent any evidence of drug problems in a particular school (Simon 2007, 17).[6] Under the No Child Left Behind (NCLB) Act of 2001, school districts receiving federal funds "must have a policy requiring that any student who brings a firearm or weapon to school will be referred to the criminal justice or juvenile delinquency system" (Cooper 2002). The Safe School Initiative, which was a collaborative research project between the U.S. Secret Service and the Department of Education to learn from previous school shootings, released a report in 2002 advocating that schools conduct "threat assessments" in conjunction with the implementation of student profiling and security systems (Casella 2006). And in the aftermath of 9/11 and of the deadly terrorist attack on a school in Beslan, Russia, in 2004, the U.S. Department of Homeland Security made grants available for schools to implement crisis management plans, coordinate with police, and purchase security equipment (Casella 2006).

Our neoliberal ideological climate plays an important role in the formation of cultures of control in public education. The general distrust of public institutions and celebration of private-sector and individual solutions to social problems nourishes control mechanisms that aggravate social inequalities (Fisher 2009; Katz 2006; Monahan 2008). This is a coupling of the so-called invisible hand of free-market solutions with the iron fist of discipline and control (Wacquant 2001). Those who are unable to embody the identity of empowered consumers taking responsibility for their own needs might be understood as failed neoliberal citizens who are subsequently targeted for punitive state interventions. Neoliberal policies are typically not aimed at achieving "small government," no matter what their proponents claim.

Instead, especially in the post-9/11 context, they inscribe new priorities for government bodies: to amplify security and military functions of the state on one hand and to serve the needs of industry on the other. In education, one can witness this trend with the judicious government funding for information technology (IT) and surveillance systems in schools that cannot afford books, supplies, furniture, classrooms, or even teachers (Casella 2006; Monahan 2005a). These schools then turn around and pay private vendors and contractors for those systems, effectively handing over to industry public funds that are sorely needed for other purposes. As noted elsewhere (Monahan 2005a), schools are placed in an almost impossible position, because if they choose not to apply for federal funds for IT or security (because they do not perceive the need for these things), they are branded as being irresponsible or incompetent "bureaucracies," which adds fuel to the school privatization movement.

Although it makes sense to locate the social control dimensions of educational neoliberalism in security equipment, police presence, and unforgiving policies for dealing with infractions, standardized tests and audits represent the most widespread forms of surveillance and social control in public schools. Standardized tests are nothing new, but they now carry harsh penalties not only for students but also for public school teachers, administrators, and districts. As mandated by NCLB, all schools receiving federal funds must annually test students in grades three through twelve for reading and math (and science after 2007–2008) (Gilliom, chapter 11 of this volume). Schools must then demonstrate improvement across all subgroups of students (for example, "English language learners," "special education," or "African American") from year to year or risk being "placed on probation" and taken over by the state.[7] Teachers and administrators are penalized if students' subgroups do not demonstrate adequate improvement, which then encourages teachers to flee from schools serving poor or immigrant students. NCLB carves out other avenues for surveillance too by requiring public schools to open their campuses to military recruiters and provide them with personal data (names, addresses, phone numbers) on all students, unless students are informed that they can opt out and choose to exercise this option (Wall, chapter 6 of this volume).[8]

As John Gilliom argues in chapter 11, NCLB institutes many layers of surveillance and restricts the autonomy of teachers and schools to craft what they feel to be appropriate curricula for their students. In this way, NCLB is a political tool that enforces a conservative curricular agenda because teachers must spend most of their time preparing students for decontextualized, "back to basics" test questions. In addition, NCLB advances a neoliberal agenda: by categorizing the neediest schools as "failing" it serves as a tacit argument for the restriction of public funds to public education and the implementation of school voucher programs to speed privatization.

NCLB, therefore, contributes to the ongoing corporatization—or marketization—of public education. It is true that school districts now effectively sell students to corporations looking to harvest consumer data through online educational "games" (Steeves, chapter 5 of this volume) or to colonize student markets in more direct ways, such as selling products in schools, placing advertising in "educational" materials, or forcing students to watch the infamous "Channel One" programs and advertising every morning in homeroom classes (Apple, chapter 10 of this volume). Less obviously, the infiltration of "audit cultures" refashions the mission of schools away from educational achievement and student learning to profits and balanced budgets (Apple 2001). Corporate structures predominate, with chief financial officers, chief information officers, and superintendents and school board members acting more like CEOs demanding a constant stream of reports in their quest for performance enhancement and accountability. With audit cultures, workplaces mutate to value that which can be documented (Strathern 2000), subsequently altering workplace practices to stress the generation of reports (such as test results) and to devalue that which cannot easily be translated into documents or databases (such as mentoring students). These documents then open organizations and the people within them to heightened surveillance through software applications that can mine data and generate reports comparing performance levels of employees, students, or schools. Seemingly, having the data necessitates comparative evaluations through software applications such as decision support systems, which then compel administrative actions to discipline "underperformers" and ensure accountability (Monahan 2005a). Thus, although audit mechanisms such as tests may not have the look and feel of harder surveillance technologies, they are clearly a form of surveillance and need to be understood as such (Haggerty and Ericson 2006).

SKETCHING THE SURVEILLANCE FIELD

As one can see, surveillance in public education implies a great deal more than watching and disciplining students. Surveillance is a dominant organizing logic of modern institutions, shaping all their operations (Lyon 2007). For the purposes of our inquiry, we define surveillance as watching, monitoring, tracking, or data analyzing for purposes of control. Surveillance, as a form of knowledge production, draws upon and thereby reifies normative categories of appearance and behavior. Surveillance is an operation of power. As Michel Foucault (1980) noted long ago, power is not simply about one person's control over another but instead signifies an entire apparatus of material, social, and symbolic relations within which human actors are caught. Power regimes constantly evolve, overlap, and reproduce themselves in iterative fashion—that is, they may repeat but always with a difference. Foucault described three such regimes: the sovereign, the disciplinary, and the biopolitical. Whereas the sovereign could indiscriminately and arbitrarily take life and render gruesome punishments upon the body, disciplinary regimes were marked by rational and efficient organizations that disciplined the soul. The panopticon, or all-seeing prison, still stands as a hegemonic metaphor of this form of organized discipline, which was reproduced by modern organizations (schools, hospitals, factories) and internalized by subjects, transforming them into self-disciplining "docile bodies" (Foucault 1977).

Unfortunately, many scholars become captivated by the decidedly alluring metaphor of the panopticon and neglect analysis of Foucault's third articulation of power, the biopolitical, which may have special relevance in today's globalized world. Biopolitical power functions on the level of population; it creates a population, as such, through mechanisms for categorizing and controlling people in aggregate. Whether with public health programs, public housing, migration, insurance, the census, or standardized testing, biopolitical power regulates populations in conjunction with disciplinary power. Foucault (1978) writes:

> The setting up, in the course of the classical age, of this great bipolar technology—anatomic and biological, individualizing and specifying, directed toward the performances of the body, with attention to the processes of life—characterized a power whose highest function was perhaps no longer to kill, but to invest life through and through. The old power of death that symbolized sovereign power was now carefully supplanted by the administration of bodies and the calculated management of life. (140)

Discipline exerts itself as a discrete and individualizing force, while biopower regularizes on the level of population. Both can be observed with the non-neutral sorting of people—as bodies—according to supposedly rational categories of risk and value. For instance, in public education, as elsewhere, police, teachers, and administrators tend to single out male youth of color for heightened scrutiny, thereby assisting in sorting those populations into the criminal justice system (Kupchik, forthcoming). And schools receiving Title I federal assistance for needy students (for example, to provide free or subsidized lunches) are more heavily scrutinized and penalized for lack of improvement on NCLB-mandated tests (Gilliom, chapter 11 of this volume). Clearly, biopower is discriminatory and racist, as Foucault saw: "It is indeed the emergence of this biopower that inscribes [racism] in the mechanisms of the State. It is at this moment that racism is inscribed as the basic mechanism of power, as it is exercised in modern States. As a result, the modern State can scarcely function without becoming involved with racism at some point" (2003, 254).

All the while, the disciplinary force of spatial design persists. Many public schools are highly fortified spaces surrounded by fences, walls, and gates, secured with bars on windows and high-tech security checkpoints, and frequently locked down like prisons. Under the rubric of "defensible space," design elements are introduced to make people in schools more visible, governable, and ostensibly more safe. Ronnie Casella explains: "[S]chools are built with more windows and skylights (to have more soothing light but also to allow for better viewing and to cut down on darkened corridors), with straighter hallways for better viewing, and with security technologies that blend in with the architecture" (2006, 29).[9] This, along with the tenacious Fordist design of standardized and compartmentalized rooms, lockers, desks, and so on render students accessible to surveillance and act as a form of "built pedagogy," teaching students values and proper comportment through constraints upon social action and interaction (Monahan 2002 and 2005a). The presence of SROs and police vehicles then complements the built pedagogy of fortification, visibility, and enclosure, communicating to students and others that school discipline will be enforced.

Space is indeed political. As Henri Lefebvre reminds us, space is never merely a container or a frame for social action; instead, it is constitutive of social relations and contexts. Lefebvre opines: "Space is social morphology: it is to lived experience what form itself is to the living organism, and just as intimately bound up with function and structure" (1991, 94). Fortified spaces, which are usually monitored by surveillance, are predicated upon logics of inclusion and exclusion that—in our current neoliberal climate—normalize the exclusion and containment of the most threatening, needy, or least economically productive members of society, such as the homeless, the elderly, the young, or the indigent (Davis 1990). The fortification and surveillance of places, ranging from gated communities, to national borders, to prisons, to schools, engenders racial divisions as well, neatly hidden most of the time behind the presumed neutrality of spatial design (Gilmore 2007; Monahan 2006a; Sorkin 2007).

In practice, fortified urban schools monitored by surveillance systems may compel students to remain on school grounds during the day but not necessarily in the classroom. Ethnographic research on schools has found that after entering the front gates, many students simply roam the hallways and grounds of schools and socialize (Monahan 2005a; Weiss, chapter 12 of this volume). Notable exceptions to this trend can be witnessed when teachers and staff round up all available students and escort them to classrooms for days when teachers administer statewide tests or schools tally "average daily attendance" (by which school funding allocations are determined). A cynical reading of this situation might be that students are correctly deciphering the codes being given to them—that keeping them off the street is the primary function of public education today. Another reading could be that students are asserting agency in the face of inattentive authority figures or systemic pressures to conform. Perhaps they are resisting or appropriating the system to the degree that they can without being criminalized, and enacting their own meaning-making practices in school space. It is likely that all these things are true to some extent. Although the modus operandi of many schools may be containment and visibility for heightened security and control, that does not necessitate a passive role for students (or teachers), as several chapters in this book make clear.

REFLECTIONS ON CULTURES OF CONTROL

We began this introduction by raising the rhetorical question of what contemporary mechanisms of control "mean" in public education contexts. Dominant discourses of school safety tend to deflect critical inquiry, which is why any serious treatment of the issues needs to bracket the promise of safety and take a more holistic and empirically grounded view of the situation. Doing so leads to many possible answers to the question of what all this means. One answer is that people are deeply afraid of violence affecting their children or children in their communities. Although fear may be healthy and inspire necessary precautions to ensure safety, the media tend to blow some dangers—such as school shootings—out of proportion to the actual likelihood of their occurrence, galvanizing extreme responses to extremely unlikely threats (Altheide 2006; Glassner 2000). Another answer is that people are convinced by the discourse of "trade-offs," such as that between security and civil liberties, leading many to conclude that any trade-offs in the name of security are worth the financial or social cost. Unfortunately, the discourse of trade-offs masks the fact that most security systems do not improve safety, just the impression of safety (Monahan 2006b). The belief in trade-offs is closely correlated with another possible answer: people have an almost unshakable belief in technological progress. Contrary to mounting evidence about the enhanced vulnerability of "tightly coupled" technological systems (Perrow 1999), where a breakdown in one sector sets off a chain reaction of further system breakdowns, many people believe that increased automation and adoption of high-tech systems will correct existing vulnerabilities without creating new ones. The sober fact, again, is that many high-tech systems do not work as intended. For example, while video surveillance cameras may give the impression that "someone is watching" and will come to the rescue if help is needed, most systems are not monitored in real time, so people may develop a false sense of security that further endangers them (Norris and Armstrong 1999; Norris, McCahill, and Wood 2004).

Another set of meanings emerges from the neoliberal matrix within which cultures of control are situated. Namely, there is a deep suspicion of public programs and the people who use them, and a misguided faith in private industry. The force of this hegemonic value system motivates school accountability regimes, such as the mandates of the No Child Left Behind Act, and zero-tolerance policies for disciplinary infractions, such as students carrying weapons or drugs (Lyons and Drew 2006). Suspicion of students also manifests in the adoption of radio-frequency identification cards or biometric fingerprinting for students entering school grounds or using school cafeterias or libraries (ACLU 2007; D'Andrade 2006). Such systems allow schools to erect a series of digital checkpoints to police student access to public services and amass data that can later be used for surveillance or accountability purposes. Apparently neutral identification systems such as these support politically biased questions about whether students availing themselves of subsidized lunches are "really" poor or are cheating the system in some way or whether undocumented immigrants are illegally accessing public education resources. Meanwhile, politicians redirect much-needed school funding to security and technology industries to provide "solutions" to the largely manufactured problems of accountability and safety in public schools. These are just a few of the meanings that lurk below the surface of discourses about surveillance, safety, and accountability in schools.

BOOK OVERVIEW

The goals of this book are to analyze contemporary arrangements in school surveillance and discipline, theorize their broader implications, and document creative forms of resistance. The book is divided into five sections, each of which tackles one major dimension of social control in public schools, ranging from police and military recruiters on school campuses, to testing and accountability regimes, to efforts by students and teachers to circumvent the most egregious forms of surveillance. Across these five sections, the book paints a detailed portrait of the emerging structures of school discipline and the practices of individuals working within and against what might be called the "maximum-security school." Although the emphasis is on examples found in the United States, chapters also specifically identify similar trends in the United Kingdom and Canada. We would expect that the themes described here would resonate with the findings of scholars studying school discipline in other countries too.

Part I, "New Disciplinary Orders," provides a disturbing overview of the presence of police officers and surveillance apparatuses in public schools. As Kupchik and Bracy's chapter stunningly describes, the majority of high schools and middle schools in the United States now have armed, uniformed police officers on campus at least part-time. These officers engage in a panoply of practices that extends well beyond the enforcement of zero-tolerance laws to include mentoring students, cultivating informants, and enforcing school policies in addition to laws, thereby socializing students to interactions with the criminal justice system and its agents. Paul Hirschfield's chapter picks up these themes to call attention to inequalities among schools with the types of discipline exercised by police and surveillance systems. For instance, as noted earlier in this introduction, students in economically depressed urban schools face invasive police searches and security screening far more often than their suburban counterparts. Students may then be arrested for ridiculous violations such as stepping out of the security-screening queue or refusing to relinquish their cell phones. Lizbet Simmons wraps up this section with a provocative mobilization of and expansion upon Foucault's writings about discipline. Drawing upon her field research on a public school housed in a prison, Simmons advances an analysis of race and gender inequality wherein one can see "an arterial power structure . . . in which power is differentially distributed and discipline is differentially experienced."

Part II, "Schools as Markets," delineates some of the ways in which the institution of public education is transformed into a market for the selling of security equipment and the purchasing of students' data and bodies. Ronnie Casella begins this section with a chapter on the success of the security industry in penetrating the public education market. Rather than view this in a conspiratorial light, Casella argues that security companies are simply engaged in routine business practices. By branding security equipment as a status symbol and taking advantage of government funding opportunities, security companies have made their systems desirable for schools across the spectrum, from wealthy private schools to poor public ones. Valerie Steeves adds another layer to this story in her chapter on the surveillance of students in online environments. Drawing upon examples from Canadian schools, she illustrates how corporations were able to dictate "access" to students' data as a condition of wiring schools for the Internet. Online surveillance of students extends well beyond school walls, of course, and is conducted by school authorities, corporations, police, and peers. Most disturbingly, Steeves describes an emerging pattern in which corporate owners of insidiously extractive and propagandistic "educational" Web sites defend themselves as altruistic providers of a "public service." Tyler Wall's chapter concludes this section with an investigation of military recruitment practices on school campuses. The chapter's title, "School Ownership Is the Goal," is taken from an official recruiting handbook and flags the problematic conflation of schools with markets and students with commodities in the "war on terror." Wall mobilizes an impressive array of ethnographic data and quotes from interviews with recruiters to problematize recruiters' surveillance and salesperson tactics without simplifying the complexity of military relations on "the home front."

Part III, "Security Cultures," critically examines national security priorities, school-based responses, and motivations behind school shootings. Richard

Matthew's chapter, "Reading, Writing, and Readiness," discusses the rise in very real threats to public safety and criticizes dominant security responses that position school actors as passive recipients of consumer products, instead of active participants and collaborators in local security provisions. Based on the data available, Matthew posits that "one might reasonably conclude that U.S. schools are very safe and that the best overall approaches to reducing the current rates of severe injuries and deaths experiences by school-age children would include poverty reduction, supervised after school care, and universal health care." Tyson Lewis's chapter probes the school-shooter phenomenon and questions the social and psychological factors contributing to such events and collective understandings of them. Lewis argues that "in an environment of latch-key children, suburban isolation from community, the panopticism of Internet surveillance, and reality TV, the imaginary no longer connects the subject to the symbolic world of social norms, prohibitions, traditions but instead locks the subject to a narcissistic fixation on the level of individaul threats, personal conspiracies, and antagonistic rivalries." The neoliberal capitalist economy propagates new forms of psychic disconnect that can, and do, manifest in violent outbursts.

Part IV, "Accountability Regimes," explores the ways in which high-stakes tests, curricular standards, and audits are reshaping educational practices and experiences, controlling students and teachers while making them "accountable" for systemic failures in public education. Pauline Lipman connects the surveillance of students and teachers under NCLB to a general neoliberal rationality that justifies the exclusion and punishment of the neediest populations in society. At the same time, and through the same mechanisms, possibilities for discussing social problems and working toward social justice are being restricted in schools, perhaps at a time when we need these things the most. In the next chapter, Michael W. Apple describes the general process of the corporatization of education through audit technologies and techniques that are inherently surveillant. He writes, "Making the state more 'business friendly' and importing business models directly into the core functions of the state such as hospitals and education—in combination with a rigorous and unforgiving ideology of individual accountability—these are the hallmarks of life today." Contrary to popular understandings of the decentering of state functions under neoliberalism, a form of "fragmented centralization" (Monahan,2005b) is taking place whereby decision-making authority is centralized while responsibility is distributed to the most vulnerable educational actors—students and teachers. This section concludes with John Gilliom's bracing chapter analyzing testing as surveillance. He asserts: "If we think of surveillance as just *watching*, we err, because surveillance is never really just watching. It's not vision, but *super*vision. It's not just sight, but *over*sight. Surveillance assumes, advances, and/or creates a relationship of domination." Given that under NCLB teachers and administrators are being held responsible for unsatisfactory levels of improvement on standardized tests, Gilliom makes a persuasive case that tests should be understood as a form of "workplace surveillance" that both disciplines teachers and diminishes their autonomy. As a logical transition to the next section of chapters on resistance, Gilliom reviews a number of ways that teachers and administrators resist or circumvent this workplace surveillance: "they manipulate state test results, remark test sheets, guide students during exams, and train students to do well on the tests."

Part V, "Everyday Resistance," charts some of the many ways in which students, teachers, and others resist mechanisms of school surveillance. Whether through artistic performances, acts of sabotage, or selective enforcement of rules, the people involved in public education routinely express their agency to challenge cultures of control. Jen Weiss proffers a number of examples of students altering their routes to circumvent scrutiny, performing for those who are watching, or appropriating the system by befriending guards and receiving favors. The workings of gender inflect these interactions in what can be troubling ways: female students most often receive special "privileges" from male guards, but in so doing they open themselves up to what can be unwanted physical attention or harassment.[10] In the final chapter, Andrew Hope documents strategies of resistance occurring in schools in the United Kingdom. He finds that rather than surveillance serving simply as a tool of social control, students intentionally test boundaries and engage in proscribed activities to savor the thrill of being watched, caught, and punished. For example, students view inappropriate content on their computers, monitor the observers, and deftly switch Web page windows before they are caught. They also break into buildings and circulate pornographic materials on the Web just to court the adrenaline rush at the prospect of being found out. Surveillance creates spaces for "empowering exhibitionism" (Koskela 2004), and sometimes being part of the spectacle can be quite enjoyable and subversive.

CONCLUDING REMARKS

Surveillance is a privileged form of modern knowledge production, organizational management, and social control. As this book makes clear, surveillance entails much more than the use of video cameras to passively monitor people. Surveillance is a mode of governance that controls access, opportunities, and life chances and even helps to channel choices, often using personal data to determine who gets what. This is clearly evident in the context of public education, where disparate surveillance mechanisms—from metal detectors to standardized tests—overlap to enmesh school actors in a larger surveillant assemblage that thrives upon the production and exchange of data and the sorting of populations based on their perceived value, potential, or risk (Haggerty and Ericson 2000). In other words, education is inseparably linked to the political economy and often serves as a battleground for ideological and material conflicts over resources, values, and rights. Surveillance is not merely a weapon in those larger contests; it actively shapes the social field upon which those contests play out.

Whereas this book initiates inquiry into contemporary surveillance and cultures of control in public education, there are many related areas in need of further critical research. For instance, it would be beneficial to know more about the processes by which laws and policies pertaining to school surveillance are determined, applied, and resisted. Like prisoners and soldiers, students have few legal rights when it comes to surveillance of their bodies, activities, possessions, or data. Research into the legal aspects of surveillance in schools could help map this terrain and identify pressure points where concerned citizens could mitigate the developments taking place. Similarly, research on how local school boards make decisions about surveillance and security issues in schools could shed light on the rationales and assumptions that undergird the adoption of surveillance equipment or the development of partnerships with law-enforcement agencies or other entities.

As the chapters in this book show, school administrators, teachers, security guards, and police actively interpret and selectively apply both law and policy. These actors serve as "citizen agents" who do not simply bend the rules but rather make informed character judgments on the ground, thereby producing normative orders, some of which may temper overly harsh treatment of students and others of which may discriminate against students perceived as delinquent (Maynard-Moody and Musheno 2003). Greater insight into the value judgments made by such citizen agents would add to our empirical understanding of the mediation of surveillance and the continual reshaping of the field of social control at local sites. Moreover, while a few chapters in this book address local tactics of resistance (especially the chapters by Gilliom, Weiss, and Hope), resistance on the level of law and policy is undoubtedly occurring but has not yet been studied systematically.

Finally, very little is known about the subjective experiences of school actors—especially students—living within, navigating, and appropriating everyday surveillance. Collectively, we should be asking, "What kind of social identities and subjectivities are being formed through constant exposure to surveillance apparatuses and personnel?" Or, "What are the long-term effects upon students of routine scrutiny, social sorting, and unequal treatment?" These are not necessarily new questions, just as surveillance of students is not a new phenomenon, but in a neoliberal context that blurs demarcations among public education, criminal justice, and corporate institutions, pursuing such questions is perhaps more pressing—and challenging—than ever.

ACKNOWLEDGMENTS

The authors thank Aaron Kupchik and participants in the Center for Community Studies reading group at Vanderbilt University for insightful comments on this introduction. We also thank Alesha Durfee for pointing us in the direction of recent statistics on violence against children. Additionally, R.T. would like to express a special note of thanks to Leo Chavez of the UC-Irvine Center for Research on Latinos in a Global Society and the Center for Unconventional Security Affairs at UC-Irvine for providing financial support to complete this volume.

NOTES

1. See Simmons (chapter 3 of this volume) for a description of such a "prison school" in New Orleans.
2. Submitting to metal detectors and security screening on a routine basis constitute what William Staples (2000) calls "meticulous rituals of power." While these rituals operate on the level of the everyday and the mundane, they nonetheless control social actors by embedding them in a vast matrix of unequal power relations, which then becomes normalized.
3. A particularly disturbing example of this occurred in 2008 when six teenage girls in Florida lured a female classmate into a house and severely beat her while two teenage boys stood on lookout. According to one news report: "The 16-year-old victim suffered a concussion, and has hearing loss in her left ear and some loss of vision in her left eye" (Celizic 2008). The brutal attack was perpetrated, apparently, in retaliation for verbal criticisms of a few of the attackers that the victim had placed on her MySpace page. The thirty-minute beating was apparently protracted because the assailants were committed to videotaping it and placing it on the Internet for others to view. As this example shows, students engage in surveillance of and performances for others, and the everyday technologies of cell phones, YouTube, and social networking sites may create new spaces and excuses for extreme forms of bullying.
4. This statistic applies to school-age youth (ages 5–18) on school grounds, even if they were not current students.
5. This is not to imply that tragedies like the shooting at Columbine directly led to current manifestations of school security systems and practices. Schools were already embracing security modalities prior to Columbine, which is one reason why that school did have surveillance cameras and a guard. Still, tragedies serve as sparks for moral panics that at the very least discourage parents and policy makers from opposing further security developments.
6. *Board of Education of Independent School District No. 91 of Potawatomie County v. Earls* (2002).
7. A similar practice of rating schools occurs in the United Kingdom, with "school league tables" used to compare schools based on students' test results (Hope, chapter 13 of this volume; Apple, chapter 10 of this volume).
8. If schools allow other groups on campus, such as those providing information about college or employment opportunities, they must allow military recruiters on campus as well.
9. Ironically, designs that heighten visibility and openness may afford students a healthy sense of connection with the world beyond the classroom (Monahan 2002). At the same time, "garrison architecture," which stresses extreme bunkerlike fortification and isolation, is an altogether different response that is currently on the rise (see Matthew, chapter 7 of this volume).
10. Devine (1996, 27, 89–91) highlights how such relationships can quickly become inappropriate and lead to sexual harassment or assault.

REFERENCES

ACLU. 2001. Safety in schools: Are we on the right track? Boulder, CO. http://www. aclu-co.org/news/letters/paper_boulderschools.htm.

———. 2007. ACLU of Massachusetts praises decision to cancel Lunch Bytes Program. http://www.aclu.org/privacy/biotech/29445prs20070419.html.

Altheide, David. 2006. *Terrorism and the politics of fear.* Lanham, MD: Altamira Press.

Apple, Michael W. 2001. *Educating the "right" way: Markets, standards, God, and inequality.* New York: RoutledgeFalmer.

Casella, Ronnie. 2006. *Selling us the fortress: The promotion of techno-security equipment for schools.* New York: Routledge.

Celizic, Mike. 2008. Teens videotape beating as revenge for online posts. *MSNBC. com,* April 8. http://today.msnbc.msn.com/id/24009077/.

Child Welfare Information Gateway. 2008. Child abuse and neglect fatalities: Statistics and interventions. Washington, DC: U.S. Department of Health and Human Services. *http://www.childwelfare.gov/pubs/factsheets/fatality.cfm#children.*

Cooper, Edith Fairman. 2002. The Safe and Drug-Free Schools and Communities Program: Background and context. Washington, DC: Congressional Research Service. https://www.policyarchive.org/bitstream/handle/10207/1009/RL30482_20020422. pdf?sequence=1.

D'Andrade, Hugh. 2006. First RFIDs, now fingerprints used to track students in schools. San Francisco: Electronic Frontier Foundation. http://www.eff.org/deep-links/2006/11/first-rfids-now-fingerprints-used-track-students-schools.

Davis, Mike. 1990. *City of quartz: Excavating the future in Los Angeles.* New York: Vintage Books.

Devine, John. 1996. *Maximum security: The culture of violence in inner-city schools.* Chicago: University of Chicago Press.

Dinkes, Rachel, Emily Forrest Cataldi, Wendy Lin-Kelly, and Thomas D. Snyder. 2007. Indicators of school crime and safety: 2007. Washington, DC: U.S. Department of Education; U.S. Department of Justice. http://nces.ed.gov//pubs2008/2008021. pdf.

Fisher, Jill A. 2009. *Medical research for hire: The political economy of pharmaceutical clinical trials.* New Brunswick, NJ: Rutgers University Press.

Foucault, Michel. 1977. *Discipline and punish: The birth of the prison.* New York: Vintage Books, Random House.

———. 1978. *The History of sexuality: An introduction.* Vol. 1. New York: Vintage.

———. 1980. *Power/knowledge: Selected interviews and other writings, 1972–1977.* Brighton, Sussex: Harvester Press.

———. 2003. *"Society must be defended": Lectures at the College de France, 1975–76.* Trans. D. Macey. New York: Picador.

Garland, David. 2001. *The culture of control: Crime and social order in contemporary society.* Chicago: University of Chicago Press.

Gilmore, Ruth Wilson. 2007. *Golden gulag: Prisons, surplus, crisis, and opposition in globalizing California.* Berkeley: University of California Press.

Glassner, Barry. 2000. *The culture of fear: Why Americans are afraid of the wrong things.* New York: Basic Books.

Gonnerman, Jennifer. 2008. Slammed. *Mother Jones* 33 (4): 44–46.

Gootman, Elissa. 2004. Police to guard 12 city schools cited as violent. *New York Times.* January 6.

Haggerty, Kevin D., and Richard V. Ericson. 2000. The surveillant assemblage. *British Journal of Sociology* 51 (4): 605–622.

———. 2006. The new politics of surveillance and visibility. In *The new politics of surveillance and visibility*, ed. K. D. Haggerty and R. V. Ericson. Toronto: University of Toronto Press, 3–25.

Katz, Cindi. 2006. The state goes home: Local hypervigilance of children and the global retreat from social reproduction. In *Surveillance and security: Technological politics and power in everyday life*, ed. T. Monahan. New York: Routledge, 27–36.

Koskela, Hille. 2004. Webcams, TV shows and mobile phones: Empowering exhibitionism. *Surveillance & Society* 2 (2/3): 199–215.

Kupchik, Aaron. Forthcoming. *Reading, writing, and rules: School discipline in an age of fear*. New York: New York University Press.

Kupchik, Aaron, and Torin Monahan. 2006. The new American school: Preparation for post-industrial discipline. *British Journal of Sociology of Education* 27 (5): 617–631.

Lefebvre, Henri. 1991. *The production of space*. Trans. D. Nicholson-Smith. Cambridge, MA: Blackwell.

Lianos, Michalis. Forthcoming. Periopticon: Control beyond freedom and coercion. In *Surveillance and democracy*, ed. K. D. Haggerty and M. Samatas. New York: Routledge.

Lyon, David. 2007. *Surveillance studies: An overview*. Cambridge, UK: Polity Press.

Lyons, William, and Julie Drew. 2006. *Punishing schools: Fear and citizenship in American public education*. Ann Arbor: University of Michigan Press.

Maynard-Moody, Steven, and Michael C. Musheno. 2003. *Cops, teachers, counselors: Stories from the front lines of public service*. Ann Arbor: University of Michigan Press.

Monahan, Torin. 2002. Flexible space & built pedagogy: Emerging IT embodiments. *Inventio* 4 (1). http://www.torinmonahan.com/papers/Inventio.html.

———. 2005a. *Globalization, technological change, and public education*. New York: Routledge.

———. 2005b. The school system as a post-Fordist organization: fragmented centralization and the emergence of IT specialists. *Critical Sociology* 3 (4): 583–615.

———. 2006a. Electronic fortification in Phoenix: Surveillance technologies and social regulation in residential communities. *Urban Affairs Review* 42 (2): 169–192.

———. 2006b. Questioning surveillance and security. In *Surveillance and security: Technological politics and power in everyday life*, ed. T. Monahan. New York: Routledge, 1–23.

———. 2006c. The surveillance curriculum: Risk management and social control in the neoliberal school. In *Surveillance and security: Technological politics and power in everyday life*, ed. T. Monahan. New York: Routledge, 109–124.

———. 2008. Editorial: Surveillance and inequality. *Surveillance & Society* 5 (3): 217–226.

Norris, Clive, and Gary Armstrong. 1999. *The maximum surveillance society: The rise of CCTV*. Oxford: Berg.

Norris, Clive, Mike McCahill, and David Wood. 2004. Editorial. The growth of CCTV: A global perspective on the international diffusion of video surveillance in publicly accessible space. *Surveillance & Society* 2 (2/3):110–135.

Perrow, Charles. 1999. *Normal accidents: Living with high-risk technologies*. Princeton, NJ: Princeton University Press.

Pew Charitable Trusts. 2007. Time for reform: Investing in prevention: Keeping children safe at home. Washington, DC: Pew Charitable Trusts. http://www. preventchildabusewv.org/docs/PEWKAWPreventioeport.FINAL.pdf.

Rand, Michael, and Shannan Catalano. 2007. Criminal victimization, 2006. Washington, DC: U.S. Department of Justice. http://www.ojp.usdoj.gov/bjs/pub/pdf/cv06. pdf.

Simon, Jonathan. 2007. *Governing through crime: How the war on crime transformed American democracy and created a culture of fear.* Oxford: Oxford University Press.

Sorkin, Michael, ed. 2007. *Indefensible space: The architecture of the national insecurity state.* New York: Routledge.

Staples, William G. 2000. *Everyday surveillance: Vigilance and visibility in postmodern Life.* Lanham, MD: Rowman & Littlefield.

Strathern, Marilyn, ed. 2000. *Audit cultures: Anthropological studies in accountability, ethics, and the academy.* New York: Routledge.

Wacquant, Loïc. 2001. Deadly symbiosis: When ghetto and prison meet and mesh. *Punishment & Society* 3 (1): 95–134.

Wald, Johanna, and Daniel J. Losen. 2003. *Deconstructing the school-to-prison pipeline: New directions for youth development, number 99.* San Francisco: Jossey-Bass.

PART ONE

New Disciplinary Orders

*Police, Surveillance, and
Inequality in the Carceral School*

CHAPTER 1

To Protect, Serve, and Mentor?

POLICE OFFICERS IN PUBLIC SCHOOLS

Aaron Kupchik and Nicole L. Bracy

A RECENT REPORT published by the New York Civil
Liberties Union (Mukherjee 2007) describes the growth in numbers of police
officers and school safety agents (who are under the control of the New
York City Police Department) in New York City public schools, and abuses
of students and school staff at the hands of these officers. The report is
disturbing—the abuses described include physical abuse and sexual harassment of students, retaliatory arrests of school staff who protect students from
abuse at the hands of police, and other offenses. After illustrating the litany
of problems associated with police in schools, the report concludes that
these officers should be better trained and supervised, that there should be a
process in place for reporting abuses by these officers, and that they should
be under the control of the schools rather than reporting only to the police
department.

The report's conclusion tells us a great deal about the rarity of critical
thought concerning whether police *ought* to be in public schools to begin
with. Perhaps some schools—such as those in high-crime neighborhoods of
New York City—need full-time officers. But are those officers necessary in
low-crime areas as well? There seems to be no discussion among educators,
policy makers, the media, or the general public about whether police in
schools might be a bad idea. This silence sharply diverges from the debates
surrounding other school initiatives such as dress codes, school vouchers, or
zero-tolerance policies. Apparently, even the New York Civil Liberties Union
has accepted the idea that it is unproblematic to extend the criminal justice
system into schools by placing armed, uniformed police officers there, so long
as they are properly supervised and trained, since their very presence goes
unquestioned within this otherwise scathing report.[1]

In this chapter we begin a critical discussion about the role of police officers within schools, and what effects their presence has. Recently, public school systems across the United States have imported officers into their schools, yet there has been very little research on what these officers do and how they interact with students and school staff (for an exception see Casella 2001). Although we have no answers to whether this policy benefits or harms students, we offer a necessary background discussion of how many officers are in schools across the United States, and how they interact with both students and school staff. In particular, we use empirical data from field research in four high schools to highlight the potential advantages and disadvantages of placing police in public schools. Our goal is to establish a foundation for future critical analyses about the role of police in schools and their effects on the school social climate.

BACKGROUND OF POLICE IN SCHOOLS

In parts of the United States, police officers have been involved with schools for at least seventy years, often in the form of isolated law enforcement positions designed to patrol specific schools with a perceived crime problem. In recent years, however, schools have turned toward a school resource officer (SRO) model for policing public schools. Though the first official SRO program began in 1958 in Flint, Michigan, it was not until the early 1990s that the program became widespread in the United States (Brown 2006; Girouard 2001), largely in response to encouragement and funding from the federal government, in three stages. First, the Safe Schools Act of 1994 facilitated the growth of school-police partnerships by allocating federal funds to schools with demonstrated severe crime problems; much of the funding could be spent to hire security or law enforcement officers (Brady et al. 2007; Stefkovich and Miller 1999). Second, a 1998 amendment to the 1968 Omnibus Crime Control and Safe Streets Act encouraged school-police partnerships through the SRO model (see Casella 2001). Third, in 2000 the Office of Community Oriented Police Services (COPS) awarded $68 million in grants to schools across the country specifically for the hiring of school resource officers.

Based on a problem-oriented community policing model, SRO programs extend the criminal justice system through school-law enforcement partnerships, with the purported goal of working together to identify and prevent crime in schools (Atkinson 2002). In some locations, one or more SROs are assigned to a single school; in other places one officer splits his or her time between two or more schools. Most SROs are armed, uniformed police officers, although some are plainclothes officers. While SROs may still report to their precincts for supervision or be involved in more traditional law enforcement duties from time to time, their schools are their officially assigned "beats."

The actual duties of SROs vary from district to district, officer to officer, and school to school, but SRO programs generally cite three overarching roles for officers: law enforcement officer, counselor, and teacher (Burke 2001; National Association of School Resource Officers n.d.). The duties SROs perform vary considerably and may include patrolling the school campus, investigating crimes that occur on campus, gathering information from students about crimes that have occurred in the community (Libby 1994), mentoring and advising students, providing drug and crime prevention programs for students, and teaching law-related classes (Vera Institute of Justice 1999).

Recently, the number of schools using SROs has grown. By 1999, more than half (54 percent) of public middle and high schools reported having security guards or assigned police officers; by 2005, this had increased to 68 percent (Dinkes et al. 2007, 61). While it is difficult to know exactly how many police officers are in place in schools across the country, the National Association for School Resource Officers claimed to have over nine thousand members in 2008 (National Association of School Resource Officers n.d.). As this number only represents SROs who belong to this particular professional organization, this should be viewed as an extremely conservative estimate of the actual number of police officers in schools.

METHODS

To understand what happens when police work in schools, we conducted research in four public high schools across two states: one southwestern and one mid-Atlantic. In each state we selected one school that includes a large proportion of low-income students and students of color and one school with mostly white middle-class students. This design allows us to consider how policing operates across diverse student bodies, as well as in different regions of the United States.

Researchers spent approximately six months collecting observational data at each school, with two to three visits per week at each school. Since each visit lasted approximately two to three hours, we logged over one hundred hours of observations at each school. While observing schools, we would either shadow a police officer or other school rule enforcer (such as security guard, dean of discipline, or administrator), observe classrooms, or observe interactions in public spaces (for example, hallways during breaks between classes, courtyards, and cafeterias at lunchtime). Our primary goal was to gain an understanding of how discipline and security work at each school, mainly by observing disciplinary interactions, such as when a police officer questions a student suspected of committing a crime. To reduce the likelihood of an observer bias, we did not record field notes while in the field; all field notes were recorded immediately after leaving the field.

We also conducted more than one hundred interviews at the four schools. We interviewed each police officer (there was one at each school) and principal, as well as assistant principals, security guards, other discipline staff (such as dean of discipline), teachers, students, and students' parents. The interviews were guided by semistructured interview protocols that left room for exploring themes as suggested by each respondent. Our focus was on how each respondent thinks about school crime, security, discipline, and police in schools, as well as his or her experiences with these issues. All interviews were professionally transcribed.

WHAT DO SROS DO?

Generally, SROs perform a range of tasks (see Vera Institute of Justice 1999). However, the diverse needs of each school as well as the individual style of various officers mean that there is no "typical" SRO. Through observations of SROs at four different high schools, we were able to see what SROs actually do on a day-to-day basis and come to a better understanding of what the job of an SRO actually entails in four very different environments. The SROs we observed spent the majority of their time watching the halls, conducting administrative police work, and investigating minor incidents. We also observed SROs attempting to mentor students and participating in (noncriminal) school discipline matters.

Watching the Halls

All of the SROs we observed spent some part of their day patrolling; this includes making rounds in the hallways, supervising the cafeterias during lunch times, and overseeing students as they board school buses at the end of the day (see Casella 2001). These patrolling activities serve two main functions—to remind students of the presence of the SRO (that is, it is a show of force) and to help school administrators watch over students.

Officers' approaches to this task varied among the four SROs, particularly whether they interacted personally with students or silently observed them. In two of the schools, the SROs silently observed students more often than they interacted with them. These SROs quietly watched students during high-traffic times such as lunch, immediately after school, and during breaks between classes. One of these SROs would occasionally drive his police car onto the school's courtyard during lunch, park it in the middle of the picnic table area where many of the students dined, and sit in his car throughout lunch; this school was an open-air campus with a central outdoor courtyard. While the presence of these officers allowed them to respond quickly to a disruption if needed, their presence seemed to be primarily a reminder (or a threat) to students and staff that they were there.

In the other two schools, the SROs had more frequent face-to-face interactions with students. In one school the SRO periodically made his way through all of the hallways of the school building, checking doors that led outside to make sure they were not ajar and demanding hall passes from students he encountered along the way. His more interactive approach in the hallways cast him in the role of a school administrator, in that he determined if students were following school rules that had no bearing on criminal laws and sent them to an administrator when they violated these rules.

Administrative Police Work

When the SROs were not patrolling the halls or responding to a particular incident that occurred on campus, we would often find them in their offices, usually with the door closed, working on administrative issues. This typically included reviewing incident reports, following up on previous cases, and completing arrest reports when a student had been arrested at school. This administrative police work demands a significant amount of time, up to half of each day, according to the SROs.

Investigating Minor Incidents

Serious criminal offenses are very rare on school campuses, both nation-wide (see Dinkes et al. 2007) and on the campuses we visited. As a result, the SROs we observed spent most of their time investigating minor on-campus incidents such as suspected thefts, fights between students, or drug or alcohol possession. For example, at one school a student's car had been broken into in the school parking lot; the SRO dusted the car for fingerprints and sent them to the police fingerprint lab to be analyzed. At another school the SRO investigated a case involving a stolen iPod that was allegedly resold by the student who had stolen it. At a third school, the SRO responded to a teacher's complaint about a student driving recklessly out of the school parking lot by tracking down the license plate number and looking it up in the school's records to determine the car's owner. Minor incidents like these arose with some regularity and composed the vast majority of the criminal offenses the SROs dealt with.

Mentoring

Most of the SROs at the schools we observed made at least some attempt to mentor students in their schools and did so in a variety of ways. One of the SROs we met, for example, was an assistant coach for the school's track team; he told us that he hoped this role would give students a chance to see him as a real person and not just a cop. Another told us that he wrote a recommendation letter for a student who had recently graduated. The following example illustrates how one SRO attempted to mentor a student:

> The SRO approached a student who he described to me as "troubled," and who was attending his first regular school. [The SRO] talked to him for a few minutes, and asked the student why he was not in class earlier. The student said that because he has ADD he can't sit through a whole class, and he has to get up sometimes. [The SRO] encouraged the student to come to his martial arts class again. They seemed to have a good rapport. He later explained to me that he teaches a martial arts class, and he gave the student some passes to come to it. (Field notes)

Not all of the SROs felt the same way about this issue, however, and some encountered difficulty with the mentoring process. One SRO said he avoids mentoring because he doesn't feel qualified to counsel students:

> INTERVIEWER: Do you ever try to mentor them or counsel them in any way?
> SRO: No, I don't try. I mean sometimes they come to me and then I've had kids come in here and say look I'm having problems with this or I wanna be a cop, or whatever and I'll shoot them in the right direction. One of the officers who's a little weird, he mentors young ladies, and that usually, that kind of concerns me, so I try to stay away from the mentoring, because I'm not qualified to mentor. So I mean, not to be a counselor or anything: I'm a cop.

In another school, the SRO was interested in mentoring but felt the administrators were resistant to it. He talked about wanting to get students to open up and feel comfortable talking to him, but then said:

> That's kind of been shot down because of the administration here, and they see things differently so . . . I guess you could probably say they wouldn't want me to be more I guess you could look at it as being touchy feely, they don't want that, they want me to just have visibility and do my job.

Helping with School Discipline

While some SROs were resolute that they only enforce criminal laws and do not get involved in school discipline matters, other SROs frequently inserted themselves in situations that were clearly school discipline matters rather than legal violations and that had little or no impact on overall school safety (for example, dress code violations or attendance policies). The SROs' involvement in these matters often escalated minor disciplinary situations. For instance, at one school, the SRO overheard a student in the halls cursing and told her to watch her language. The student responded by repeating the curse word several times. The SRO turned the situation over to an administrator, who instructed the student to write an apology letter to the SRO and planned to give the student one day of in-school suspension as punishment. When the administrator brought the apology letter to the SRO, however, the SRO called for a more severe punishment:

> [Administrator] called over to [SRO] and handed him an apology letter ... he told [SRO] he had her rewrite it several times until it was good enough. [SRO] took the letter and asked what [student's] punishment was going to be. [Administrator] said because she wrote the apology letter he was just going to give her one day of in-school suspension. [SRO] said he thinks her punishment needs to be more severe than that. He said because of the circumstances of this particular situation, he wanted her suspended out of school. [Administrator] said "OK," that he would give her a day of out-of-school suspension. [SRO] repeated that he thinks this is necessary because of "the way it went down." (Field notes)

The SRO's call for harsher punishment of this student is outside the realm of his job. Moreover, the student received a harsher punishment than she would have otherwise received, only because the adult involved in the situation was a police officer.

What Are the Benefits of Having Police in Schools?

Whether SROs are a benefit to schools depends entirely on how one defines benefit, and who one focuses on as the recipient of the benefit. Their presence has very different consequences for different stakeholder groups (students, teachers, administrators, and the police department).

Benefits to the School Administration

There is no question that the presence of a police officer benefits school administrators. The principals at the schools we studied each rely on their SRO as a legal advisor of sorts. Contemporary laws require school officials to know the law, since state laws mandate that schools report certain criminal offenses to the police or the state, although without legal training it might be unclear how particular behaviors should be officially classified. For example, a principal may be uncertain whether a Swiss Army knife qualifies as a "deadly weapon," or whether a student found with somebody else's prescription drugs should be prosecuted as a drug offender. Police officers, on the other hand, are accustomed to making decisions about whether a crime has been committed, thus school administrators often seek their advice on these matters.

Similarly, school administrators use SROs to advise them on security matters. For example, during one visit to a school we observed administrators respond to a bomb threat:

> A student had reported graffiti in the girls' bathroom that said: "Bomb. You better get out, cuz there in the school." There was also a similar message written in the boys' bathroom the day before. To help determine whether these messages should be considered legitimate threats, the principal consulted with the SRO. The SRO examined the messages written on the stalls and together the principal and SRO determined that not only were the two messages written by different people, but that each message was written in stages—this suggested to them that a benign message was successively reshaped by several students, rather than representing a legitimate threat made by a single student. The principal decided not to evacuate the building or end the school day early. (Field notes)

The presence of SROs also helps school administrators by lending legitimacy to their school safety initiatives. If questioned by a concerned parent, schools can highlight the presence of an SRO as evidence of how seriously they take school security threats. When students are caught violating school rules in ways that the school defines as criminal, the SRO can explain to parents why their child is being arrested and absolve an administrator from having to defend this harsh response; we observed this in cases when students were arrested for fighting on school grounds, for example. Furthermore, by outsourcing part of the job of school security to an SRO, school administrators are somewhat insulated from public indignation and accusations of incompetence if a violent incident does occur on campus.

Finally, the presence of an SRO helps administrators if they wish to target certain behaviors for particularly harsh consequences. At one school we studied, all students caught fighting were arrested, regardless of the severity of the fight or who the instigator was. The presence of the SRO at this school allowed the school administration to prescribe punishments for actions that are typical among adolescents yet go beyond the school's portfolio of sanctions. Furthermore, administrators know that they can implement policies that may be unpopular and coercive, and that they have recourse to a police officer if students rebel against these rules. For example, the school in our study with the highest suspension rate demanded that a parent accompany a student on his/her return to school following a suspension. When students and parents disobeyed, the school asked the SRO to arrest these students for trespassing, since technically they are still suspended until a parent accompanies them, and thus they are trespassing if they enter school grounds before then. The presence of the SRO allowed the school to follow a very strict policy, since the SRO, not a school administrator, was responsible for dealing with students who violated the policy.

Despite these advantages to the school administration, the presence of an SRO can be problematic for the school administrators, since it may result in administrative role confusion. Because SROs typically are not supervised or evaluated formally by anyone at the school, there may be questions as to whose authority is greater—the SRO or the school principal—and who should prevail in a conflict over school discipline (see Devine 1996; Mukherjee 2007). Moreover, some research suggests that police power in schools may be overtaking that of teachers, administrators, and other school staff, undermining the school's authority, and shifting discipline responsibilities away from teachers and administrators (Bazemore et al. 2004; Beger 2002).

Benefits to the Police Department

Although this was not a primary focus of our research (we did not interview police command or other, non-SRO police officers), it became apparent from observations of and discussions with SROs how having a representative in the school benefits the police department. Prior research shows that police organizations view school-embedded officers as opportunities to foster legal socialization by building relationships with youth; this view presumes that through regular and casual interaction with school police officers, students will gain a better understanding of and greater respect for law enforcement (Jackson 2002) and will view police officers as resources or allies rather than adversaries (Hopkins 1994). Although we did not observe this benefit to the police, we did note how the presence of SROs facilitates police surveillance and community policing in other ways.

SROs facilitate community policing because they are constant fixtures within one of the most important community institutions. They get to know many of the students and thereby learn about these students' families (and their families' problems), as well as the needs and problems the community faces. Since the SROs are still members of police precincts and report to these precincts regularly, they can easily share this information with other officers, who can act on it. Additionally, to the extent that the officers can befriend some students and reduce fears of police, they may help lower the boundaries that separate community members from the police department, and thereby facilitate future police investigations.[2] The SRO at one school stated:

I don't enforce the school rules, because I don't wanna be the bad guy, but I hold them accountable when they break the laws. And if anyone needs anything I'm here for them, and I'm supposed to teach classes, and every time I teach a class I've got thirty new best friends, well probably about twenty-seven and then three of them still just hate cops, but people that were, are more apt to [know] me than [to] just say "hi." . . . it's cool because I'm creating informants for later on.[3]

SROs also help gather information that can be used by the police department to detect and respond to crimes occurring outside of school. In one school, for example, the SRO commonly viewed students' MySpace pages. When asked what he learned from this, he said that he often found out about parties that are planned for the weekends; he then told other officers, who broke up the parties if alcohol was being served. Here, the SRO used his knowledge about the students (who they are, and that they have MySpace accounts) to expand the police department's surveillance of youth, thereby facilitating police work that occurs during the weekend and off school grounds.

Enhanced surveillance can also occur in a more open way, however. In another of our four schools, a current student and a recent student were both murdered, execution-style, while working together at a local fast food restaurant. The incident was covered prominently by the local news. Since the SRO at this school knew the victims and many of their friends, and since he had a great deal of knowledge about the community, generally, he was in a good position to help solve the crime. He spoke to students about what they knew, and, according to school administrators, his investigative work helped the police department solve the case.

Benefits to Students?

Though the presence of SROs clearly benefits administrators and the police department, it is less clear whether it benefits students. The existing evaluative research shows some support for the argument that SROs can prevent crime (Johnson 1999; Schuiteman 2001), but these studies are relatively inconclusive and rest on weak methodological grounds.[4] Yet there are other potential advantages to having SROs, such as whether students feel safer because an officer is present, and whether SROs can effectively mentor students.

When we began this research, we expected students to feel alienated by officers and hostile to their presence. We were surprised to find that almost all students whom we interviewed liked having an officer present. Their stated reasons varied: some believe an SRO's presence is a deterrent to crime, while others stated that an SRO is helpful in case there is a crisis situation at the school. Responses about whether the campus is safer with an SRO than without one varied considerably as well.

Some respondents did express reservations about having an SRO, such as stating that a police car out front of the school can make students or community members believe that the school is dangerous, or that having an SRO can be invasive in students' lives. Yet even when respondents made critical claims, they usually countered by noting the benefits of an SRO's presence, as well. For example:

> An officer at school, at times one feels like, like he's looking at you in a bad way and one feels, like, under scrutiny or bad, but one also has to realize that it's for our own safety, it's for our security that in case there is an accident or a person that has a gun. Then in that sense it is good.

Overall, students reported being pleased that their schools had police officers, even when they didn't believe that the SRO's presence decreased school crime. This result is important, regardless of its empirical basis. That is, even if SROs do not make schools safer, if students *feel* safer, this has positive consequences on its own. Students who feel safer may be less likely than others to avoid school activities or locations within the school (Dinkes et al. 2007); thus feeling safe can contribute to a positive school climate.

SROs seem far less successful at helping students when it comes to mentoring them, however. Although most school staff members and parents whom we interviewed believed that the SRO at their school is a good mentor to students, the students themselves were less positive about this aspect of the SRO program; some did talk about SROs as a positive presence, although others disagreed.

Based on our observations, we saw several ways that SROs are limited in their capacity to mentor students effectively. All the SROs we observed sincerely tried to help students by being a positive, supportive influence, but the role of mentor can conflict with their obligations as police officers. This is especially apparent when a student confides in the SRO about illegal actions that either they or their friends may have committed—here the SRO has an obligation to take legal action, even if it means betraying the student's trust and subjecting the student to arrest or ridicule (for betraying peers). This was particularly acute in one of the schools we studied, in an area with a large number of Mexican immigrants, many of whom were undocumented (as reported to us by the principal). For example, one student there told us that he would not talk to the SRO about a problem he was having: "Well, because of legal matters. I've heard that police officers also have the right to call immigration and so, no."

More commonly, though, SROs are in the position to interact with students in an informal mentoring role rather than act as confidants. Yet here, too, the role of police officer can conflict with the role of mentor/role model.

Police officers are trained in conflict and deal with conflict on a daily basis; shifting gears and adopting a "softer side" was not a strength of the SROs we observed. Consider, for example, the following interaction with a student that an SRO described to us:

> The other day a student on the track team [which the SRO helped coach] was messing around during practice, so [the SRO] made him run two laps. Instead of running, the student walked the two laps. So, [the SRO] said he told him to leave practice; the student said he wasn't going to leave and [the SRO] couldn't make him. They got into an argument and the student called [the SRO] "a bitch." [The SRO] told me that in his training as a police officer he is taught to not back down from situations or to walk away. He said they are supposed to go toward problems and do what needs to be done to resolve them. [The SRO] then said he told the student that if he had something to say to him to "be a man" and say it to his face instead of mumble it under his breath. The student said to him "What are you going to do—hit me?" [The SRO] replied "Why would I need to hit you?" The student said if [the SRO] hit him he would sue him. [The SRO] told me that this let him know that the student was just running his mouth and didn't really want to engage in a confrontation with him. He said he kicked the student off the track team. (Field notes)

Here the SRO seemed proud of the fact that he "put a student in his place" by asserting his own authority, eventually kicking the student off the track team for being disobedient. The training one receives as a police officer—to assert authority and not back down—conflicts in this case with a conflict-resolution approach to dealing with a student's behavior problem. Although the SRO may have wanted to help—he was volunteering his spare time to be an assistant coach for the track team—his role and training as an officer made him a less than ideal mentor in this case.

Occasionally, the SROs' attempts to mentor or counsel students resulted in inappropriate interactions. For example, we observed an SRO advise a student on how to talk to her probation officer. This student came to the SRO's office to update him on her case, during which:

> [The SRO] chatted with the student a bit, and gave her a lot of encouraging feedback (for example, "that's terrific," "good for you") when she said that she was going to take extra classes to graduate early, work for a year, then go to college to be a veterinarian. He said to her, "I think this is going to be a good year for you." Then, when she was leaving, he called out to her "I love you" in a very fatherly way. (Field notes)

This SRO was clearly trying to mentor the student by advising her about her probation case, giving positive feedback regarding her future plans, and letting her know that he cares. However, telling her that he loves her was entirely inappropriate considering his position in the school. Clearly, mentoring students is a challenge for some police officers, for which their training and experiences leave them ill-prepared.

Police presence in schools also disadvantages students by criminalizing behaviors that are not actually threatening to school safety (Beger 2003). Police involvement in disciplinary matters means that some behaviors that would have led only to school punishment had an officer not been present now result in arrest because an officer is present. Earlier in this chapter we discuss this in relation to fights among students. The 2007 New York Civil Liberties Union report (Mukherjee 2007), which examined police activities in New York City schools, documented officers' enforcement of dress codes and confiscation of cell phones and other electronic devices, with arrests following student resistance to these officers' arbitrary and inconsistent enforcement of school rules.

The ability of SROs to help students is also limited by the fact that the presence of a police officer can infringe on students' rights. When it comes to questioning students about a crime or searching students, school administrators and SROs are bound to different standards under the law. School administrators can search a student with "reasonable suspicion," for example, while SROs must meet the higher legal standard of "probable cause." However, in their partnership, we observed schools and SROs finding ways to get around this legal impediment of police control. For example, at one school we observed a student being sent to an administrator's office to be searched because the student was caught reentering the school building during school hours, which is a violation of the school's closed-campus policy. The student's rule violation constitutes reasonable suspicion for an administrator to search yet falls short of probable cause that a criminal offense has been committed; thus the SRO had no legal authority to search the student. However, the administrator asked the SRO to observe the search as the administrator physically conducted it. Had the administrator found any contraband such as drugs or alcohol, there would have been—only at that point—probable cause for the SRO to intervene directly, continue the search, and arrest the student. Thus, although the SRO was legally prohibited from conducting the search, the SRO's presence meant that the student did not receive the protections the law intended her to receive. With the infusion of police into public schools, it is increasingly likely that schools and police will partner in ways that put students' rights in jeopardy.

Finally, the presence of SROs negatively affects students by socializing them to expect a law enforcement presence in their lives. One student told us that he does not object to the penalties for possessing drugs or alcohol, or for fighting (each of which is automatic arrest and suspension or expulsion), because:

> I mean it's like, if you, in order to have freedom you have to have restrictions. So, in order to be able to do whatever you want in this school basically, to do whatever club you want, to choose your classes, you have to have the restrictions of: no, you can't get in a fight, and if you do, these are the consequences, and everyone knows that. So you signed the code of conduct, if you don't sign the code of conduct you don't have to go here, transfer to another school. The security's fine here.

The fact that growing numbers of children will go to schools that have full-time police officers on campus is likely to make views like this even more common (Casella 2001). Over time, fewer students will view police presence as objectionable or even unusual, since they will be accustomed to it. This growing normalization of law enforcement is consistent with the trends toward increasing punitiveness and centrality of law enforcement in everyday affairs, as noted by scholars such as David Garland (2001) and Jonathan Simon (2007), and contributes to problems like mass incarceration.

CONCLUSIONS

BY DESCRIBING HOW police work within schools, we illustrate in this chapter how the introduction of police officers into schools very clearly represents an area of convergence between schools and formal criminal justice systems. In growing numbers, schools across the United States are inviting police officers to join their ranks as staff members. Through serving as legal advisors and disciplinary resources, these officers reshape school discipline, thereby causing schools to borrow from policing mentalities and practices. Moreover, the presence of these officers in the school augments the police department's ability to gather information about students, their families, and their communities.

It is clear that SROs help school administrators run the school and help the police department police communities, enhancing the school's control over students and police department's surveillance of communities, yet it is not at all clear whether SROs help students, their primary constituents. Some limited benefits are apparent, particularly reduced fears and greater comfort among students knowing that an officer is there. Yet how these benefits stack up against the potential for serious harms—the erosion of students' rights, escalation of punishments, growing surveillance over students and communities, the inability of SROs to mentor students, and the socialization of students to expect a law enforcement presence in their lives—requires normative considerations that are beyond the scope of this chapter. Importantly, these potential harms to students are an institutional problem rather than individual problems; they stem from the official role, obligations, and training of police officers, not from deficits of individual SROs.

With so little prior thought dedicated to how police interact within schools, the goal of this chapter has been to describe this interaction and lay the foundation for future critical analyses that weigh the apparent costs and potential benefits of the SRO program. Perhaps the most important future direction is to pursue a better understanding of whether the presence of police in schools disproportionately affects racial/ethnic minority youth or lower-income youth. It is extremely likely that this is the case, given that prior research very clearly illustrates that students of color are disproportionately subjected to school punishments (for example, Ferguson 2000; Wu et al. 1982), and that research also shows how youth of color, generally, are more likely than whites to draw the suspicion of police officers and be subjected to police intervention (see, for example, Conley 1994). As a result, the growth of SRO programs may add to the disadvantages faced by youth who are already marginalized within subpar schools (Kozol 2005).

The popularity and rapid growth of SRO programs suggests that they will only increase in number—at least as long as local and federal funding for them continues. Our hope is that schools and communities begin to engage in discussions about whether police in schools actually serve their needs, rather than blindly incorporating them into their schools without any critical thought.

ACKNOWLEDGMENTS

This material is based upon work supported by the National Science Foundation under grant no. SES-0550208. Any opinions, findings, and conclusions or recommendations expressed in this material are those of the authors and do not necessarily reflect the views of the National Science Foundation.

NOTES

1. While discussing a model example of a school with effective school security, the report does state that only school safety agents, not police officers, police the school (Mukherjee 2007, 24). However, other school districts that do have police officers in schools, such as Fairfax County, Virginia, and Orange County, Florida, are praised as having effective school resource officer programs that "create a symbiosis between the security officers and the schools" (25). Chicago, as well, is praised for how principals can hire and evaluate the part-time law enforcement officers who work in the school (25–26). Moreover, the report's policy recommendations all involve police but seek to effectively supervise and train them, rather than questioning whether they ought to be in the school.
2. It is important that recent research questions the effectiveness of SRO programs at improving students' perceptions of police (see Hopkins 1994; Jackson 2002). Although student bodies overall may not shift their thinking about officers, it is

clear from our research that at least some students do befriend SROs and provide them with information that assists police work.

3. Teaching classes is one of the primary SRO duties we outline in this chapter, based on program goals. However, we observed very few instances of this in our four schools. As a result we do not include it among SROs' observed routine activities.

4. These studies have relied on opinions of stakeholders or trends in crime, but without adequate comparisons such as a control group. For example, when evaluating the effect of police officers on offense rates in Birmingham, Alabama, schools, Johnson (1999) finds that offense rates were lower for some offense categories following placement of full-time SROs in school, but higher in others, and concludes that SROs deter offenses. Significantly, however, these data were collected at a time of unprecedented decreases in juvenile crime, nationally, and the research includes no comparison/control group, which substantially raises questions about the validity of the results.

REFERENCES

Atkinson, Anne J. 2002. *Fostering school-law enforcement partnerships*. In Safe and secure: Guides to creating safer schools (research report series). Portland, OR: Northwest Regional Educational Laboratory.

Bazemore, Gordon, Jeanne B. Stinchcomb, and Leslie A. Leip. 2004. Scared smart or bored straight? Testing deterrence logic in an evaluation of police-led truancy intervention. *Justice Quarterly* 21:269–299.

Beger, Randall R. 2002. Expansion of police power in public schools and the vanishing rights of students. *Social Justice* 29:119–130.

———. 2003. The "worst of both worlds": School security and the disappearing fourth amendment rights of students. *Criminal Justice Review* 28:336–354.

Brady, Kevin P., Sharon Balmer, and Deinya Phenix. 2007. School-police partnership effectiveness in urban schools: An analysis of New York City's impact schools initiative. *Education and Urban Society* 39:455–478.

Brown, Ben. 2006. Understanding and assessing school police officers: A conceptual and methodological comment. *Journal of Criminal Justice* 34:591–604.

Burke, Sean. 2001. The advantages of a school resource officer. *Law and Order* 49:73–75.

Casella, Ronnie. 2001. *Being down: Challenging violence in urban schools*. New York: Teachers College Press.

Conley, Darlene J. 1994. Adding color to a black and white picture: Using qualitative data to explain racial disproportionality in the juvenile justice system. *Journal of Research in Crime and Delinquency* 31:135–148.

Devine, John. 1996. *Maximum security: The culture of violence in inner-city schools*. Chicago: University of Chicago Press.

Dinkes, Rachel, Emily Forrest Cataldi, and Wendy Lin-Kelly. 2007. *Indicators of school crime and safety: 2007*. Washington, DC: National Center for Education Statistics.

Ferguson, Ann. 2000. *Bad boys: Public schools in the making of black masculinity*. Ann Arbor: The University of Michigan Press.

Garland, David. 2001. *The culture of control: Crime and social order in contemporary society*. Chicago: University of Chicago Press.

Girouard, Cathy. 2001. School resource officer training program (FS 200105). Washington, DC: U.S. Department of Justice, Office of Justice Programs, Office of Juvenile Justice and Delinquency Prevention.

Hopkins, Nick. 1994. School pupils' perceptions of the police that visit schools: Not all police are "pigs." *Journal of Community & Applied Social Psychology* 4:189–207.

Jackson, Arrick. 2002. Police–school resource officers' and students' perception of the police and offending. *Policing: An International Journal of Police Strategies and Management* 25:631–650.

Johnson, Ida M. 1999. School violence: The effectiveness of a school resource officer program in a southern city. *Journal of Criminal Justice* 27:173–192.

Kozol, Jonathan. 2005. *The shame of the nation: The restoration of apartheid schooling in America*. New York: Crown.

Libby, Dana S. 1994. Preventing school violence. *FBI Law Enforcement Bulletin* 63:20–24.

Mukherjee, Elora. 2007. *Criminalizing the classroom: The over-policing of New York City schools*. New York: New York Civil Liberties Union.

National Association of School Resource Officers. n.d. Introduction. http://www.nasro.org/about_nasro.asp (accessed May 1, 2008).

Noguera, Pedro A. 2003. Schools, prisons, and social implications of punishment: Rethinking disciplinary practices. *Theory into Practice* 42:341–350.

Schiraldi, Vincent, and Jason Ziedenberg. 2001. *Schools and suspensions: Self-reported crime and the growing use of suspension*. Washington, DC: Justice Policy Institute.

Schuiteman, John G. 2001. *Second Annual Evaluation of DCJS Funded School Resource Officer Program*. Richmond: Virginia State Department of Criminal Justice Services.

Simon, Jonathan. 2007. *Governing through crime: How the war on crime transformed American democracy and created a culture of fear*. New York: Oxford University Press.

Stefkovich, Jacqueline A., and Judith A. Miller. 1999. Law enforcement officers in public schools: Student citizens in safe havens? *Brigham Young University Education and Law Journal* 99:25–68.

Skiba, Russ, and Reece Peterson. 1999. The dark side of zero tolerance: Can punishment lead to safe schools? *Phi Delta Kappan* 80:372–382.

Vera Institute of Justice. 1999. *Approaches to school safety in America's largest cities*. New York: Vera Institute of Justice.

Wu, Shi-Chang, William Pink, Robert Crain, and Oliver Moles. 1982. Student suspension: A critical reappraisal. *Urban Review* 14:245–303.

CHAPTER 2

School Surveillance in America

DISPARATE AND UNEQUAL

Paul Hirschfield

THE IMPORTATION OF SURVEILLANCE TACTICS from criminal justice and the military into schools is most commonly attributed to elevated fears of school violence and a growing realization that "it *can* happen here." Interestingly, however, the rural and suburban schools where the most extreme forms of violence *did* happen tend to avoid the relatively invasive surveillance and control methods (such as metal detectors and personal searches) that have become commonplace in the largest and poorest urban school districts (Hirschfield 2008). For example, in late summer of 1999 when the Littleton, Colorado, community was mourning the April in-school massacre of thirteen of its members, Columbine High School officials, with community support, refused to subject their students to any invasive search procedures, including metal detectors. They opted instead to add more and better surveillance cameras and confront the negative social climate that led to the tragedy (*New York Times* 1999). Likewise, Heath High School in West Paducah, Kentucky, which lost three of its students to a "rampage" shooting in 1997, actively avoids methods that treat students like criminal suspects or prisoners. The school resource officer (SRO) was hired primarily to be a "positive role model" and to "build trusting relationships with students"; detecting crime and arresting delinquents are secondary (Pascopella, 2005). Unlike Columbine's largely upper-middle class students, Heath's predominantly working-class students do have to submit to cursory weapons searches (bag searches and pat-downs by teachers), but even this ritual is couched in a way that rejects the rhetoric of coercion and criminalization. The school principal asserts, "We've tried to make it a Wal-Mart greeter situation. Rather than, 'I'm searching your book bag,' we try to make it a positive experience" (Pascopella 2005).

The transformation of costly school surveillance methods from a necessary evil to a sleek consumer commodity (Casella 2006) and a "positive experience" helps explain why nonurban "markets" do indeed sustain the continuous expansion of school surveillance. According to recent national survey-based estimates (2005–2006), 46 percent of schools in communities located in "the urban fringe" and "towns" used surveillance cameras, compared to 41 percent in cities and rural areas (Dinkes et al. 2007). Likewise, my analysis of the publicly available data from the 2003–2004 version of the same survey indicates that 39 percent of schools in towns and suburbs employed sworn police officers on a regular basis compared to 35.4 percent of urban schools (Guerino et al. 2006). School security/police forces in towns and suburbs are far more likely (81 versus 63 percent) to be armed compared to their urban counterparts, and the police officers stationed there are equally likely to be on campus full-time.

Such surprising patterns have led various scholars to posit that schools across America's fragmented social landscape are experiencing qualitatively similar intensifications in school surveillance. Their work suggests a number of interrelated explanations for isomorphic patterns, including the government-subsidized expansion of the techno-security industry and its aggressive marketing to school safety administrators (Casella 2006), technology-based fortification as a middle-class coping response to endemic social anxiety and social inequality (Casella 2006; Simon 2007; Staples 2000), widespread fears of violence and discipline-related litigation (Casella 2006; Hirschfield 2008), preparation for and educational policy accommodation to a neo-liberal political order and a postindustrial and penal-industrial economy (Hirschfield 2008; Kupchik and Monahan 2006), and the ascendancy of crime and punishment as a template for school governance and "school accountability" (Simon 2007).

The rapid penetration of law enforcement personnel and technology into urban, suburban, and rural schools is certainly a curious historical development worthy of theoretical and empirical attention. Data showing schools' widespread adoption of cameras and police invites causal narratives that transcend race, class, and geography. However, homology of form does not dictate uniformity in substance, etiology, or function. The camera systems and school police officers in suburban Cherry Creek, Colorado (see Kennedy 2002) probably diverge in purpose and operation from their counterparts in Denver proper (see Advancement Project 2005). Systematic interschool and intercommunity differences in modes, origins, and techniques of surveillance not only limit the scope of any "general theories" of school surveillance but also have important social consequences. For example, the uneven use of surveillance practices for the purposes of punishment and exclusion can reinforce racial, gender, and socioeconomic disparities in arrests and suspensions, educational attainment, and school safety (Brooks et al. 1999).

This chapter, in keeping with critical social reproduction traditions within the sociology of education (Bowles and Gintis 1976), highlights and theorizes stratification in school surveillance practices across school districts and schools. Empirical work demonstrates that school security practices, even when implemented under the same federal funding initiative, are highly variable across social contexts (Coon 2007; Gottfredson et al. 2000). From a critical social reproduction perspective, the resultant disproportionate policing and surveillance of urban minority students functions to prepare such students for their rightful positions in the postindustrial order, whether as prisoners, soldiers, or service sector workers (Duncan 2000; Noguera 2003; Nolan and Anyon 2004; Wacquant 2001). The "school-to-prison pipeline" finds support in evidence that inner-city students are more often subject to carceral rituals at school such as bodily and metal detector searches and arrest (Florida State Conference NAACP et al. 2006; New York Civil Liberties Union and American Civil Liberties Union 2007; hereafter NYCLU and ACLU). Concordant data from the National School Survey on Crime and Safety, 2003–2004 (Guerino et al. 2006), show that urban schools composed largely of minority students made up 14 percent of the nation's middle and high schools yet represent 75 percent of the surveyed middle and high schools (n = 59) that scan their students with metal detectors daily (Guerino et al. 2006).[1]

The primary drawback of the social reproduction approach to understanding variations in school surveillance is that the accounts it fosters rarely specify the intermediary social and political processes that link structural and cultural shifts and constraints to school surveillance practices. Myriad social actors participate in these processes, including elected officials, centralized school policy makers, school-level administrators, teachers, parents, students, and outside organizations. To understand why schools in some contexts, such as "inner-city" neighborhoods, manifest more aggressive and coercive surveillance than schools in other contexts requires an understanding of how contextual forces and factors condition the interests, values, and preferences of each of these groups. Interrogating how such forces set and shift the balance of power among competing groups is also critical, because these social and political configurations sustain whichever security apparatus is in place or in formation. These intellectual tasks give aim and structure to this chapter.

THEORIZING SCHOOL SURVEILLANCE POLICY AND PRACTICE

The few studies that examine contextual patterns and sources of variation in surveillance and security practices focus on general characteristics of schools (size, attendance, racial composition) and communities (urbanicity, crime levels) (Coon 2007; Dinkes et al. 2007). The values, perceptions, attitudes, and milieu-specific political dynamics, which weigh more heavily and proximately in decisions about school surveillance, have, therefore, eluded careful consideration. The abundance of pertinent values, stakeholders, and surveillance practices precludes my attempting anything resembling a comprehensive etiological analysis. Rather, I focus on four pairs of often conflicting values, whose corresponding policy and political imperatives form critical fault lines in battles over school security reforms. Although each of these value conflicts weighs on all stakeholders (albeit unevenly), I focus on the contextually variant importance of each in relation to the preferences of only one stakeholder group, uneasily lumping parents and students together. Furthermore, I limit inquiry to the surveillance tactics that are most common, costly, or controversial (cameras, police, and metal detectors).

Central versus Localized Governance

Each sensationalized school shooting lends school safety more salience as a political issue. School districts throughout the United States face political and legal pressure to devise and implement strategies for preventing and responding swiftly and decisively to actual and potential threats. School districts vary greatly, however, in the nature and intensity of this pressure and in the social and political parameters that condition their response. In the large majority of schools and school districts, school violence has never been a serious or frequent problem. In such districts, investing in technologies and personnel that sustain *perceptions* of safety and preparedness is arguably more politically profitable than adopting demonstrably effective crime prevention methods. Accordingly, a survey of 41 school districts conducted shortly after the Columbine tragedy found that 90 percent had purchased surveillance cameras and 55 percent had metal detectors, mostly handheld (Garcia 2003). Merely making high-tech surveillance equipment available to schools or hiring police officers demonstrates policy makers' commitment to school safety (Cantor et al. 2002; Casella 2006); the actual use of these devices in schools may be a secondary consideration, at least until a serious violent incident occurs. Field research involving forty middle and high schools suggests that lax oversight by school districts contributes to partial and haphazard implementation (Gottfredson et al. 2000).

By contrast, the minority of school districts that administer some schools plagued by violence, gang activity, truancy, and academic failure take issues of oversight and implementation very seriously. Chaotic and failing schools are a source of political embarrassment to elected officials, school superintendents, and school boards. At the same time, the politicization of school violence has strengthened and spawned various mechanisms through which centralized school policy actors can exert more control over schools (Simon 2007).

Struggles over centralized control help explain why permanent metal detectors are concentrated in large urban school districts. From 1985 through

1991, juvenile homicides surged in most major cities, including Chicago. Strikingly, only one Chicago homicide apparently took place inside a Chicago public school. Nonetheless, gang-related neighborhood tensions often erupted in the schools, and some students brought weapons for protection: 800 weapons were confiscated in Chicago public schools between January 1987 and October 1990 (Hagan et al. 2003). At the same time, the Mayor's office and the school board were literally losing control over the schools. In 1988 the Illinois legislature passed landmark decentralization reform, which handed discretion over the implementation of school policy, including security, to local school councils. Elected in 1989, Mayor Richard M. Daley, a former prosecutor, seized upon the hot-button school safety issue, in part as a means to regain some mayoral control of the schools. In 1990 Daley successfully pushed the creation of the School Patrol Unit, which greatly intensified the presence of the Chicago Police Department in the public schools. The unit made 9,822 arrests (8 percent of them for index crimes) in its first year alone (Chicago Police Department 2001). Armed with police-generated data on weapons arrests and confiscations, Mayor Daley, with the school board's assent, purchased walk-through metal detectors for all of the city's high schools in June 1992. Months later, more than a third of these schools, often citing staffing concerns, refused the metal detectors, and many others operated them sporadically. The mayor publicly blasted each of the defiant schools at a news conference, implying that the blame for any weapons-related school injuries would rest with school administrators. Indeed, after three students were shot, one fatally, at Tilden High School in November 1992, the mayor blamed the principal for not operating the metal detectors every day. The deputy chief of the police department's School Patrol Unit at the time asserts that, after this incident, all school principals, albeit with variable enthusiasm, complied with the metal detector program (Hagan et al. 2003).

Chicago's school policing and metal detector programs, whereby all high schools—regardless of their individual needs and preferences—implemented the same untested surveillance tactics under the watchful eye of the Chicago Police Department, provided a template for centralized control within a "decentralized" policy context (Simon 2007). These programs were the first two of a series of school security and disciplinary mandates that the mayor, school superintendent, and/or school board successfully imposed on Chicago public schools. The metal detectors sternly remind teachers and school administrators each morning of the power that central administration wields over the daily affairs of their schools.

Some may dismiss Chicago schools as an outlier, given the particularities of their gang problems and governing structure. However, struggles over centralized control also help explain New York City's adoption of similar school surveillance tactics. In New York City, Mayor Rudolph Giuliani also sought greater control over schools that stood out nationally as underperforming and unsafe. A significant step en route to the mayoral takeover of the New York City public schools was the transfer of authority over the school safety agents (SSAs) from the New York City Bureau of Education (BOE) to the New York Police Department (NYPD), which the mayor goaded the BOE into passing unanimously in 1998 (NYCLU and ACLU 2007). Once school security was under the NYPD's jurisdiction, it became harder for schools to keep disciplinary matters in-house. According to the NYCLU, "Fighting in the hallway is classified as assault; swiping a classmate's pencil case can be classified as a property crime; and talking back to an SSA or being late to class is disorderly conduct" (2007, 17). Since SSAs report to off-site supervisors in the NYPD—a national leader in aggressive policing—arrests are a natural and important indicator of their productivity.

Other centrally initiated and mandated surveillance technologies, like metal detectors and surveillance cameras, aid SSAs in their efforts to find "crime." The operation of this equipment by police employees, as opposed to school employees, is probably a source of cross-contextual variation in how these methods are used and how they are perceived by other stakeholders. Since the police who operate metal detectors cannot be disciplined by school officials and are encouraged to make and tally arrests and seizures of contraband, metal detectors facilitate surveillance that extends far beyond weapons. An NYCLU survey of over 1,000 high school students at schools with permanent metal detectors finds that 53 percent of students reported that officers at the metal detectors had frisked them and searched their pockets and 58 percent had to remove or lift up clothing other than belts and shoes. Intensive scrutiny at the metal detectors routinely nets "cell phones, iPods, food, school supplies, and other personal items" (NYCLU and ACLU 2007, 6). Students are subject to arrest or the threat of arrest for refusing to turn over cell phones, for stepping out of line, and for refusing to be scanned. Overall, 77 percent of officially recorded police interventions are for noncriminal incidents such as these. Moreover, schools with permanent metal detectors report twice as many noncriminal police incidents as do "typical similarly-sized schools" (20). The SSAs also have real-time access to Internet Protocol Digital Video Surveillance (IPDVS) systems, which are now installed in 163 schools (Winston 2007). According to the chief operating officer of a major vendor of digital school surveillance systems, this exemplifies a major difference between camera installations in large urban schools and affluent suburbs (interview, name withheld, 2008). Affluent and nonurban schools generally store their surveillance footage in-house and do very little real-time viewing. Urban school districts like those of Austin, Texas, Newark, New Jersey, and New York

City feed live video directly to centralized district command centers, perhaps reinforcing the ideology of centralized coordination and control.

I single out Chicago and New York City because they epitomize the top-down initiation and administration of school surveillance. The installation of surveillance practices like cameras and police in these giant cities follows distinct developmental pathways. In smaller jurisdictions, such practices are more likely to accord with expressed or tacit demands of the impacted community. Ernest Logan, the president of the Council of School Supervisors and Administrators in New York City, the union representing New York City's school principals and assistant principals, asserts, "Many principals resent the idea of metal detectors in their schools and often feel pressured to have them installed" (Logan 2008). School principals may decry such top-down surveillance methods not only because they make schools seem more like correctional facilities and principals like wardens but also because they are wary of the broader shifts toward centralized governance they signal and facilitate (Simon 2007). Police-generated information on crime incidents may be viewed by policy makers and evaluators as an indicator of "school safety" that is less subject to manipulation by school administrators. Following legislative and administrative guidelines, centralized actors do, in fact, use this information to make normalizing judgments and impose a specific program of reform on errant schools (Foucault 1977; Simon 2007). In New York City, schools with high rates of reported crime risk being labeled as "Impact Schools," which doubles their police presence and imposes zero tolerance for repeat student rule-violators (Drum Major Institute 2005). The mere threat of the dangerous label is likely to promote greater conformity on the part of school administrators.

Securing compliance from disadvantaged urban schools in this fashion is in keeping with wider state and federal "school accountability" initiatives. The Safe and Drug-free Schools Act, as described by Simon (2007), is one example. It encourages tighter surveillance of schools, first by allocating money partly on the basis of a demonstrated crime problem and second by encouraging the purchase of surveillance equipment with program funds. Another even more pertinent and timely example is the No Child Left Behind Act (NCLB). One provision of NCLB mandates that states, in collaboration with school districts, define and report "persistently dangerous schools" and give their students the option of transferring (King 2007). Like Operation Impact in New York City, NCLB grants school districts greater leverage over the most troubled schools. I suspect that principals of schools that approach state thresholds for persistent dangerousness are less likely to resist central school surveillance mandates. In most states, this provision affects only poor urban schools, as they tend to be the schools that persistently rank highest on official indicators of "dangerousness" (King 2007).

Inclusionary versus Exclusionary Ethos

Schools vary in their surveillance practices, even in pursuit of the same district mandates. This variation depends on the particular constraints facing schools and the orientation and preferences of key decision makers and stakeholders. A key issue that all schools confront is how to respond to low-performing and disruptive students. Inclusionary approaches aim to accord full-member status to these students and offer extra attention and services to help them become productive members of the school. Exclusionary approaches push such students out of school, to make more resources available to students who stand a better chance of success. Where school administrators fall between these two divergent approaches plays a pivotal role in their preferences for particular surveillance practices and the manner of their execution.

An unfortunate reality is that most public schools lack sufficient resources to save all struggling and troubled students. Students whose conduct impedes the performance of their teachers and peers directly or indirectly (through usurping resources) are a particular liability, and the imperative to exclude such students from mainstream classrooms and schools is nearly universal (Bowditch 1993; Riehl 1999). This imperative weighs more heavily on administrators in resource-poor schools, who fear further cuts or even demotion should they fail to improve levels of student achievement, truancy, and crime. Overcrowded conditions are also conducive to selective exclusionary practices; trimming "surplus" students can improve safety and achievement without forcing cuts in key personnel.

Inclusionary and exclusionary value orientations correspond to inclusionary and exclusionary modes of surveillance. In practice, both modes are manifest, although in varying degrees, within the same schools and even in the same technologies. The distinction between them is as much one of function as one of form. An inclusive system of surveillance emphasizes reducing or obscuring differences among subjects, whereas an exclusionary system magnifies deviant subjects for the purpose of exploiting or purging them (see Young 1999 for a parallel discussion of inclusive and exclusive societies). Inclusionary surveillance systems are more likely to be operative in small, relatively cohesive schools and in schools that are predominantly middle class and affluent. Inclusionary surveillance is a tool of disciplinary power, as described by Foucault (1977). Surveillance cameras, at least in theory, articulate a disciplinary logic, as they entail continuous, hierarchical observation to encourage students to direct their bodies toward normal, orderly, and productive action. Ubiquitous in contemporary society, surveillance cameras do not single out students as a special class of deviants. To inclusionary and exclusionary school principals alike, they are marketed as a natural and essential fixture in any "future-oriented" high school and an important symbol of their professional competence and clout (Casella 2006).

School police, although not a natural embodiment of disciplinary power, can also function within inclusionary systems of surveillance. Suburban and rural school districts emphasize SROs' counseling and educational functions and pursue SROs who act as "role models" and will "get to know" and "earn the trust" of students (Kennedy 2002). This rhetoric suggests that SROs aim to reform minor troublemakers rather than to remove them. Relatively affluent schools strive to assimilate school security and police into the school culture, which, in cohesive schools, orients them more toward discipline and inclusion than exclusion. As the director of Facilities Support of Cherry Creek School District in Colorado states, the school police are "part of the fabric of the school district . . . Most students are comfortable with them" (Kennedy 2002, 9). School principals in these districts are also relatively comfortable, because they exercise more power over the selection and management of their schools' police. Most suburban and rural SRO's were hired under a designated federal funding stream (COPS in Schools) awarded to and administered by the school district (Pascopella 2005). On the other hand, inclusionary principals are natural foes of metal detectors. Principals commonly complain that metal detectors treat students with suspicion, sour students' attitudes toward school and school authorities, and undermine a positive, respectful academic environment (Ascher and Maguire 2008; Astor et al. 1999)—all of which undermine an inclusionary ethos. Metal detectors—a formidable physical barrier between students and their schools and a frequent cause of disunity or discord within the school community—are, in some respects, inherently anti-inclusionary (Brown 2005; Santos 2005).

By contrast, school administrators with exclusionary aims may direct or welcome the use of metal detectors, police, and cameras as exclusionary surveillance. Exclusionary surveillance facilitates the detection and removal of rule breakers and other less desirable students. Surveillance technologies are particularly effective as exclusionary tools when "outside" police are instrumental to their operation. As mentioned earlier, metal detectors and associated procedures make rule violations more visible. They can also invite confrontations with police that escalate into arrests and subsequent suspensions (NYCLU and ACLU 2007). Metal detectors and school police/security forces help keep the students who are least academically engaged but most academically needy out of classrooms, mostly urban ones, through several other means: (1) sending students home for tardiness or violating the dress code; (2) causing late entrants into the metal detector line to miss classes; and (3) sweeping the halls after the bell rings, sending straggling students to detention rooms or even handcuffing them (Sullivan 2007). Indeed, school attendance in some underperforming schools slips markedly on the days they are selected for the NYPD's random metal detector program (NYCLU and ACLU 2007; Sullivan 2007). Whereas many principals bemoan "heavy-handed" police surveillance (Logan 2008), others welcome and facilitate proactive and aggressive school policing (Rimer 2004). In one Los Angeles school, the principal reportedly "announced over the loudspeaker that anyone socializing in the hallways in between periods or caught standing still in groups in the hallway would be ticketed by police and/or suspended" (Sullivan 2007, 42). In Chicago, the director of the Office of Safety and Security of the Chicago Public Schools blames excessive school arrests on school principals who are "too willing to call the police for minor infractions" (Mendell 2006).

Surveillance cameras also pack considerable exclusionary power. In nearly all schools that have them, surveillance cameras provide archival evidence that can help suspend, expel, or prosecute accused students. Naturally, their use for these purposes is greater where there are more suspensions, arrests, and incidents reported to the police. However, I have uncovered few examples of authorities' using school cameras to detect violations as they occur, which may reflect the inefficiency of real-time monitoring or cameras' deterrent value. That said, one example illustrates how cameras can forward a criminalization agenda and, perhaps, challenge the benign image that the techno-security industry carefully cultivates among school professionals and in the wider school community (Casella 2006). A high school principal in Goose Creek, South Carolina, claimed that images of drug transactions that he observed with school surveillance cameras led him to invite police to conduct a drug raid on his school (McRoberts 2004). African American students make up only 25 percent of the school's population but represented a majority of the 107 students who were subject to the raid, during which police pointed guns at prostrate students' heads. The raid uncovered no arrest-worthy offenses but did exact a $1.6 million court settlement (Smith 2006). Ironically, the same cameras that apparently emboldened the principal to summon these extreme exclusionary measures captured disturbing images of the raid that hastened his own removal from the school.

Exclusionary and inclusionary aims and strategies depend not only on individual administrators' philosophy and management styles but also on the social and political contexts in which they are embedded. Broadly speaking, principals who run schools with a reputation for chaos and failure have a greater incentive to implement exclusionary surveillance. Aggressive, "no-nonsense" surveillance suggests that they are serious about turning their schools around and offers a means of weeding out the students who are giving their schools a bad name. For schools with a reputation for being safe, cohesive, nurturing, and academically focused, the political calculus is completely different. Administrators of these schools mainly pursue technologies (for example, video cameras) that will make their schools appear safe, technologically advanced, and efficient and will prevent problems from occurring (Casella 2006). Surveillance tactics like metal detectors and authoritarian guards that convey danger, uncover more than a token amount of problem behavior, and foment and highlight social divisions that threaten the standing of the school and the principal (Newbart 2005). Especially in small towns and suburbs, the entire community has a stake in maintaining a veneer of safety and harmony in its schools (Newman et al. 2005), since real estate values and derivative quality-of-life issues are closely tied to the schools' reputations (Hu 2006).

Discipline and Control versus Academics

Teachers wield less influence over school surveillance policy and practice than district- and school-level officials do. However, teacher's unions, especially in larger jurisdictions, carry a powerful and distinctive voice into policy debates over school surveillance, and individual teachers often play a key role in the execution of surveillance practices. According to Devine (1995), the formidable New York City teacher's union was the driving force behind the development of the largest school police force ever recorded. Often victimized by students and fearful of being sued or injured for intervening in student altercations, teachers demanded delegation of frontline disciplinary responsibilities to other personnel. Devine (1995, 176) reports that once the security apparatus was in place, guards complained that some "teachers call them into the classroom for the least little thing." Likewise, teachers sometimes resent or resist uninvited police interventions that disrupt their lessons (NYCLU and ACLU 2007).

Levels of concern over threats to personal safety or teaching effectiveness are probably overriding explanations of teachers' individual and collective support of tighter surveillance. However, teachers, like principals, vary in their orientation toward particular categories of students in ways that probably bear independently on their dispositions toward surveillance. Teachers, far more thoroughly and directly than principals, are charged with socializing and training students to become productive and responsible adults. The desired content of socialization and training depends on the adult future that teachers envision for particular students. Aside from personal safety and performance enhancement, therefore, teachers also judge surveillance practices in relation to the values, cultural capital, and curricular content that they feel schools should pursue and instill. Teachers who believe in teaching students that they are valued citizens whose individual rights must be protected may take issue with intrusive electronic surveillance. "I think it sends a really negative message," one teacher reported to Astor, Meyer, and Behre. "It's like a prison . . . when you have to have cameras in your cell" (1999, 29). Another former teacher opposed to cameras remarked, "You are raising a generation of people who believe the Fourth Amendment has no meaning and no significance anywhere" (Hetzner 2001). Academically demanding teachers are perhaps the most vehement in their opposition to metal detectors, given that long lines at the metal detectors can cut severely into the teachers' instructional time and can keep even the most engaged students out of class. Finally, teachers focused on preparing students to graduate and pursue higher education may question whether expensive surveillance equipment—which neither observes nor addresses classroom problems—should take budgetary precedence over instructional support, guidance counselors, and other direct benefits to students (Cantor et al. 2002).

Sociologists of education have long observed, however, that some teachers in some schools place far more value on students' autonomy, individuality, and intellectual development than others (Bowles and Gintis 1976). In some schools, the overriding pedagogical goal is instilling docility. According to Kozol (2005, 64), a "pedagogy of direct command and absolute control" can articulate both with administrative imperatives for standardized test improvements and the adult futures that teachers (and corporations) envision for their students. Ferguson (2000) observes that many teachers are particularly concerned about black males' precarious standing in relation to the labor market, the police, and other mainstream institutions. For African-American boys, Ferguson asserts, "the enactment of docility is a preparation for adult racialized survival rituals of which the African-American adults in the school are especially cognizant" (87). Teachers who aim to prepare students for an economic and criminal justice system that tightly monitors and subordinates them may register less opposition to more intrusive forms of school surveillance. Judged against this goal, morning rituals of submission at the metal detector may even hold some pedagogical value.

Safety versus Dignity

Student leaders and parent advocates often seem miles apart from educational professionals on issues of school surveillance. This reflects the fact that the benefits that flow to the key architects and managers of school surveillance do not always trickle down to students and may even be seen as a cost. For example, a principal who learns how to operate a high-tech surveillance system and uses the school's security force to purge the school of chronic miscreants may appear to peers and superiors as competent, innovative, strong, and committed to "safety" (Casella 2006). To students and concerned parents, however, these accomplishments are basically worthless unless students are safer or feel safer. If improved safety does not result, it is difficult for students to see how added surveillance is worth costs such a loss of privacy, time, self-esteem, motivation, and school spirit (NYCLU and ACLU 2007).

Thus, for students and parents the effectiveness of surveillance technology in reducing crime and fear is paramount. Following gunfire in one of Boston's high schools, the district's fifty-member Student Advisory Council submitted a proposal for *stricter* metal detector screenings, claiming students frequently escaped thorough electronic screenings. On the other hand, a half dozen parents and students from the Roxbury alternative school that experienced the gunfire publicly argued that "the detectors would alienate students and make the tight-knit school appear more dangerous than it is" (Jan 2005).

It appears that much of the student discourse on surveillance technologies weighs any added safety benefits against their social and psychological costs. Because I was not able to find any data comparing students' attitudes toward or reactions to surveillance strategies across contexts, I can only speculate about whether and how these attitudes and their political influence vary. I suspect that metal detectors are only accepted where weapons are perceived as a serious threat and scans are seen as effective and efficient. However, some of the same factors that foster violence may also make metal detectors less effective and efficient. For example, overcrowded schools suffer from excessively long lines, and it is easier to smuggle weapons into older schools, which feature many entrances and windows. A student in a high school whose working metal detector failed to thwart a stabbing complained, "You can't get an MP3 player or a cell phone in, but you can get a knife in" (Paddock and Melago 2008). Excessively long lines triggered a mass walkout of 1,500 of 4,600 enrolled students at DeWitt Clinton High School in the Bronx, who marched to the Department of Education and unsuccessfully demanded the removal of both metal detectors and security cameras (Santos 2005). Student and parental opposition to metal detectors appears more vocal and effective in middle-class schools where students are less accustomed to criminalization and where parents of valued students may credibly threaten to transfer their children or otherwise generate flak (Cantor et al. 2002; De Vise 2008).

On the other hand, surveillance cameras spark little resistance among students and parents, and even less in the suburbs. In resource-rich school districts, expensive surveillance equipment is less likely to require skimping on other important expenses. To some status- and safety-conscious parents, the fact that the district has the surplus cash and know-how to purchase and install state-of-the-art surveillance may even be comforting (Casella 2006). In resource-poor school districts where violence is legitimately a serious concern, such equipment is likely viewed as a worthwhile investment only if it improves safety. One of these districts, in Brownsville, Texas (91 percent Hispanic), features school video cameras operated by its own school district police force. A semi-random survey of 230 Brownsville high school students suggests that student valuations are divided; 54 percent of respondents agree that "video surveillance cameras help reduce crime" (Brown 2005). This tepid support is not too surprising given that cameras afford students no protection in bathrooms, locker rooms, and most parking lots (Garcia 2003); nor do they discern common, harmful behaviors like taunts, threats, and harassment (by students and police). I suspect that cameras in poor or urban districts are also more likely to be viewed as a threat to student dignity, because, as the case of DeWitt Clinton High School illustrates, they are embedded within a security apparatus that demeans, criminalizes, and excludes many students. In advantaged communities, cameras are largely blunt instruments and mundane fixtures. Accordingly, they no longer evoke an image of Big Brother, himself a less ominous figure nowadays (Casella 2006). Rather, to children growing up in the age of camera phones, Webcams, and YouTube, video cameras symbolize individual expression as much as repression and control (Koskela 2004). Such flexible connotations may actually hinder cameras' effectiveness as a social control device and, possibly, undermine their desirability in relatively violent schools. As one student reported to Astor, Meyer, and Behre (1999, 29), "All the cameras are gonna do is videotape, you know what I'm saying? They'll fight right in front of the camera too . . . some of them they'll be asking, 'Can I get that tape?'"

CONCLUSION

It is noteworthy that the surveillance methods that are popular in largely white towns and suburbs appear designed to affirm and preserve student individuality and dignity. SROs are trained to "get to know" students. Cameras are not used to hunt rule breakers, but function largely as an extension of the human eyes that observe them or ignore them all day long. They provide only a daily log of bodily movements through school and, in that respect, are the functional equivalents of the systems that unobtrusively track phone calls, cash withdrawals, and food purchases. By contrast, metal detectors, which are rarely found in these schools, forcibly align student bodies and dictate highly choreographed rituals of submission (such as standing spread-eagled). Although their official purpose—preventing weapons from entering the schools—is laudable, to thousands of bitter and anxious students forced to pass through them every day, metal detectors stand as a daily reminder of how little power students have over those in whom they entrust their futures and, in turn, how powerless their trusted guardians are to secure for the students a dignified, timely, and safe passage into school (and adulthood). On the other hand, all stakeholders have limits regarding acceptable vigor or laxity of surveillance, which they will defend when transgressed. I hope this chapter inspires further inquiry into how these limits are set, how they vary by social group, and whose limits most shape policy and practice. Such insights can inform both efforts to maintain these thresholds and efforts to shift them.

NOTE

1. This rate is 71 percent when the fifty-nine schools are weighted by their chances
   of sample selection. However, this sample is too small to constitute a probability
   sample of schools with metal detectors.

REFERENCES

Advancement Project. 2005. *Education on lockdown: The schoolhouse to jailhouse track.*
Washington, DC: Advancement Project.

Ascher, Carol, and Cindy Maguire. 2008. Beating the odds. *Voices in Urban Education*
no. 19. http://www.annenberginstitute.org/VUE/spring08/Ascher.php (accessed
April 2, 2009).

Astor, Ron Avi, Heather Ann Meyer, and William J. Behre. 1999. Unowned places and
times: Maps and interviews about violence in high schools. *American Educational
Research Journal* 36 (1): 3–42.

Bowditch, Christine. 1993. Getting rid of troublemakers: High school disciplinary
procedures and the production of dropouts. *Social Problems* 40:493–509.

Bowles, Samuel, and Herbert Gintis. 1976. *Schooling in capitalist America: Educational
reform and the contradictions of economic life.* New York: Basic Books.

Brooks, Kim, Vincent Schiraldi, and Jason Ziedenberg. 1999. *School house hype: Two
years later.* San Francisco: Center on Juvenile and Criminal Justice.

Brown, Ben. 2005. Controlling crime and delinquency in the schools: An exploratory
study of student perceptions of school security measures. *Journal of School Violence*
4 (4): 105–125.

Casella, Ronnie. 2006. *Selling us the fortress: The promotion of techno-security equipment
for schools.* New York: Routledge.

Cantor, David, Scott Crosse, Carol A. Hagen, Michael J. Mason, Amy J. Siler, and
Adrienne von Glatz. 2002. *A closer look at drug and violence prevention efforts in
American schools. Report on the study on school violence and prevention.* Washington,
DC: US Department of Education, Planning and Evaluation Service.

Chicago Police Department. 2001. Unpublished data. Police Headquarters, Chicago.

Coon, Julie K. 2007. *Security technology in U.S. public schools.* New York: LFB Scholarly
Publishing.

De Vise, Daniel. 2008. U.S. suburban schools reject metal Detectors. *Washington Post.*
April 18, A01.

Devine, John. 1995. Can metal detectors replace the panopticon? *Cultural Anthropology*
10 (2): 171–195.

Dinkes, Rachel, Emily Forrest Cataldi, and Wendy Link-Kelly. 2007. *Indicators of school
crime and safety.* Washington, DC: National Center for Education Statistics, Institute
of Education Sciences, U.S. Department of Education, Bureau of Justice Statistics,
Office of Justice Programs, and U.S. Department of Justice.

Drum Major Institute. 2005. *A look at the impact schools. A Drum Major Institute for
Public. Policy data brief.* New York: Drum Major Institute.

Duncan, Garrett A. 2000. Urban pedagogies and the celling of adolescents of color.
Social Justice 27 (3): 29–42.

Ferguson, Ann A. 2000. *Bad boys: Public schools in the making of black masculinity.* Ann
Arbor: University of Michigan Press.

Florida State Conference NAACP, Advancement Project, and NAACP Legal Defense
and Educational Fund Inc. 2006. *Arresting development: Addressing the school discipline*

crisis in Florida. http://www.advancementproject.org/reports/ArstdDvpm_SM.pdf (accessed April 2, 2009).

Foucault, Michel. 1977. *Discipline and punish: The birth of the prison.* New York: Pantheon Books.

Garcia, Crystal A. 2003. School safety technology in America: Current use and perceived effectiveness. *Criminal Justice Policy Review* 14 (1): 30–54.

Gottfredson, Gary D., Denice C. Gottfredson, Ellen R. Czeh, David Cantor, Scott B. Crosse, and Irene Hantman. 2000. *A national study of delinquency prevention in school: Final report.* Ellicott City, MD: Gottfredson Associates.

Guerino, Paul, Michael D. Hurwitz, Sarah M. Kaffenberger, David C. Hoaglin, and Kristine Burnaska. 2006. *School survey on crime and safety. 2003–04.* Washington, DC: National Center for Education Statistics.

Hagan, John, Paul J. Hirschfield, and Carla Shedd. 2003. Shooting at Tilden High: Causes and consequences. In *Deadly lessons: Understanding lethal school violence,* ed. Mark H. Moore, Carol V. Petrie, Anthony A. Braga, and Brenda L. McLaughlin, 143–174. Washington, DC: National Research Council.

Hetzner, Amy. 2001. Am I on campus camera? *Milwaukee Journal Sentinel.* May 28. http://www.jsonline.com/news/wauk/may01/secure29052801a.asp.

Hirschfield, Paul J. 2008. Preparing for prison? The criminalization of school discipline in the USA. *Theoretical Criminology* 12 (1): 79–101.

Hu, Winnie. 2006. A very violent school, or just very honest? *New York Times.* October 8.

Jan, Tracy. 2005. Students want weapon screenings: Advisory group seeks stricter school policies. *Boston Globe.* December 12, A1.

Kennedy, Mike. 2002. Balancing security and learning: School security supplement. *American School & University* 74 (6): 8, 10–11.

King, Ledyard. 2007. Program to identify most dangerous schools misses mark. *USA Today.* January 18. http://www.usatoday.com/news/education/2007–01–18-dangerousschools_x.htm.

Koskela, Hille. 2004. Webcams, TV shows and mobile phones: Empowering exhibitionism. *Surveillance & Society* 2 (2/3): 199–215.

Kozol, Jonathan. 2005. *The shame of the nation: The restoration of apartheid schooling in America.* New York: Crown.

Kupchik, Aaron, and Torin Monahan. 2006. The new American school: Preparation for post-industrial discipline. *British Journal of Sociology of Education* 27 (5): 617–631.

Logan, Ernest. 2008. Personal communication to author. June 10.

McRoberts, Flynn. 2004. High school drug raid rattles town race is subtext as ex-Chicagoan joins lawsuit accusing SC officials of violating students' rights. *Chicago Tribune.* February 15.

Mendell, David. 2006. Schools, cops aim to curtail arrests. *Chicago Tribune.* February 6.

Newbart, Dave. 2004. Teacher say principals need to get tough on violence. *Chicago Tribune.* April 25.

Newman, Katherine S., Cybelle Fox, Wendy Roth, Jal Mehta, and David Harding. 2004. *Rampage: The social roots of school shootings.* New York: Basic Books.

New York Civil Liberties Union and the American Civil Liberties Union. 2007. *Criminalizing the classroom: The over-policing of New York City schools.* New York: New York Civil Liberties Union and the American Civil Liberties Union.

New York Times. 1999. Back to Columbine. Editorial. August 17.

Noguera, Pedro A. 2003. Schools, prisons, and social implications of punishment: Rethinking disciplinary practices. *Theory into Practice* 42 (4): 341–350.

Nolan, Kathleen, and Jean Anyon. 2004. Learning to do time: Willis' cultural reproduction model in an era of deindustrialization, globalization, and the mass incarceration of people of Color. In *Learning to labor in new times*, ed. Nadine Dolby, Greg Dimitriadis, and Paul Willis, 133–149. New York: Routledge.

Paddock, Barry, and Carrie Melago. 2008. Coach helps save stabbed student. *New York Daily News.* March 29. http://www.nydailynews.com/ny_local/brooklyn/2008/03/29/2008-03-29_untitled__2stab29m.html.

Pascopella, Angela. 2005. Money makes security go around. *District Administration* 41 (7): 47–53.

Riehl, Carolyn. 1999. Labeling and letting go: An organizational analysis of how high school students are discharged as dropouts. *Research in sociology of education and socialization* 12:231-268. New York: JAI Press.

Rimer, Sara. 2004. Unruly students facing arrest, not detention. *New York Times.* January 4, A1.

Santos, Fernanda. 2005. Protest over metal detectors gains legs: Students walk out. *New York Times.* September 2.

Simon, Jonathan. 2007. *Governing through crime: How the war on crime transformed American democracy and created a culture of fear.* New York: Oxford University Press.

Smith, Jordan. 2006. Weed watch: Goose Creek police geese. *Austin Chronicle.* July 21.

http://www.austinchronicle.com/gyrobase/Issue/story?oid=oid%3A388477.

Staples, William G. 2000. *Vigilance and visibility in postmodern life.* Lanham, MD: Rowman & Littlefield.

Sullivan, Elizabeth. 2007. *Deprived of dignity: Degrading treatment and abusive discipline in New York City & Los Angeles public schools.* New York: National Economic and Social Rights Initiative.

Wacquant, Loïc. 2001. Deadly symbiosis: When ghetto and prison meet and mesh. In *Mass imprisonment: Social causes and consequences*, ed. David W. Garland, 82–120. London: Sage.

Winston, Ali. 2007. Students on camera: Schools under watch. *City Limits Weekly.* April 9. http://www.citylimits.org/content/articles/viewarticle.cfm?article_id=3304.

Young, Jock. 1999. *The exclusive society: Social exclusion, crime and difference in late modernity.* Thousand Oaks, CA: Sage.

CHAPTER 3

The Docile Body in School Space

Lizbet Simmons

IN *DISCIPLINE AND PUNISH: The Birth of the Prison* (1979), Michel Foucault establishes the particularities of modern power and the practice of punishment by tracing their institutionalization in the prison system. With the prison as his ultimate example, Foucault argues that modern power is embedded and advanced in the disciplines, a set of practices that organizes individuals and the spaces they occupy for the production of docile bodies. The disciplines work to manipulate individuals by the technologies of modern power, which proceed, remarkably, without force. Foucault suggests that this shift toward a more subtle authority happened at the end of the eighteenth century and offered new opportunities for power and new ways of managing the body and persuading the soul. That reconfiguration of power, as he saw it, penetrated the prison and other disciplinary institutions by transforming the actual techniques and materials of discipline such that they penetrated the human body, and more significantly, the social body.

I turn to Foucault to locate disciplinary power relations as they operate in school space, managing students and orchestrating their daily engagements. I focus on everyday expressions of control and governance—the practices embedded in typical school architecture and routine curricular arrangements—not to diminish the significance of high-tech control networks and surveillance systems, but rather to show how they are historically situated and instituted. Although they find new expression and new reach in surveillance technology, disciplinary power relations are embedded in the very foundation of the American public school system. As such, it is not merely a matter of technological capacity or a matter of current political expediency that schools are laboratories for cultures of control (Noguera 1995). As disciplinary strategies expand in the public school landscape, with armed guards, security cameras, metal detectors, and identification practices, there is a need to trace this emergence and to situate these strategies within embedded power relations.

Foucault provides one of the most detailed accounts of power in its operation, and in the chapter entitled "Docile Bodies" within *Discipline and Punish*, he delineates how power operates in space as an "art of distributions." This art is made manifest in several spatially significant forms: (1) by the practice of *enclosure*, which limits the parameters of movement; (2) by *partitioning* individual bodies, which disaggregates groups of individuals; (3) through *functioning sites*, for which each site has a particular function; and (4) by *rank*, which organizes individuals in relation to each other. By locating modern power in its physical arrangement, this schema points to the way in which the body is regulated in the negotiation of space.

A number of educational theorists and historians (Tyack 1974; Bowles and Gintis 1976; Oakes 1985) have offered studies of distribution as a social control practice, but this work has not been adequately examined in light of Foucault's disciplinary typology, which precisely articulates the practices as they enable power relations. John Devine's book on school discipline, *Maximum Security* (1996), does deal directly with Foucault, but Devine's critique of the text is focused on the panopticon, Jeremy Bentham's design for a surveillance-controlled prison. The panopticon is the primary figure of Foucault's analysis of power in *Discipline and Punish*, and it has rightfully been central to discussions of the text. The panopticon represents the way in which a physical structure is functional in the production of docile bodies. In the panoptic prison, inmates are arranged in a ring of cells and are surveilled by authorities positioned at the ring's center. The panoptic sphere disallows private space and private movement, because the inmate is either being watched or, even more important, is imagining himself being watched. The unremitting and objectifying gaze contributes to what Foucault calls the "power/knowledge regime." As it enables the constant visibility of the subject, the gaze produces a knowledge about the subject that benefits the management of individuals and thus bolsters the workings of power (Fraser 1989).

The figure of the panopticon is a familiar one in the consideration of school security (and security in general). More often than not, the panoptic concept is employed as a catch-all trope to conveniently gloss anecdotes of surveillance. Devine suggests, however, that we might be too quick to accept Foucault's panopticon as the modus operandi for school discipline. Ultimately, he argues against the concept, suggesting that an "anti-panopticon" is operational in many public schools, as teachers have stopped observing their students and have turned their disciplinary powers over to school security guards instead. This critique is well-founded in Devine's work, even if he might go too far in his oppositional stance. Schools rely on established disciplinary networks made up not only of security guards but also of teachers, administrators, students, and parents, who pay rigorous attention to the meticulous details of students' bodies and students' behavior using the mechanisms of high-tech surveillance or the gaze of embodied observation. Indeed, the geometries of discipline that facilitate the operation of power and house surveillance strategies are—though not always panoptic—so fully integrated into school design, curriculum, and culture that they are normalized and easily taken for granted.

I aim to read into Foucault's *Discipline and Punish* to reveal analyses that have been overshadowed by the figure of the panopticon but nonetheless constitute its underpinnings. I am interested in Foucault's ideas about the very mechanics of power, which he provides by parsing spatialized operation and enumerating its contribution to the power relations of organized experience. By grounding the discussion of discipline in the physical landscape of the school, this essay provides a necessary framework for understanding social control in educational practice. I extend this analysis with an interpretive case study of a school that opened in the Orleans Parish Prison, at which the disciplined body was a primary investment. This case is an expression of Foucault's disciplinary claims but also exposes their most significant limitation. It was a necessary condition of his genealogical method that Foucault mapped a modern power arrangement as it penetrates both the human body and operates at "every level of the social body" (Foucault 1979, 303). Through the writing of a common history, though, Foucault dealt in production rather than prohibition, in normalization rather than repression, in micro rather than macro politics, and in genealogy rather than sociology (Fraser 1989). Theorizing from my case study, I seek to mediate these dichotomies and offer a methodological corrective that allows us to consider the critical and ethical dimension of race within power relations.

THE ART OF DISTRIBUTIONS

In "the art of distributions" Foucault articulates four distinct disciplinary techniques—enclosure, partitioning, functional sites, and rank—that have significant aspects in common. "These were always meticulous, often minute, techniques," he writes, and "they defined a certain mode of detailed political investment of the body" (1979, 139). With a characterization of the disciplines as "a political anatomy of detail" in which "no detail is unimportant," Foucault makes a general claim for the ubiquity of disciplinary power as it is borne through meticulous precision (139, 140). He argues that this detail is captured in the capillary structure of modern power, which operates through minute spaces and has extensive reach. Consequently, Foucault argues, a capillary power structure has the capacity to "cover the entire social body" (139). Foucault presents this coverage in examinations of the church, the military, the factory, and the school, acknowledging their respective disciplinary elements while suggesting that they form a general pattern, or "blueprint," of discipline (145). From his perspective, the disciplines take shape in "extensive architectural arrangements" within these institutions and configure the structure of modern power, which operates without the need for extensive "restraining measures or rigid confinement" (148).

Controlled concentration is, in Foucault's estimation, the eminent goal of enclosure, and the monastery is his model for its application. In confined spaces, the disciplines can operate "to maximum advantages and to neutralize the inconveniences (thefts, interruptions of work, disturbances and 'cabals'), as the forces of production become more concentrated; to protect materials and tools and to master the labour force" (142). Under one roof, there is greater opportunity for the assertion of authority, organizing labor toward purpose. This spatial order can be established by separation, architecture, surveillance, and fortification. In schools, students are managed within a restricted space that delineates the distinction between inside and outside, here and there, us and them. As a disciplinary strategy, enclosure serves both an endo-cultural function and an exo-cultural one; it organizes individuals within and without—homogenously within the enclosure but heterogeneously to those outside. This dual delineation begins to explain why Foucault describes the enclosure as a "place of disciplinary monotony" and "the specification of a place heterogeneous to all others" (141). While the school building, or the fence that surrounds it, may mark the territory as a place of education for those inside, it may conversely designate the outlying territory as other. This borderline is significant when considering the role the school serves for their greater constituency, and it raises questions about how responsive the school might be to community concerns or initiatives.

Enclosure is fully integrated as a design concept in educational institutions across the United States. Public schools are commonly set apart by campus borders, drug-free zones, surveillance networks, fencing, barbed wire, barred windows, metal detectors, identification check points, school security officer patrols, and, increasingly, police patrols. The degree of enclosure can be extended, however, beyond the edge of the border if the school is built at a remove from the larger community. Henry Barnard, a leading educator in the earliest American schools, proposes this precise strategy in a treatise entitled *School Architecture*:

> The location [of the school] should be dry, quiet, pleasant, and in every respect healthy. To secure these points and avoid the evils which must inevitably result from a low and damp, or a bleak and unsheltered site, noisy and dirty thoroughfares, or the vicinity of places idle and dissipated resort, it will sometimes be necessary to select a location a little removed from the territorial center of the district. (Barnard 1854)

Barnard expresses the urge to isolate the school from the depravities of the larger society, a sentiment not uncommon among the early reformists, including Horace Mann and Jacob Riis, who struggled with the exponential influx of immigrants in the early nineteenth century and thought the "new" Americans were in need of a civilizing institution (Tyack 1974). In their minds, enclosed schools, separated from the ostensible vices of their immigrant community, served to order and discipline the masses.

School architects in contemporary Tucson, Arizona, designed the Desert View High School as an enclosure that enforces a disciplined internal focus. Designed with no windows, the Desert View High School was, paradoxically, built with no desert view, orchestrating instead an inward gaze (Wilkinson 1992). It also kept outsiders at a distance by designating a single entry to the school and forming this opening with reinforced steel set into solid concrete block. The defensive stance of the school enclosure is shored up architecturally, as Joseph Wilkinson explains, when "[t]he school, accessible by only a single gate, presents an impregnable face to the world." In this design the school formalizes an "educational regime," setting up a binary order of internal homogeneity and external differentiation (Foucault 1979).

In many schools, the "educational regime" elaborates and extends racial and ethnic subjugation. John Devine suggests in his book *Maximum Security* that underperforming New York City public schools are ostensibly correctional institutions for urban minority youth (Devine 1996). Cordoned off with chain-link fences and single-entry enclosures, and guarded by security personnel, the New York City schools are fortressed in his estimation to a degree only comparable to prisons. As has been well established in the literature on the "school-to-prison pipeline," minority students disproportionately experience prisonlike conditions at school and bear the brunt of criminalizing policies, such as zero tolerance (Brown 2003; Casella 2003; Simmons 2007; Skiba 2001). In *Discipline and Punish* Foucault links schools and prisons as disciplinary institutions, but an analysis of a racialized experience of discipline in these institutions is absent.

Following his discussion of enclosure, Foucault's next move is to illuminate the concept of partitioning, the disciplinary mechanism that furthers the powers of enclosure by working at the level of the individual body. Disciplinary partitioning resonates with that of enclosure because it operates on the spatial notion of controlled confinement. The difference is that enclosure confines the group, whereas partitioning confines the individual. Foucault writes: "Each individual has his own place; and each place its individual" (1979, 143). Foucault takes as his main example the monastic cell, where "space tends to be divided into as many sections as there are bodies or elements to be distributed." "Partitioning" separates individuals from each other, diminishing social ties and any power that could be developed in a collective. In their "elementary location[s]," individuals are more responsive to the disciplinary regime as subjects.

Randolph Bourne's description of the American classroom in 1915 dramatizes the historical role of disciplinary partitioning in schools:

> Here were these thirty children. . . . forced, in accordance with some principle of order, to sit at these stiff little desks, equidistantly apart, and prevented under penalty from communicating with each other. All the lines between them were to be broken. Each existed for the teacher alone. . . . These children were spending the sunniest hours of their whole lives, five days a week, in preparing themselves, I assume by the acquisition of knowledge, to take their places in a modern world of industry, ideas, and business. (Bourne 1977)

Bourne's description of the turn-of-the-century classroom, as alarmist as it may seem, is not anomalous. Other education theorists have similarly observed the correspondence of industrial mechanization and classroom systemization as it is expressed by individual partitioning, such as in the graded school, where students are "grouped by age and proficiency" (Bowles and Gintis 1976). These descriptions of the classroom respond to the position of the school in the context of newly emerging industrial relationships in the early part of the twentieth century. Modern industry modeled an adherence to the efficiency model originally championed for factories by Frederick Winslow Taylor, and schools were caught up in the fervor that surrounded this production method. The "cult of efficiency" exerted enormous pressure on "schools [to] be organized and operated in a more businesslike way" (Callahan 1962).

To demonstrate the design of efficient student participation, we might consider the tablet arm desk, which is widely used in school settings. This desk—a small writing surface that is bracketed, typically on the right side, to a molded plastic seat—is geared to serve students of average build who are right-handed. The design is restrictive, preventing the seated student from facing any direction but forward. In some classrooms these desks are bolted to the floor and thus cannot be rearranged. The form of the tablet arm desk figures the enforcement of spatial separation in the classroom. The desk designates a student's place on the floor and controls the student's angle of view. Sight and, therefore, communication is limited by the architecture of the desk itself and ultimately serves, by way of the disciplinary apparatus, to enforce the authority of the instructor.

The cubicle has a similar disciplinary effect. It organizes students in a cellular pattern with the goal of limiting distractions, advancing concentration, and maximizing space utilization. While students may find solitude in this kind of space and achieve a focus there that supports their intellectual endeavors (much like Foucault's example of the monastics who were encouraged by their confinement in religious cells), the design also dictates a single site for each individual and precludes interactions and organizations that could threaten the chain of command.

The spatial unit of the cubicle functions as a disciplinary mechanism in prisons, as Foucault indicates. He documents the carceral incarnation of the cubicle with a photograph of the prison at Fresnes (1979, 169–170). The image shows the prison auditorium and tall cubicles that are arranged on tiers facing a lecturer. Each cubicle holds one standing inmate who peers out a small forward-facing cubicle window to view the lecturer, who, as Foucault briefly annotates, is denouncing alcoholism. From the cubicle window, the inmates can see and hear the lecturer but likely little else. In this scenario, the disciplinary effect of partitioning is displayed in its most unmitigated form: "[E]ach individual has his own place; and each place its individual" (143).

The partitioning of individuals by way of separation and designated arrangement is a highly organized use of space that is officially dictated. By partitioning individuals, Foucault argues, authorities are addressing the necessity of efficient government to "establish presences and absences, to know where and how to locate individuals, to set up useful communications, to interrupt others, to be able at each moment to supervise the conduct of each individual, to assess it, to judge it, to calculate its qualities or merits. It [is] a procedure, therefore, aimed, at knowing, mastering and using" (143). In schools, teachers may rely on partitioning to designate student positions, supervise and assess participation, and direct attention, while fracturing lines of unwanted communication. The disciplinary effect of partitioning individual bodies could be furthered by the reorganization of space such that each space corresponds to a particular activity and each individual partitioned in that space has a clearly defined task. Foucault's analysis extends in this direction with a discussion of what he calls "functional sites."

Foucault's notion of "functional sites" translates in education to various prescriptions for architectural form and detailed spatial designations for students. In America the shift from the one-room schoolhouse begins the specialization of instructional spaces. As student populations grew in the urban centers along with immigration, learning spaces and activities were separated and systematized in an effort to accommodate them. Teachers began to specialize in certain aspects of the curriculum and were no longer required to be the "jack-of-all-trades" in a one-room schoolhouse of years past (Tyack 1974).

A new demand for functional spaces corresponded to this shift in teacher specialization. The architect John Philbrick designed "the egg crate school" in the mid-1800s with the idea of lending form to function. As the architect describes the school, "Every teacher had a separate classroom for the one grade she taught, each scholar his own desk. The scholars, he said, should be divided according to their tested proficiency, and 'all in the same class [should] attend precisely the same branches of study'" (quoted in Tyack 1974). This kind of specialization affected schools so quickly that one adult reminiscing about their school experiences in the nineteenth century reported that "by 1860 the schools of most of the cities and large towns were graded. By 1870 the pendulum had swung from no system to nothing but system" (Tyack 1974). School spaces that could largely be considered fungible in 1860 were significantly tipped toward functional use a decade later.

Callahan, writing in *Education and the Cult of Efficiency*, refers to an efficiency theorist who marvels at the new order of schools in the image of factories. As on the efficient production floor, a supervisor in the efficient school had a new authority by virtue of the redesigned educational spaces. The order was so great, he exclaims, that one could tell "almost at a glance whether pupils or rooms are making proper progress" (quoted in Callahan 1962). Callahan furthers this analysis of productive space by presenting the shift in relation to growing concerns regarding class tensions in a society expanding with industry and large-scale immigration. Between 1865 and 1900, as Callahan explains, over fourteen million immigrants came to the United States, and this mass immigration continued into the twentieth century. It was thought that to manage this new American population schools would need to operate with industrial precision. Callahan suggest that the immigrants, many of them poor, semiliterate in their native tongue, and non–English speaking, "constituted an educational problem unparalleled in human history" (Callahan 1962). Tyack indicates that teachers faced with this newly diverse student population established order in the classroom primarily by "keeping each child busy at a specific task every minute." As in the factory, these tasks demanded discipline from students who were otherwise perceived as dangerously out of control. With the rigid organization of individuals in space, the schools assimilated students to the American order of things—an order that depended on spatial and social hierarchizing.

Rank is the fourth and final technique of discipline elucidated in Foucault's exegesis. Foucault presents rank as a concept that is differentiated from the previous disciplinary techniques but also integrates them. Enclosure establishes homogeneity of groups in cellular spaces; partitioning delineates individual positions; and functional sites designate particular tasks to occupy individuals. Rank marks status and embeds the previously discussed spatial orders with a hierarchical logic (1979, 147). Unlike the other strategies outlined in Foucault's typology, rank is not solely expressed in material terms but depends on comparisons of individuals—made easier by enclosure, partitioning, and functional sites. While rank can have a real effect on the organization of individuals in space, as a disciplinary technique it expresses social meaning. In schools, rank is designated by levels of classroom instruction, the hierarchy of pupils within the classroom, and the status of pupil performance after any given test or exam. Foucault suggests that rank as a relative designation is potentially a category in flux. This dynamic underscores a motivation for competition, and students in this system are encouraged to jockey for higher position in the educational hierarchy. Also, rank serves as its own reward; those who achieve within rank establish their value within the given order.

In his discussion, Foucault refers to the use of ranking as a system that "guarantee[d] the obedience of individuals," and he turns to the writing of Jean-Baptiste de La Salle to relay its processes at work in school.

> In every class there will be places assigned for all the pupils of the lessons, so that all those attending the highest lessons will always occupy the same place. Pupils attending the highest lessons will be placed in the benches closest to the wall, followed by others according to the order of the lessons moving toward the middle of the classroom. . . . Each of the pupils will have his place assigned to him and none of them will leave it or change it except on the order or with the consent of the school inspector. (Quoted in Foucault 1979, 147)

As La Salle describes, rank enforces the partitioned spaces and functional sites that separate individuals and arranges those individuals by task. A ranking system may serve to assign students not only to a particular desk or a particular task, such as mathematics, but they also may be assigned to engage in a particular level of mathematical study at their individual desk. Further, as students are assigned to ever more specified tasks, the aberration of any one student is immediately observable by a supervisor, such as a teacher or instructional aide. Foucault writes that this makes "the educational space function like a learning machine, but also as a machine for supervising, hierarchizing, rewarding" (147).

Foucault alludes to this tightly controlled ranking system as a kind of mechanical production. While this is in keeping with the industrial context within which schooling emerged, the analogy of mechanization is disrupted when social dynamics and their possible role in these processes are considered. Foucault himself accepts that ranking may achieve more than an automatic and quantitative distinction of merit. It may also constitute a qualitative measure designating "a whole series of distinctions at once: according to the pupil's progress, worth, character, application, cleanliness and parents' fortune" (147).

Foucault returns again to the writings of La Salle, who uniquely attests to the social aspects of the ranking system: "Things must be so arranged that 'those whose parents are neglectful and verminous must be separated from those who are careful and clean; that the unruly and frivolous pupil should be placed between two who are well behaved and serious, a libertine either alone or between two pious pupils'" (quoted in Foucault 1979, 147). Even though Foucault offers this description of the ranking system, he stops short of a full-scale sociological analysis. Other authors, however, have examined the social and cultural factors that influence educational ranking systems more carefully.

Jeannie Oakes considers the use of a ranking system in schools with the practice of tracking and suggests that the phenomenon is informed by elements of socioeconomic reproduction. The practice of "tracking" students into "ability groups" is probably the clearest example of the ranking system as it operates in schools (Oakes 1985). School officials—sometimes teachers and sometimes administrators—sort students into class division based on their perceived potential. Students of similar "ability" are placed in the same classroom, spatially separated from students who are alternately designated. Frequently, students in the lower tracks who need remedial help are assigned to classrooms isolated from the rest of the students in the school (Ferguson 2000). Although Foucault presents rank as a fluid classification system, Oakes finds that rankings are influenced by students' entrenched social status and are, therefore, more fixed than not. She argues that "poor and minority kids end up more often in the bottom [academic] groups; middle- and upper-class whites more often at the top" (1985, 13). She hypothesizes that these ranking placements are "influenced by race and class—dress, speech patterns, ways of interacting with adults, and other behaviors," resulting in the disproportionate placement of marginal youth in marginal ranks and pointing to the socially reproductive mechanism of the ranking system itself (ibid.).

Oakes's study of tracking suggests that ranking is not similarly experienced by all individuals within modern society as Foucault would have us believe. It is worth mentioning again, however, that Foucault's concern is how discipline operates, not for whom it operates. I turn now to a consideration of this particular point. I have suggested that there is a limitation to Foucault's method, which yields this focus on *how* discipline operates. In the section that follows, I confront this limitation with a case study that clearly demonstrates the uneven experience of disciplinary power along the axis of race.

RACE AND DISCIPLINARY POWER

The great and unparalleled strength of Foucault's work is his examination of how mechanisms of power operate in disciplinary space. Ultimately, however, this strength is also a shortcoming. By focusing, with Neitzschean genealogical fervor, on the how of penality, the subject—the whom—is abandoned. Foucault speaks of docile bodies, but to whose docile bodies does he refer? If we know and control, who is it that is known and controlled? Similarly, power in Foucault's work is uniquely dislocated from its agent (Deleuze 1988). While the dislocation of power allows the latitude necessary for Foucault's particular methodological endeavor, the absence of a critical engagement with privilege problematizes the effort to apply Foucault.

Here, it may be helpful to distinguish between the conception of a capillary distribution of power relations and a capillary organization of power itself: it is the latter that is inconceivable. Foucault's egalitarian conception of capillary power relations elides a recognition of an arterial structure in which power is motivated along certain pathways that align with privilege. Foucault's effort was to map power as it extended through the entire social body, but if the unit of investigation is particular rather than general, and in this regard homogenous rather than heterogeneous, trajectories of privilege are likely to appear in relief. One could look at any American school and see Foucault's precepts at work in establishing disciplinary space. They are remarkably ordinary disciplinary techniques. In New Orleans, Louisiana, however, these techniques are made manifest in extraordinary ways to reveal, in stark geometries, the relationship between disciplinary strategy and the production of docile bodies and to highlight, quintessentially, the coordination of the prison and the school as disciplinary institutions.

In 2002, I began an eighteen-month interpretive case study of a public school set on the grounds of a prison compound in New Orleans. In many ways, the "prison school," as locals called it, was a striking manifestation of Foucault's disciplinary precepts. Notably, the youth sent to the "prison school" were not juvenile delinquents. They were public school students who had broken the zero-tolerance disciplinary code at their traditional public schools for committing minor infractions such as tardiness, absenteeism, and disrespectful behavior.

The "prison school" operated with strict principles of disciplinary enclosure. It was located in a twenty-square-block area of New Orleans referred to as the "sheriff's city within a city," a correctional space separate and distinct from the New Orleans known by tourists. The space of the school itself had formerly been used for prison inmates, and the vestiges of this past remained intact (as did an enormous mural of the Confederate flag, painted on the roof of the prison itself). A tall fence and gate surrounded the one-story school building. The windows, visible just above the fence, were fortified with thick bands of steel barring, and a set of surveillance cameras ran along the exterior walls. Students were taken into the school once in the early morning and released twelve hours later when the perimeter gate was unlocked. As one student explained, "The school is locked down. Can't get outside unless they open the door [pause, deep sigh]." Inside the building the surveillance network was extensive; every room, including the bathroom, which lacked privacy stalls, was under closed-circuit observation. The images captured by the closed-circuit cameras were fed to a bank of monitors that was manned by two or three deputies. Here, we might recall the critical import of the panopticon to Foucault's reading of discipline.

Students who were deemed to be disruptive while at the "prison school" were taken to what one student described as a "dark" and "black " room with "no lights" and "cages running around [it]." In an interview I asked the student to explain how the disciplinary trajectory might lead to this enclosure and isolation.

L: What would you have to do to be put in that room?
S: Like if you don't have no pencil or else if you are going to sleep, or else if you talk bad, like if you be fussing with one of the teachers, something like that.

In a generous interpretation, the youth enclosed in this space were experiencing a time-out, but because the space is a correctional one and the room is dark, surrounded by cages, monitored by uniformed and armed guards, and experienced by youth singularly, it seems more to suggest a partitioning that functions as a space of correctional solitary confinement. Both interpretations fold into Foucault's concepts of disciplinary enclosure and partitioning, but the second allows for an analysis of these within the dominating sphere of carceral power.

In the space of the classroom, the students were given what one youth informant called "little desks." The classroom teacher assigned remedial tasks to the students to be completed at these desks, and some of the lessons were designed to prepare students to take standardized tests. The lessons kept the students occupied, but the content was disconnected from the students' actual curricular needs. One student explained that the curriculum was "stuff I knew already." An outside consultant for the "prison school," who was a professor at a local university observed one of the math lessons, and remarked that the instruction being given to the students was inaccurate. Describing this incident, he said:

I don't have any blooming idea what [the teacher's] perception of the world was. One of them was teaching [how to find] the area of a rect-angle. . . . He said there is no trouble with this you just add [it] up. . . . This is a four by six by four by six. Four by six is half and four by six is half. It's twenty! And I am going, "I think we just set some people back a little bit." And if it had been one thing that was o.k., and [another consultant] would go in the evenings and say it was just a mistake. And we would say yeah, it sure was. But none of it.... It didn't get any better from there. (Author interview with informant September 16, 2003)

In this instance, the teacher had taught the students how to find the perimeter rather than the area of a four-by-six rectangle, which was the intended lesson. As the consultant suggests, this example of poor instruction was not anomalous but part of a pattern that raised concerns for him about the overall quality of the education the students were receiving. This example is stunning, not least for the misinformation transmitted from teacher to student but for the way in which it articulates the disciplinary rather than the pedagogical function of the site. One student explained, "We didn't really study like say: all we mostly done is go to school every day, making sure that we are on time every day, early in the morning." The space of the prison school contained the students and prevented the tardiness and absenteeism that had been their downfall in their traditional schools. The remedial tasks, which were assigned to keep them busy and diminish their capacity to resist the structure imposed on them, had no instructive content beyond discipline.

Significantly, the teacher at the "prison school" taught many lessons designed to prepare the students for the Louisiana Educational Assessment Program (LEAP) test, a standardized test administered to Louisiana middle school students. The LEAP test is intended to measure student mastery in major curricular content areas and rank students according to their skill. Although the students at the "prison school" were ostensibly assigned there because of disruptive behavior, all of them had correlated academic difficulties and remedial skills that arguably shaped their behavior in the first place. The "prison school" itself was thus a materialization of the students' remedial rank. Also, the school's administrators suggested to students that the ability to graduate was predicated on good behavior and advancement in rank, so students could garner a reward that would ultimately justify compliance and competition and thus fulfill the disciplinary goals of the program.

While Foucault's "Art of Distributions" helps explain how disciplinary power operates in the space of the "prison school," it does not help us understand the disparate experiences within disciplinary power structures. When the school opened in 2002, all the students assigned there were African American males, the youngest of whom was twelve. Because over 90 percent of New Orleans public school students in 2002 were African American, any program serving local public school students necessarily culled from a largely African American population. Even so, the matriculation of solely African American students at a disciplinary educational program must be understood as racialized. In what community with a 90 percent white student population would disruptive but noncriminal youth be sent to a public school at a prison?

We also see the gendered aspects of this specific disciplinary phenomenon and the way in which race and gender conflate as intersecting axes of oppression. The students at the "prison school" were keenly aware of how their status as minority males contributed to their matriculation in a disciplinary program. One student explained that his first school suspension was for kissing a girl on the playground, and although the girl was, in his estimation, an equal partner in the encounter, only he was penalized. Racialized and gendered power relations such as these are unattended to in Foucault's critique of discipline.

Foucault was fully aware of racial disparity, and in his first visit to Attica Prison in 1972—just three years before the French publication of *Discipline and Punish*—he noted the disproportionate number of incarcerated black men with some dismay (Davis 1998). "In the United States," he comments, "there must be one out of 30 or 40 black men in prison: it is here that one can see the function of massive elimination in the American prison" (quoted in Davis 1998). As Angela Davis points out, if Foucault could have returned to a United States prison in the later part of the century, the racial disparities would have been even more pronounced. By 1999, studies show that more than one in five black men had been to prison by the time they reached their early thirties (Western et al. 2002). Consequently, it is increasingly important to tie the awareness of racialized and gendered power structures to analyses of discipline and power.

CONCLUSION

Foucault's omission of a racialized dynamic in *Discipline and Punish* is, perhaps, somewhat curious. His critics have indicated that this failure to recognize social difference and related experiential differences stems from his presentation of a neutral and dislocated power. This neutrality benefits Foucault's notion that power penetrates the social body through capillary extension. A capillary structure presents the image of equivalents and not the image of disparity. It also presents a nonevaluative stance on power relations: modern power is neither good nor bad but simply is. Fraser finds Foucault's claim to neutrality specious and notes that his language of "domination," "subjugation," and "subjection," which is used throughout *Discipline and Punish,* is ominously inflected and suggestive of judgment (Fraser 1989). Also, if we are to take Foucault at his word and accept his nonevaluative stance, his construction offers little hope for agency, since a motivated resistance to power would require, first, a critique of power. Best and Kellner (1991) suggest, however, that despite Foucault's failure to outline the space for resistance within his study of power, he does discover a new terrain in which considerations of power can be examined. In other words, Foucault provides the tools for investigating the complex arrangement of power in a nuanced way, and though his own study of power does not balance the study of domination with a study of resistance, it does lay the ground for that work. In this vein, Foucault's scholarship remains significant for a consideration of modern power and its operation.

My aim has been to map the landscape of spatialized power in education. Distribution is but one vector of educational power relations, but these geometries undergird the multiple layers of power formation that are productive of docile bodies. In turning to this dimension of Foucault's analysis I also intend to point to surveillance capacities that are embedded in architectural and organization schema and that further enable the operation of surveillance technologies. In other words, advanced technologies of surveillance in education build upon a foundation of supervision and social control that is established in more primary techniques of student assignation.

My effort to put Foucault's disciplinary analyses to work in revealing this context ultimately yields a series of questions about how to understand these operations as having a capillary distribution and neutral aspect when we narrow our perspective to any one site, such as the "prison school." With these parameters, an arterial power structure emerges in which power is differentially distributed and discipline is differentially experienced. The racialized and gendered relations extant at the "prison school" are testament to this. It is necessary, then, to build on Foucault's analysis of disciplinary power by both examining the dimensions of discipline and critiquing oppressive power relations. I turn away from a genealogy and toward situated analyses of power relations to advance this effort. I have proceeded with a Foucauldian reading of schooling for its potential to shed light on the workings of power within space, but I have taken up a sociological reading of Foucault that concentrates on racialized discipline. The case of the "prison school" speaks to both the need for an analysis that understands schools in the context of carceral structures of discipline and punishment and the need to rethink these structures in terms of their pointed effect on the individual body, marked by race and gender.

REFERENCES

Barnard, Henry. 1854. *School architecture.* New York: C. B. Norton.

Best, Steven, and Douglas Kellner. 1991. *Postmodern theory: Critical interrogations.* New York: Guilford Press.

Bourne, Randolph. 1977. *The radical will.* New York: Urizen Books.

Bowles, Samuel, and Gintis, Herbert. 1976. *Schooling in capitalist America.* New York: Basic Books.

Brown, Enora. 2003. Freedom for some, discipline for others. In *Education as enforcement: The militarization and corporatization of schools,* ed. Kenneth Saltman and David Gabbard, 127–152. New York: RoutledgeFalmer Press.

Callahan, Raymond. E. 1962. *Education and the cult of efficiency: A study of the social forces that have shaped the administration of the public schools.* Chicago: University of Chicago Press.

Casella, Ronnie. 2003. Punishing dangerousness through preventive detention: Illustrating the institutional link between school and prison. *New Directions for Youth Development: Deconstructing the School-to Prison Pipeline* 99 (Fall): 55–70.

Davis, Angela. 1998. Racialized punishment and prison abolition. In *The Angela Y. Davis reader*, ed. Joy James, 96–107. Malden, MA: Blackwell Publishers.

Deleuze, Gilles. 1988. *Foucault*. Minneapolis: University of Minnesota Press.

Devine, John. 1996. *Maximum security: The culture of violence in inner-city schools*. Chicago: University of Chicago Press.

Ferguson, Anne. 2000. *Bad boys: Public schools in the making of black masculinity*. Ann Arbor: University of Michigan Press.

Foucault, Michel. 1979. *Discipline and punish: The birth of the prison*. Trans. Alan Sheridan. New York: Vintage Books.

Fraser, Nancy. 1989. *Unruly practices: Power, discourse and gender in contemporary theory*. Minneapolis: University of Minnesota Press.

Noguera, Pedro. 1995. Preventing and producing violence: A critical analysis of responses to school violence. *Harvard Educational Review* 65, no. 2 (Summer): 189–213.

Oakes, Jeannie. 1985. *Keeping track*. New Haven, CT: Yale University Press.

Simmons, Lizbet. 2007. Research off limits and underground: Street corner methods for finding invisible students. *Urban Review* 39 (3): 319–347.

Skiba, Russell. 2001. When is disproportionality discrimination? In *Zero tolerance: Resisting the drive for punishment in our schools*, ed. William Ayers, Bernardine Dohrn, and Rick Ayers, 176–187. New York: New Press.

Tyack, David. 1974. *The one best system: A history of American urban education*. Cambridge, MA: Harvard University Press.

Western, Bruce, Becky Petit, and Josh Guetzkow. 2002. Black economic progress in the era of mass imprisonment. In *Invisible punishment: The collateral consequences of mass imprisonment*, ed. Marc Mauer and Meda Chesney-Lind, 165–180. New York: New Press.

Wilkinson, Joseph. F. 1992. Designing against malice. *Architectural Record* 180 (11): 111.

PART TWO

Schools as Markets

Selling Security, Buying Students

CHAPTER 4

Safety or Social Control?

THE SECURITY FORTIFICATION
OF SCHOOLS IN A CAPITALIST SOCIETY

Ronnie Casella

IMAGINE YOU ARE A YOUNG PERSON entering a school. This
may be the series of events that unfolds: even before entering, you may
be recorded by surveillance cameras that have the ability to zoom in and
archive the footage that is taken; you may be required to scan an ID card
that retrieves information about you and is able to track your whereabouts
through a radio-frequency identification (RFID) system; you may pass through
an upright metal detector; or have your body scanned, perhaps your face, iris,
or palm, by a device that checks your biometric reading against a database
of collected readings. Now that you have entered school, you may continue
to be on surveillance cameras during the day and have your movements
monitored through the RFID chip in your ID card. And even after you leave
for the day, you may still be tracked and on surveillance cameras on the bus
that takes you home.

It has become quite clear that the use of security equipment in schools
is becoming more prevalent in the United States and other countries (Smith
2003).[1] In the United States, this shift is partly a response to incidents of
horrific school shootings as well as threats of terrorism, especially when
schools were identified as potential terrorist sites following the 2001 attacks on
New York City and Washington, DC. This made schools eligible for "homeland
security" grants to purchase security equipment and to coordinate with police
departments.[2]

The trend to outfit schools with security equipment is also a way of
controlling youths and, increasingly, teachers and parents (Devine 1996;
McCormick 2004). It is an example of how technology and telecommuni-
cations development in the 1990s aided the success of businesses involved

in surveillance, detection, identification, and database technologies. Judicial rulings also paved the way for security fortification by establishing the legal use of random surveillance in public places such as schools (Stefkovich 2002; Sher 1996). Add into the mix governments throughout the world, especially in the United States and England, that pump extraordinary amounts of money into security equipment development at research labs such as School Security Technology and Resource Center at Sandia National Laboratories in the United States, and we see that security fortification is also the result of governments that have bankrolled the creation of the equipment (Casella 2006; Parenti 2003; Green 1999). Federal-agency financial support that goes directly to schools, including the Matching Grant Program for School Security (which provides matching grants to schools that purchase security equipment), has made it possible for school administrators and school board members even in poor districts to purchase equipment (see H.R. 2685). Corporations that offer perks, incentives, and pro bono installation work have had the same effect.

While there is much promoting of school fortification, this chapter examines one aspect of this fortification process: the selling of security equipment to schools.[3] The fortification of schools is primarily a business response to safety. Safety has become a commodity that is sold by security professionals whose purpose, after all, is to make money and to create profit for the security companies for which they work. While we may hear that security equipment is used in order to create a "safe environment" or, on the other hand, for "social control," these claims miss a significant aspect of school fortification: that the installation of security equipment in schools is foremost a corporate transaction led not by people who can guarantee us safety, and not by tyrants imposing social control, but rather by business people who convince us that products they have for sale will give us peace of mind.

The popularity of security devices marks a new era in school safety. To some extent school administrators have given up on violence prevention and conflict resolution programs. By the first decade of the twenty-first century it was clear that newer efforts involving school safety would focus on using security equipment. Certainly, school shootings and terrorism spurred this movement, but the school security market has been developing since the 1970s, especially in urban school districts where youths of color have long been policed and monitored. However, the public school system, especially when we take into account rural and suburban schools, is a relatively new market. It is also a lucrative one. Imagine the opportunity to outfit all public (and perhaps private) schools in the country with security equipment that can cost several hundred thousands of dollars for initial setup and more with ongoing upgrades and service. Include in this mix day-care centers and colleges and universities, and for international companies, schools in countries around the globe.

The fortification of schools is in large part the result of the expanding international market for security equipment in public places and, more specifically, the targeting of the public school sector by security businesses. School administrators enter into deals with vendors and take away a product designed to provide safety but geared to making customers want to buy more and better technologies as newer devices come out. This keeps the security industry flush and contributes to a kind of consumer security: people are expected to invest in their own safety and companies are expected to provide for this social need. What we are talking about here does not involve safety, and it is not really about social control; it is about private enterprise, the opening up of the public school market to businesses, and the success that security vendors have had in penetrating this market.

SECURITY TECHNOLOGY
AND THE WIDENING-EFFECT

The two popular discourses—"security as safety" and "security as control"—do not really offer adequate explanations for why we see a surge in the use of security devices in schools. To some extent, security professionals use these discourses to sell equipment; they wish customers to know that the equipment will make them safer and that it can be used to control people and their behaviors. But their use of these discourses is always tempered, especially as they attempt to tap into the sector of white, middle-class schools. Because their motivation is profit, security professionals attempt to increase the numbers of individuals using the equipment. But in order to do this, greater numbers of people have to agree to have the equipment used on them. If security equipment were advertised and sold to schools only for its potential to control individuals, many critical people would be wary. So security professionals shy away from discussions of how the equipment can be used to control populations or how it can be used *on* people or *against* people.

They also, ironically, shy away from the idea that security makes us safer. Security dealers can not sell safety, they can only sell equipment. They may be able to guarantee that a surveillance camera can zoom in on a person's face from a mile away, but they cannot guarantee that this will make a place any safer. Also, security people want people who already feel safe to buy the equipment. As one vendor for Extreme CCTV explained, "You don't buy the equipment just to feel safe, you buy it because you know this is the way of the future."

What security professionals offer is cutting-edge technology that we are expected to assume will make us safer. In order to appeal to mostly middle- and upper-class individuals—this relatively new market of school officials and professionals—they also offer a lifestyle image that is meant to demonstrate the professionalism of the individual or institution using the equipment.

Security professionals convince consumers that security equipment is a sign
of being up-to-date, professional, and even high status.

In advertisements for school security equipment we do not learn much
about the safety of equipment or about its capabilities to control people;
instead, we learn what it means to be part of a successful, middle-class life,
which naturally includes the use of security technologies. Fargo is a security
company that markets to schools, and its advertisement for its school ID
system is typical. There is no indication that the cards will make students safer;
and certainly no mention that the cards can be used to control individuals.
We see, instead, a cherub-faced boy, with props (soccer ball, lunch, books)
indicating that he is the ideal student. He seems only too happy to have an
image of his face affixed to a student ID. The clever layout design also conveys
the naturalness of having an ID card, for the boy seems to mesh easily with
the card to the point where the boy and the card are one. The advertisement
makes ID-ing seem appealing not just for people who use it but also for
people who have it used on them; we see, for example, that ID-ing is not just
for villains, but even for our best-looking middle-class white youths. This is
how security businesses expand their market, ultimately broadening the use
of the equipment to include suburban, white, and upper-class schools, and,
ultimately, even the adults in those schools—not by forcing it on them, but
by making it so appealing that people welcome the equipment.

In another advertisement for the Fargo school ID system, we are given an
image of an entirely different person: an adult superintendent who is African
American. The advertisement conveys to potential buyers that the ID card
system is not just for kids, but for everybody in the school system, including
the superintendent. But although an entirely different person is portrayed,
there are similarities between the two advertisements. The model playing
the part of the "superintendent" is cherub-faced (like the boy) and the ideal
professional with his props: leather brief case, dark suit, crisp white shirt,
and tie; he also wears a wedding band, letting us know he is a family man.
The purposeful use of an African American model may be Fargo's attempt
to market to urban school districts. But whether urban or suburban, using a
black model or a white one, Fargo attempts in both these ads to increase sales
by appealing to middle-class professionals with models that look good and
present to us images of success, of wholesomeness, and of upward mobility.
The two advertisements also demonstrate how the security industry urges
youths and adults alike to buy into the security fortification of schools. The
superintendent advertisement makes not-so-subtle reference to this as well
in the question prominently placed at the top of the page: "How far do you
need your photo ID system to go?" It also makes reference to this in its sales
statement at the bottom of the page, stating:

No matter how far you need your ID system to go, your budget goes farther with FARGO. From simple photo ID badges to complete, one-card solutions, FARGO photo ID systems help your schools run more securely and cost-effectively. Our reliable, easy-to-use card printers integrate with virtually any photo ID software to produce the industry's most durable cards in seconds. And, with our add-on encoding and lamination modules, you can rest easy knowing your FARGO photo ID system is ready to go farther when you are. (Fargo 2003, 15)

We can expect that teachers, superintendents—all adults—will gladly "go farther." One vendor for TempBadge told me, "In the old days we would get a school—usually a university—to start with student ID-ing, then up it a notch to workers and teachers. Now, we just go in for the whole unit [sell a package that involves both youth and adult ID-ing]." But in addition to expanding the use of the equipment, when the advertisement asks, "How far do you need your photo ID system to go?" it is also referring to the extent of the technology. The "add-on encoding and lamination modules" mentioned in the Fargo advertisement, for example, will make it possible to hook up card scanners to databases that will record information about individuals and can be used to track their whereabouts.

The use of security equipment is expanding to include suburban and rural as well as urban districts and, perhaps most significantly, adults and youths alike. Consider, for example, public schools in Albuquerque, New Mexico, where school officials have implemented security systems that use hand scanners to identify parents and guardians of children (Kennedy 2001). In Philadelphia, similar technology is used on teachers, where several hundred finger scanners (rather than palm scanners) were installed in 2003. In schools in Plumsted Township, New Jersey, a similar system, called T-PASS (Teacher Parent Authorization Security System), is used by teachers and by parents to gain access to schools, and in the case of parents, to leave with their children (Uchida et al. 2004).

It is logical that parents would accept the requirement that they have special ID cards and submit to finger scanning to enter their children's schools. Most adults already carry some form of ID and are used to it being requested, and as school officials in Philadelphia stated, finger scanners are only (presumably) an updated form of the punch-in/punch-out machines that many people already use. But these assumptions neglect to recognize how the equipment has advanced: finger scanners are much more high-tech than punch-in/punch-out machines, and new ID cards are quite different from everyday "identification" cards. New cards use technology developed by scientists who worked on President Ronald Reagan's Star Wars program, using global positioning systems so that authorities can track the bearers of the ID cards, get continuous information, and even know how fast individuals are traveling (Monmonier 2002). The Spring Independent School District in Texas, for example, equipped 28,000 ID cards with built-in tracking devices based on radio frequency identification. RFID uses a computer chip that contains a micro-antenna that transmits information to the school district main office and local police department. When students board and exit school buses they must scan their cards, and in school and police centers an icon appears on a map showing the position of the cardholder (Richtel 2004). The technology is not new—a version of it has been used by companies to track livestock and inventory, and it is similar to the systems used to keep tabs on truckers (Parenti 2003). But the Spring Independent School District is one of the first to use it on children. It was first introduced in an elementary school and promoted as a way of keeping track of little children who could get lost or kidnapped. Other schools are also using the technology. In 2004 a school in Phoenix started using ID cards with a biometric scanning device to keep track of students getting on and off buses. In 2003 a school in Buffalo, New York, started keeping track of attendance with microchip-equipped ID cards. When students entered the school, they passed a scanner that registered their attendance in a main database (Richtel 2004).

School surveillance cameras have also been used to document adults, and what we see with IDs (the naturalness with which adults agree to be on the receiving end of them) we also see, for example, with cameras in school classrooms and on school buses. Beginning in 2001, all classrooms in the Biloxi, Mississippi, school system were equipped with surveillance cameras, which school officials claimed would help deter violence and vandalism and raise test scores, becoming a kind of built pedagogy of the school, integral to maintenance as well as teaching and learning (Dillon 2003; Monahan 2005). The cameras were installed to watch over students, but they also record teachers. School bus surveillance cameras, installed in Pennsylvania, Connecticut, Texas, California, and other states, operate in a similar fashion. Once used mostly to deter vandalism and usually mounted in school bus depots, with the advent of wireless networks in the 1980s surveillance cameras were moved inside buses in order to oversee students, and more recent systems also include cameras focused on bus drivers.

In an advertisement for Honeywell's Digital Chaperone surveillance system, reference is made to the fact that bus surveillance cameras are meant to oversee not just the students but also the drivers ("Securing the Bus Ride" 2003). In the advertisement, we see a close-up of a pretty blonde girl, about seven years old, presumably waving good-bye to a parent through the window of a school bus. The advertisement tells us: "Get the coverage you require to monitor the security of your passengers, drivers, and buses with the new Digital Chaperone DDR system by Honeywell Video Systems." Again, we see reoccurring messages: the cherub-faced white child—another image of successful middle-class living and wholesomeness—and the use of the equipment on adults (bus drivers) so that we are urged once again to understand that the equipment is for everybody. As one vendor for Honeywell told me, "We all know the bus driver has to keep his eyes on the road, and he can't be doing that if he's watching out for kids in the back who may be up to no good or destroying property." But he also added:

> And there is also nothing wrong with having an extra set of eyes on the bus driver. This also protects him from litigation, for we will have archival footage in the event that there is an investigation into some episode or tragedy. But it also lets parents and everybody else involved know that the bus driver is doing his job, that he is on the job, and we can even call this information up on our own computers and tune in to the cameras. . . . Because the images are digital, more can be stored with less space, so we can add more cameras, even to the outside of the school bus if we wanted, let's say, bus stop images—we could have detailed digitalized archives of who is picking up kids, who is at bus stops, whatever you want. This is what the Chaperone offers to our customers.

The name "chaperone" itself is meant to comfort people who feel that it is only logical—a matter of being a good parent—that we would "chaperone" our children with such devices. But the name of the Honeywell system betrays the sophistication of the device; what we are expected to purchase is more than your everyday friendly chaperone. The Digital Chaperone DDR system uses GPS for wireless networking and real-time monitoring, can include up to four cameras per bus, and can be hooked up to an alarm system that can turn on the cameras for recording when the buses are not in service.

Security professionals work hard to increase their market, and they know that in order to do this in a capitalist, democratic society, they must make the products appealing to consumers. Security equipment has become ubiquitous in the United States in the same way other technologies have: through people's sheer will to buy the products and make them a part of their lives. Fortification occurs not only because humans want to be safer and so authorities can spy—although these are part of it; it occurs because customers such as school officials and parents have been convinced that security equipment is an invaluable part of creating a successful school. Using security equipment and having it used on you is a sign of being forward-thinking and modern. The more high-tech the equipment, the more prestige one is liable to get—it represents being cutting-edge, and makes individuals such as school officials and institutions such as schools more competitive and appealing in a world where technology (including security technology) is a sign of advancement.

That techno-security equipment in schools is increasingly used on adults is something that could be thought about as a widening effect. Most of the technology used in school security equipment was first developed for military purposes—this is true of lasers, micro- and nanotechnology, digitalization, computers, the Internet, and so on (Fay 1993; Petersen 2000). In the 1980s, as the technology revolution helped popularize the devices, they were adopted by other organizations besides the military, including federal agencies (social services) and urban police departments, and finally by homeowners, by city council members gentrifying downtown districts, by library administrators, and naturally by school officials (Nunn 2001; Scarbrough and Corbett 1992; Staples 1997). As the equipment gets used in more public contexts and across more institutions, increasing numbers of people end up using it and having it used on them. Even within institutions, the use of the devices is likely to expand: the ID card system originally developed for students will often be expanded to include teachers; several security cameras installed to oversee a particularly dark outside portion of a school (the far corner of a parking lot, for example) will eventually be upgraded to include more cameras in more areas of the school.

By the early twenty-first century, security equipment had become integrated with other building management systems and had therefore become a common and integral component of buildings. Surveillance cameras, for example, can be coordinated with automatic locks, and facility management systems in schools that control lights, the thermostat, and other utilities can also control detection devices. Increasingly, security is becoming integral to architecture and the daily business of running a facility or living one's life; it is becoming a life accessory and a professional tool for people looking to get ahead. Security devices in schools will one day be totally integrated with office, social service, and police databases, lighting, bookkeeping, ID-ing, scheduling, and will be part of parking lots, hallways, classrooms, and the engineering of the buildings. Those who fear that schools will become like military states have a valid case, but they sometimes forget how stylish security devices can be, and with greater technological advancements comes the potential for equipment to be even more appealing and less intrusive. With more advanced lasers, for example, we can take readings without people even knowing it. We can jack up the "flow" of metal detectors. A nice-looking ID card will act as a tracking and bookkeeping device and make taking attendance easier. There are no backroom interrogations here, just people going about their day. Schools will exude "security," but they will do so in a clean and quaint way. Companies are quite capable of making surveillance cameras for schools the size of a pencil eraser so that nobody would see them. Why do we still see cameras? Partly to deter violence, but also because they look good. Additionally, covert cameras may seem too totalitarian; better to have people see the cameras and like what they see.

When the Fargo advertisement asks "How far do you need your photo ID system to go?" we should take its wording seriously. The issue is not how far do we let others go; rather, how far do *we* go? You want that nice house in the suburbs or that fancy apartment in the trendy neighborhood—it has a built-in surveillance system which you end up paying for with your mortgage or rent or co-op fees. You want that cell phone? It comes with a GPS system that can be used to locate its bearer so worried parents can keep tabs on their kids—a technology initially developed so soldiers could home in on a cell phone–carrying enemy, sometimes for a missile strike. You want to attend a nice public school? You will find it well secured, with security equipment networked into the management system of the entire school—your tax dollars at work. Of course, there are times when security is put in place against our will or without us knowing about it, but the idea that some authoritarian organization above us is setting up the equipment to keep down little people is a single-dimensional way of looking at security fortification. In some ways, security businesses must love the Big Brother story. What better way to divert attention. While the critics are clamoring about government oppression and a surveillance society gone awry, businesspeople are trotting out their wares for thousands of willing customers.

The Security Commodity

Safety has become a commodity. Items such as metal detectors and surveillance cameras are sold not so much for their protective qualities, and not just for their abilities to control populations, but for the fact that they appeal to people and give them the boost of self-confidence that we associate with ownership of advanced equipment. Middle- and upper-class people invest in security, and in doing so they follow in the footsteps of other free market agents in capitalist societies who use their buying power to acquire the newest accessories necessary to attain and give the impression of attaining a higher level of social and economic well-being. As with all commodities, security equipment is presumed to meet a basic need, but in order to be appealing security equipment must be invested with meanings that offer more than simple utility (Barthes 1972; Spitzer 1987). It is not enough that a surveillance camera record images in the dark or zoom in to record a car license number from a mile away. It also has to look good, give us a sense of power, and be a symbol of upward mobility. This is how security equipment becomes prevalent in our schools: through the concerted efforts of businesspeople to give security technology an aura that makes it appealing to those who already buy technology for economic and social advancement. Along with this, government funding, the stoking of fears, and the affordability of the newer equipment also boost business and promote the security equipment—yet none of this has anything to do with being safe.

In security equipment advertisements, we see the secret to getting a school fortified: creating an image that associates security equipment with success and contentedness, equipment that is owned by good-looking, wholesome, and successful professionals. Security professionals attempt to convince individuals that they must invest in their own security, and in time they make it an expectation that any person of social and economic worth would welcome security equipment—not only would they accept it, they would pay for it. For security businesses consulting with school officials (as well as with real estate developers, architects, urban renewal authorities, and homeowners), fortification is a way of selling a commodity to individuals with certain lifestyle expectations, who use the equipment to feel good about their status in life. School officials buy the equipment to get recognition from the community and to create an environment that is inevitably described by school officials and security professional alike as "advanced," "cutting-edge," and "high-tech," but rarely "safer." Security professionals know that they do not have to convince buyers that the equipment will make their buildings safer; they have to present images that convey to individuals that they and/or the fortified buildings will have greater worth and appeal when the equipment is utilized.

If we were to ask people why security equipment has become so prevalent in the United States, we would be likely to hear the popular discourses: by the proponents, because the equipment makes us safer, and by the critics, because the equipment is foisted on us by authorities to control and spy. As mentioned earlier in this chapter, there is some truth in both of these assertions. But they miss a crucial point. What about the people who invest in the equipment and welcome it in their kids' schools, and even seek out circumstances (going to well-secured malls, living in gated communities) where they know they will be on the receiving end of security? Most of these people are already safe. Whereas metal detectors were first used in urban schools in the 1970s, by the early twenty-first century, suburban and middle- to upper-class schools were often the first to use the most sophisticated and costly equipment, such as the T-PASS iris-scanning system used in the schools of New Jersey's Plumsted Township; the schools are 95 percent white and the township's median household income ($61,357) is higher than the median income in both New Jersey ($55,146) and in the United States ($41,994) (Uchida et al. 2004). Increasingly, security equipment is becoming another accruement that upwardly mobile people—family men, professionals, working women—use to distinguish themselves. In their children's schools, it is a sign of being advanced and modern.

If businesspeople were just selling safety, they would not be able to sell to people who are already rather safe; and if they were to focus on social control, they would not be able to broaden their market to include those people who are wary of such intentions. People have bought into security and have justified it not only on the basis of needs (we buy it because we need to protect ourselves), but also on the basis of free will and choice (we buy it because we have the choice to do so). Individuals look for safety in the same way that they look for a new style, prestige, and love—through their buying power. When people fret about a world overrun by security they envision a police state, robots that track our movements, cameras that watch everything we do, and computers that contain all information about us. But if this has happened—and to some extent it has—what has also happened is that individuals have accepted the terms of security businesses even while fretting about a world overrun with their stuff.

Security businesses have been successful tapping into urban, suburban, and rural public school sectors. To do this, they have had to redefine the equipment that they sell; rather than getting clunky mechanisms of war, we are getting cutting-edge technology and clearly articulated messages telling us that it is only natural that we would use such equipment. This is the engine for fortification when the private sector is involved; it is not imposed as much as sold. The equipment's use expands across institutions (from the military to police departments to schools, for example) and expands within institutions (from students to teachers to parents, and so on) as more people are persuaded that the equipment is essential to their lives and to the workings of buildings and organizations. This is the business dream come true: imagine that equipment once used only by the military is now becoming an essential element of even safe, middle-class schools. Sales representatives do not even have to demonstrate that a school is dangerous, or that the equipment will make the school safer even if it were dangerous; all they have to do is make the equipment look good and market it as you would any other piece of technology—by appealing to people's sense of self-worth and their yearnings for power, prestige, and thrills.

School fortification occurs because it benefits business and because school officials have been convinced that the purchasing of equipment will make the school a more desirable and efficient place. Additionally, schools have become more receptive to vendors in general, so to some extent techno-security equipment is nothing more than another item in a long line of items that businesspeople sell to schools. For the security industry, it is fortuitous that in the last two decades of the twentieth century public schools became more receptive to private enterprise at the same time that security businesses began moving into the public school market. We see the inroads that private companies have already made in schools not only in security, but in food, textbook, curricula, and other services, as well as in many voucher programs, in school "takeovers" by businesses, and in the development of some charter schools (Molnar 1996 and 2005). Many writers have discussed the privatization of education, and my point is not to recap this material but rather to point out that school security is also a part of this. The U.S. public school system is one of the last frontiers in the free market march for privatization, something the security industry knows well.

Schools are an example of how institutions are likely to fortify in technology-based capitalist countries. Security will become integral to the boosting of a place in an open marketplace; it will be used to "sell" a school—or neighborhood, or house, or mall, or community, for that matter. Advanced security equipment brings schools into the twenty-first century not only technologically but also ideologically. We hear the same old free market story: for various reasons public officials cannot provide safety, or the safety they provide is inferior to what the private sector can provide, so the private sector must step in and pick up the slack. And security business-people step in with gusto—since the 1990s, hundreds of security businesses focusing on schools have formed, and already-established businesses have created their own school security divisions. Salespeople who once sold only to prison officials and facility managers of government buildings, warehouses, and office buildings are now in touch with school facility managers. They work to convince each and every person investing in security that we must solve our own problems, that professionals in the private sector (our own "security consultants"), and not our public sector—not our police or fellow citizens—are the ones who can protect us. This is really about private enterprise and the workings of capitalist societies that inevitably turn social needs, such as safety, into commodities sold to people with the resources to afford them. Once we recognize this, we have a better grasp of what is promoting the security fortification of schools, and, therefore, what we should or should not do about it. It is almost beside the point to argue about the benefits/disadvantages of the equipment in relation to safety; no doubt the equipment can make us safer sometimes. It can also be ineffective, have unintended consequences, or be oppressive. It is also beside the point to talk about social control when it is people with budgets behind them—and often the will of taxpayers—who are paying the bill for the fortification of schools to watch over their own children. Rather than argue about safety and social control, what we need to determine is whether we want businesses to provide for all our needs. It should make us wary not that Big Brother is watching us, but that our safety comes with a price tag.

NOTES

1. See also New York Civil Liberties Union and American Civil Liberties Union (2007) and National Center for Education Statistics (1997 and 1999–2000).
2. See "Homeland Security Grants and Funding FY03" May 28, 2003, www.grant-writing.com/hsu2.html; also H.R. 2685, Reauthorization of Matching Grant Program for School Security, October 7, 2003.
3. The research was based on the analysis of advertisements from seventy-five security businesses that market to schools and interviews with security professionals. For details on the research procedures and methodology see Casella 2006.

REFERENCES

Barthes, Roland. 1972. *Mythologies.* New York: Farrar, Straus, and Giroux.

Casella, Ronnie. 2006. *Selling us the fortress: The promotion of techno-security equipment for schools.* New York and London: RoutledgeFalmer.

Devine, J. 1996. *Maximum security: The culture of violence in inner-city schools.* Chicago: University of Chicago Press.

Dillon, Sam. 2003. Cameras monitoring students, especially in Biloxi. *New York Times.* September 24. www.nytimes.com/2003/09/24/education.

Fargo. 2003. Fargo Card Personalization Systems advertisement. *American School & University* 76 (February): 15.

Fay, John. 1993. *Encyclopedia of security management: Techniques and technology.* Boston: Butterworth-Heinemann.

Green, Mary. 1999. *the appropriate and effective use of security technologies in U.S. schools: A guide for schools and law enforcement agencies.* National Institute of Justice and Sandia National Laboratories. Washington, DC: U.S. Department of Justice.

H.R. 2685. 2003. Reauthorization of matching grant program for school security. October 7.

Kennedy, Mike. 2001. Security: Making contact. *American School & University* 74 (February): 1–3.

McCormick, J. 2004. *Writing in the asylum: Student poets in New York City schools.* New York: Teachers College Press.

Molnar, Alex. 1996. *Giving kids the business: The commercialization of America's schools.* Boulder, CO: Westview.

———. 2005. *School commercialism: From democratic ideal to market commodity.* New York and London: RoutledgeFalmer.

Monahan, Torin. 2005. *Globalization, technological change, and public education.* New York: RoutledgeFalmer.

Monmonier, Mark. 2002. *Spying with maps: Surveillance technologies and the future of privacy.* Chicago: University of Chicago Press.

National Center for Education Statistics. 1997. U.S. Department of Education, Fast Response Survey System (FRSS), Principal/school disciplinary survey on school violence, FRSS Form no. 63. Washington, DC: U.S. Department of Education.

National Center for Education Statistics. 1999–2000. U.S. Department of Education, Public and public charter school surveys, Schools and Staffing Survey (SASS) (Washington, DC: U.S. Department of Education.

New York Civil Liberties Union and American Civil Liberties Union. 2007. *Criminalizing the classroom: The over-policing of New York City schools.* New York: New York Civil Liberties Union and American Civil Liberties Union.

Nunn, Samuel. 2001. Police technology in cities: Changes and challenges. *Technology in Society* 23:11–27.

Parenti, Christian. 2003. *The soft cage: Surveillance in America from slavery to the war on terror.* New York: Basic Books.

Petersen, Julie K. 2000. *Understanding surveillance technologies: Spy devices, their origins & applications,* ed. Saba Zamir. New York: CRC Press.

Richtel, Matt. 2004. A student ID that can also take roll. *New York Times.* November 17, A24.

Scarbrough, Harry, and J. Martin Corbett. 1992. *Technology and organization: Power, meaning, and design.* London and New York: Routledge.

Securing the bus ride: Digital recording systems save money and improve security. 2003. School security supplement, *American School & University* 76 (September): SS16.

Sher, Scott. 1996. Continuous video surveillance and its legal consequences. Public Law Research Institute, Working Papers Series, University of California Hastings College of the Law San Francisco.

Smith, Peter. 2003. *Violence in Schools: The response in Europe.* London and New York: RoutledgeFalmer.

Spitzer, Steven. 1987. Security and control in capitalist societies: The fetishism of security and the secret thereof. In *Transcarceration: Essays in the sociology of social control,* ed. J. Lowman, R. Menzies, and T. Palys. Brookfield, VT: Gower Publishing.

Staples, Williams. 1997. *The culture of surveillance: Discipline and social control in the United States.* New York: St. Martin's Press.

Stefkovich, Jacqueline 2002. Search and seizure of students in public schools: 2002 update of Fourth Amendment cases." In *Balancing rights: Education law in a brave new world, conference papers 2002,* ed. Education Law Association, 301–313. Dayton, Ohio: Education Law Association.

Uchida, Craig, Edward Maguire, Shellie E. Solomon, and Megan Gantley. 2004. Safe kids, safe schools: Evaluating the use of iris recognition technology in New Egypt, NJ. Washington, DC: U.S. Department of Justice, December 2004. www.ncjrs.org.

CHAPTER 5

Online Surveillance
in Canadian Schools

Valerie Steeves

FIFTEEN YEARS AGO, I met a music teacher who was about to receive an award for his innovative use of "new technologies" in the classroom. The teacher was being recognized for using video recording equipment to provide his music students with feedback on performances. He prefaced the discussion of his work by saying that of course the best thing about the technology was that he could leave it on all the time. Although the students were unaware of the fact, he used the cameras to take attendance and to monitor them when he was out of the classroom so he could discipline them when they broke the rules.

This chapter explores the ways in which the networked versions of those cameras have introduced a host of surveillance practices and dependencies that have in turn reshaped the Canadian educational experience. Canada is an interesting exemplar of what is, in fact, an international trend: it is at the forefront of embedding communications technologies into everyday teaching and learning. There is also a good body of research detailing the ways in which Canadian students use and experience the technologies they use in the classroom.

Interestingly, when Canada became the first country in the world to connect all of its publicly funded schools to the Internet in 1999, the $82 million price tag paid by the federal government (Shade and Deschief 2005, 136) came with promises that the wired classroom would help Canadian children become the "skilled techno-entrepreneurs" of tomorrow (Shaw 1998), in turn ensuring that Canada would remain competitive in the knowledge economy. The upbeat rhetoric of the time uncritically celebrated the child's facility with interactive media and naturalized the role of the child as computer user. Universal Internet access in schools was therefore expected to deepen the educational experience and provide children with the tools they would need to succeed in the work force of the future (Shade and Deschief 2005, 143).

A decade later, the Internet is now arguably the preferred medium of a large majority of Canadian children and networked computers are a ubiquitous presence in many Canadian classrooms. Yet many of the assumptions of the 1990s have proven false. Although children do see the Internet as a useful learning tool (Media Awareness Network 2005, 19), to them the Internet is primarily a social space. The wired child is not an isolated child or a technical entrepreneur, but a child who has integrated the Internet fully into his or her social life (Steeves 2005, 8). With the advent of videophones, YouTube, and social networking sites, the lines between the classroom and the rest of children's lives have blurred, complicating the learning environment in unexpected ways.

As children have woven the Internet into more of their daily activities—both in and out of school—a growing number of their interactions is being captured by others with an interest in monitoring their behavior, including teachers, school administrators, corporations, and government authorities. This chapter explores the ways in which this monitoring is reconstructing the student's experience as a learner, a consumer, and a citizen. I argue that although the surveillance capacities of networked computing have been used to deepen the neoliberal tendency to treat students as suspects, the effect of this on the social relationships in the classroom has been ambiguous, and the wired classroom remains a contested site in which students can resist the teacher's authority. The advent of computers in schools has also exposed children to a variety of corporate initiatives that are designed to "'commercialize one of the last and largest unexploited markets in the world' . . . the K-12 sector" (Moll 2001). This online corporatization has done more than open up the school as a potential marketplace; it has naturalized surveillance in the lives of young people and restructured their experience of trust and democratic action in ways that facilitate the needs of the information economy. Accordingly, online surveillance in the classroom has disrupted the social relationships that support learning and provided corporations with an unprecedented opportunity to mine the education system and steer what children learn.

THE PROMISE OF CANADA'S
SCHOOLNET PROGRAM

The federal government first committed itself to wiring all of Canada's seventeen thousand public schools to the Internet in 1994, when it announced its *Building a More Innovative Economy* (Industry Canada 1994) strategy. The umbrella organization responsible for implementing this mandate was Canada's SchoolNet. This federal initiative was run by Industry Canada in tandem with sixty corporate partners, including multinational giants like Microsoft, AOL, Cisco, Aliant, and Imperial Oil (Shade and Dechief 2005, 137). Between 1994 and 2004, SchoolNet delivered refurbished private sector computer equipment directly to schools, linked schools and libraries to the Net, developed an online collection of lesson plans in a variety of subjects, and financially rewarded schools that created and shared innovative online curricular materials on the SchoolNet Web site (ibid., 136). Its objectives in 1994 were to:

- Provide access to educational resources in order to enhance the learning process
- Facilitate the development and delivery of electronic-based learning software in order to significantly improve learning performance
- Enable students and teachers from across the country to participate in shared learning experiences
- Provide students with "key employability skills" for a knowledge-based economy
- Stimulate the development of new market opportunities for Canadian IT and multimedia businesses (Mappin 1995, 94)

This early vision was predicated upon a belief that children "loved" technology and the Internet would give them an enhanced learning experience that would build on their facility with multimedia in general (Shade and Dechief 2005, 137). This vision was also shared by many parents and educators. Many parents believed online access would give their children an advantage in school and help prepare them for the workplace (Media Awareness Network 2000). Great results were expected because children were perceived as natural technology users who would be able to "roam the world on Internet, through SchoolNet they can consult experts, share ideas" (Warwick 1995). Access was all that was required; in the words of one teacher, "The most important thing I do is get out of [the students'] way" (Keenan 2000).

By 2004, the views of government, parents, and educators had shifted in interesting ways. SchoolNet had succeeded in wiring classrooms, but there was no evidence that doing so had actually improved the quality of education (Shade and Dechief 2005, 138). Moreover, the educational goals embodied in the objectives of 1994 had lost their currency. A government-funded review of the SchoolNet program recast its mandate narrowly, "to work with Canadian learning partners to increase access to and the integration of information and communication technologies (ICTs) into the learning environment in order to develop an ICT-skilled population, capable of participating in the knowledge economy" (Schoolnet 2004, 1). The emphasis on the development of educational materials and the facilitation of online communication between teachers and students disappeared, as many of the most popular SchoolNet initiatives were dropped from the 2004 federal budget (Shade and Deschief 2005, 144).[1]

SchoolNet's management concluded that two things would be necessary for the program to move forward. First, there would have to be "whole school change" in order to allow the "learning system" to make "an irreversible transition to ICT-enabled learning" (Schoolnet 2004, 4). Second, research was required "to understand the appropriate business model and incentives to engage the private sector in future [SchoolNet] initiatives" (ibid., 6). Interestingly, these new objectives were not informed by research into the effectiveness of the Internet as a learning tool, but rather by the fact that the relationships between SchoolNet and several of its corporate partners were "in danger of collapse due to a lack of sufficient program funding, and lack of co-ordination and vision" (KPMG 2000).Parents' perceptions had done a similar 180-degree turn, but for very different reasons. By 2004, the Internet was no longer seen as a panacea, but as a scourge (Media Awareness Network 2004, 9). Although close to three-quarters of students in grades 4 through 11 (75 percent of girls and 68 percent of boys) reported that they used the Web for homework on an average school day (Media Awareness Network 2005, 19), parents saw the Internet as a source of conflict in their households. From their point of view, their children were "wasting their time" playing games and chatting with friends, and their "obsession" with online communication was interfering with family activities. They were also concerned that their children were being exposed to offensive content, and they were looking for ways to monitor their children's online activities in order to "keep them safe."

Teachers were beginning to report similar disruptions in the classroom (see, for example, Lajeunesse 2008). Plagiarism facilitated by easy access to online archives of student essays had become a growing problem, and a number of school boards were thinking about banning networked communication technologies like social networking sites, instant messaging, and cell phones from their schools because their use was interfering with classroom learning activities (*Alphonso* 2007). Early concerns about protecting children from access to offensive content were superseded by concerns about student postings on sites like Rate My Teacher, and monitoring and filtering software had become commonplace on school networks.

To date, the jury is still out on whether the wired classroom has had any effect—good or bad—on student academic performance, but the presence of networked technology has provided schools with an excellent tool to extend its surveillance of student behavior, and ostensibly given them plenty of reasons to do so.

SCHOOLS WATCHING STUDENTS

Concerns about the dangers and pitfalls of student Internet use were emerging at a time when, across North America, the number of school rules about appropriate student behavior in the off-line world was increasing. As Morris notes, by 2004 disciplinary action was no longer restricted to incidents of violence, threats, disrespect, or substance abuse but was increasingly used to control student dress and mannerisms (Morris 2005, 25–48). In order to manage this larger disciplinary burden, many schools increased their monitoring and supervision of student spaces (Adams 2000, 140–156).

A number of scholars link this increased surveillance to neoliberal forms of governance that privilege the privatization of public institutions and use market logics to respond to social problems (Saltman and Gabbard 2003). Kupchik and Monahan argue that surveillance in schools reinforces postindustrial mechanisms of social control that seek to "socialize youth into relationships of dependency, inequality and instability vis-à-vis the contemporary power dynamics of the post-industrial labor market and the neoliberal state" (Kupchik and Monahan 2006, 617). Giroux argues that the neoliberal student is "increasingly isolated, treated with suspicion, and subjected to diminished rights to privacy and personal liberties" (Giroux 2003, 553) within the school environment, leading to the creation of a "generation of suspects" (ibid., 556). As such, online surveillance of students is contextualized by a broader trend in which "[s]chools increasingly resemble prisons, and students begin to look more like criminal suspects who need to be searched, tested, and observed under the watchful eye of administrators who appear to be less concerned with educating them than with policing their every move" (ibid., 554).

In the Canadian context, the desire to use surveillance to protect children from virtual hate mongers and predators was quickly turned against students who *might* use school computers to intentionally access inappropriate content. As Caplan notes, young people's behaviors are often the source of moral panic, and children's Internet use is no exception (Caplan 2003, 115). However, policy responses in the early 2000s were complicated by school shootings in Columbine and Tabor, Alberta (Canadian Broadcasting Corporation 1999). The resulting moral panic over youth violence combined with the moral panic over the Internet and brought about "an intense and pervasive" clampdown on students who used online forums to express opinions that school authorities deemed threatening (Caplan 2003, 117).

As part of this clampdown, schools developed acceptable use policies that entrenched monitoring of students' online activities. The acceptable use agreement form used by the Ottawa-Carleton District School Board (2008) is typical. It tells students that they are not allowed to access online information that is "inappropriate" or to use the Internet "for political purposes." It gives the school board "the right to monitor all electronic communications" and warns students that "your failure to live up to this agreement will have consequences that must be accepted. You also clearly understand that there may not be a second chance." Potential consequences include suspension of computing privileges, payments for damages or repairs, suspension or expulsion from school, and civil or criminal liability. Every student (and parent of a child under eighteen) must sign this agreement before students are given an Internet account.

It is difficult to say how much monitoring actually takes place in Canadian schools. Lawson and Comber report that, in the United Kingdom, little monitoring occurs unless a teacher's suspicions have been aroused, because individual monitoring is both difficult and time-consuming (Lawson and Comber 2000, 282). Schools routinely threaten children with monitoring, however, telling them that their online activities are recorded and that teachers can check to see every site they visit on the Web (ibid., 281–282). This fear has done much to shape the student experience in the classroom. Children report an anxiety about monitoring, particularly because they feel they will not be able to prove their innocence if they are accused of inappropriate behavior (Media Awareness Network 2005).

Pornographic pop-ups that appear on the screen without any intervention from the user were a particular concern for the children who participated in the *Young Canadians in a Wired World* study in 2004 (Media Awareness Network 2005). These pop-ups were worrisome not because of the content but because the children believed that the school tracking software would record their presence and associate it with the student. Even though pop-ups are commonplace, the students worried that they would not have enough "evidence" to prove they had done nothing wrong, and that their school computer accounts would be suspended. This was a serious problem for them, not because they needed access to the Web for their schooling but because it was how they kept in contact with their friends throughout the school day; losing access to the school network would therefore cut them off from their social network.

Interestingly, the students found adults' reactions to online pornography difficult to understand. They argued that pornography was "everywhere"—in the movies they watch, the advertisements they peruse, the music they listen to—and that if adults wanted children to take their worries about online porn seriously, they should start addressing pornography as a whole. To most, online pornography was a mundane fact of life. One thirteen-year-old boy in Toronto recounted how he had "discovered" online porn at the age of eleven and become "quite interested" in it, but he was older now and had given it up because it was "kids' stuff." However, most students in the study, especially the girls, indicated they would prefer to avoid it. But they did not want adults censoring their online activities. Instead, they asked for explicit content advisories so they could make informed decisions about the information they accessed.

Typically, schools have not responded to pornography or other online content issues by empowering the student and reinforcing the student's ability to make choices. Although most teachers prefer an educational approach that provides students with the skills they need to evaluate online information (see, for example, Lajeunesse 2008; Lawson and Comber 2000; and Fabos 2004), school administrators have tended to rely upon draconian use policies, filtering software, and monitoring. By making surveillance the default response, schools have accordingly lost the opportunity to help students develop the skills of citizenship and reinforced the neoliberal view of student as suspect.

This approach has put schools under pressure to extend the disciplinary net beyond the confines of the school itself. Since all online activities leave a digital trail, many student interactions that were previously invisible to schools are now routinely captured and archived on the Web. As such, they can become flashpoints for administrators who are committed to controlling inappropriate online behavior both in school and beyond the schoolyard. In 2005, for example, three students were expelled from an exclusive private boys' school in Toronto after they hosted an online "party" in which they made a number of highly offensive anti-Semitic comments (Canadian Broadcasting Corporation 2005). The boys, one of whom was Jewish, set up the group from their home computers and hosted the online discussion after school hours. Although there was no connection between the party and the school itself, school administrators stepped in to discipline the students' conduct.[2]

The digital trail involved in online communications also feeds into the general tendency on the part of school authorities to exaggerate the seriousness of student threats (Cornell 2003, 705–719). In 2007, two boys in grade eight were expelled from school by the Western Quebec School Board for sending anonymous e-mails to teachers. The e-mails were insulting, singling out one teacher, for example, for her "fat ass" (Lofaro 2007). It is not surprising that the school board decided to discipline the boys for disrespectful behavior, but what makes the case interesting is the level of the discipline accorded. The boys were not just expelled from their own school; they were expelled from every school in the board's jurisdiction. Although they could reapply to attend school the following academic year, the board retained the discretion to refuse their application, potentially cutting off their access to public education in their geographic region.

It is hard to imagine that the same punishment would have been meted out if the boys had insulted their teachers verbally. As Cornell notes, many of the inappropriate comments uttered by students are merely fleeting expressions of anger or frustration or immature attempts at humor, made without any sustained intention to cause someone harm (Cornell 2003). When these comments are expressed online, however, a digital copy is generated that captures the words but none of the social context or "tone" that would apply in face-to-face dialogue. The very fact the Internet creates a record of student speech exacerbates the tendency to privilege the production of documents over social interaction (Kupchik and Monahan 2006, 626) and, like surveillance based on classmate informants, weakens the barriers between students' private conversations and the knowledge of authority figures (ibid., 622).

The resulting emphasis on surveillance as a method of control carries a number of potential messages for students: that "they are always being watched, that they are embedded in relations of distrust and that they should behave out of fear of negative repercussions, not because it is morally right" (Kupchick and Monahan 2006, 627). In Giroux's words, "Trust and respect now give way to fear, disdain, and suspicion" (Giroux 2003, 554). Interestingly, Kerr and Stattin (Kerr and Stattin 2000, 366–380) report that there is no relationship between monitoring and pro-social behavior in children; pro-social behavior instead occurs when children voluntarily disclose information to adults with whom they share a bond of trust. Online surveillance may therefore actually work against the kind of social trust that is likely to encourage children to comply with school rules.

The breakdown of this trust is even more problematic because electronic media provide students with opportunities to actively resist the teacher's authority (Hope 2005, 359–373). Two incidents in Quebec are illustrative. In the first, students at École Secondaire Charles-Gravel in Chicoutimi provoked a teacher into losing her temper during class. Another student recorded the event on a cell phone and later posted the tape on YouTube. A few weeks later, two thirteen-year-old girls attending École Secondaire Mont-Bleu in Gatineau provoked another teacher and recorded his loss of temper on a compact video recorder. That tape also showed up on YouTube.

The Mont Bleu teacher—a thirty-two-year veteran of the classroom with a solid reputation—was so embarrassed by the incident that he refused to return to work. The two girls were suspended, and the school banned all electronic devices, including cell phones and MP3 players, from the school. This, in turn, put pressure on the school to increase surveillance to detect newly defined "contraband" devices, which proved difficult because "we don't have metal detectors in the classrooms" (Austen 2006). As one student told journalists, "If they even see an earbud coming out of your shirt, they're going to take it away" (Canadian Broadcasting Corporation 2006).

Both schools called in the police to investigate, illustrating Kupchik and Monahan's point that "[p]roblems faced by schools or students are now more likely to be defined as 'criminal' problems rather than as social or counseling problems" (Kupchick and Monahan 2006, 623). The student responsible for posting the Chicoutimi video has not been identified, but the police have stated that they will charge him or her with defamatory libel, once they do so (Canadian Broadcasting Corporation 2006).[3]

Clearly, both schools pulled out all the stops and used aggressive disciplinary measures to reassert a sense of control. However, given the complexities of the social relationship between the student and the teacher in the classroom, the schools' actions may be counterproductive. I would suggest that opening up the classroom to surveillance is problematic for both students and teachers because it disrupts the roles of all the parties and creates an atmosphere of fear. Suspension and criminal charges are likely to exacerbate that fear for students. Moreover, the attendant loss of privacy may interfere with the student's ability to learn. Davis argues,

> To discern and to "own" appropriate connections and justifications requires a certain kind of "privacy" from the teacher. That is, the teacher, as authoritative source of knowledge, needs to be distanced in some measure from the processes through which this discernment and owner-ship is acquired. In some measure the teacher must lack detailed access to the child's thinking processes, at least for some of the time, and the child must be aware that the teacher lacks this access [emphasis in original]. (Davis 2001, 252)

On the other hand, in the words of a spokesman for the teachers' union in the Gatineau incident, networked media have disrupted the teacher's role as "master of the class" by invading what would otherwise be a "closed class and confidential" space (Canadian Broadcasting Corporation 2006). In spite of student suspensions and criminal charges, the teachers at École Secondaire Mont-Bleu still feel vulnerable because the privacy of the classroom has been breached (ibid). They share the same concerns with other teachers across Quebec who have reported that they no longer "feel safe" acting as authority figures because their students might use networked media to embarrass or harass them (Lajeunesse 2008).

Electronic surveillance in the classroom is a double-edged sword. Online monitoring may or may not lead to compliance with school rules, but it clearly reconstructs the classroom and interferes with the relationships that are at the heart of learning. Like other forms of in-class surveillance, it erodes the trust that is central to the learning process and detracts from democratic socialization. It is a particularly invasive form of monitoring because children do not separate their online activities, often doing school work, surfing sites of personal interest, expressing themselves, and communicating with friends, all at the same time (Steeves 2005). On the other hand, the medium itself provides students with opportunities to negotiate and resist authority. Draconian disciplinary responses are therefore likely to transform online expressions of student identity into "a mode of subversive opposition" (Morris 2005), making the wired classroom a contested site of surveillance.

CORPORATIONS WATCHING STUDENTS

Canada's SchoolNet program did more than introduce electronic monitoring on the part of school authorities. It also created an opportunity for corporations to monitor, and potentially influence, student behavior. This was not unintentional. SchoolNet's corporate partners participated in the program in exchange for tax breaks, and a chance to market directly to schools and to develop brand loyalty among a captive audience of impressionable young people (Shade and Dechief 2005, 137).

This type of corporate marketing is no longer unusual in Canadian classrooms. The Canadian Teachers Federation reports that 55 percent of Canadian high schools allow commercial advertising on school property, and 22 percent sell advertising space directly to advertisers (Canadian Teachers Federation 2006, 7). Schools are also not the only place where corporations court the elusive youth market. Companies spend approximately $15 billion per year marketing to kids, hoping to attract some of the $2.9 billion Canadian kids spend—and the $20 billion in family spending they influence—each year (ibid.).

The commercialization of the school network is particularly problematic because it entails much more than exposing children to traditional marketing messages. The interactive nature of the medium means that corporations can surreptitiously watch children as they go about their schoolwork, instant-message their friends, and surf for fun; corporations then use the information they collect to shape the online environment in ways that promote a particular view of the child's place in the world. Marketers present this as "enriching" the child's learning environment by delivering "fun and great products" (Hastings 2005), but a more critical examination demonstrates that it provides corporations with an unparalleled opportunity to steer what the child learns.

The crux of the system rests on surveillance. In the words of marketing guru Rob Graham, "There's no way to sugar coat this. In order to learn more about individual consumers, marketers have to resort to 'spying'" (Graham 2006, 47). By collecting the minute details of children's online activities—the sites they visit, the terms they search, the profiles they post, the links they click on, the names of their friends on social networking sites—marketers are able to construct detailed profiles of individual consumers. Each child is categorized according to patterns of behavior he or she shares with others, then fed information in order to change his or her behavior (Steeves 2005, 134). From the industry's perspective, "The beauty of [behavioral targeting] is that it allows publishers and advertisers to learn more about their customers not as group, but as individuals. Rather than sifting through mountains of data meant to encapsulate the buying patterns of groups of people, [behavioral targeting is] a way to look into the minds of a single, potential customer" (Estrin 2007). The school network is therefore not just "branded" by a sponsor, it becomes a window into the daily life of the students who use it. Corporate educational initiatives are therefore highly valuable properties because "schools are where the children are.... Nowhere else can marketers expect to have such a broad reach for their commercial messages" (Molnar and Boninger 2007)—or a better way to track them.

The commercial nature of many of these corporate initiatives is often masked with kid-friendly and teacher-friendly educational lingo. World Maths Day, for example, invites students from around the world to solve math problems. In 2008, more than a million students from over 150 countries "unite[d] in their quest to set a world record in answering as many questions as possible" in a "global celebration of numbers" (World Maths Day 2008). Teachers were encouraged to register their class because "[t]his is a truly unique event and a fantastic way to promote numeracy within your school. The students will make significant improvements in their mental arithmetic skills and have a great deal of fun in the process!" (ibid.). What is harder to see is that the event also enables 3P Learning, the company that owns the site, to track each students' progress, correlate the information by age, school, and class, and generate a database that can then be used to sell product to specific teachers and schools.[4] Interestingly, the World Maths Day privacy policy focuses on the importance of the "safety and security of our registered users" (ibid.), but does little to enlighten teachers or parents about the commercial value of the information collected from students. The surveillance itself is deproblematized because, even though each child is directly identified by name, age, and class location, the corporation only uses "anonymous" information to "enhance the learning resources" and "personal information" is not sold to advertisers or third parties. Instead, the policy underlines other risks of participating, most notably the possibility that students might communicate with each other and that predators might use the site to identify a child's name and address. The second risk is mitigated by the fact that the corporation does not post student surnames, and the first is dealt with by making it technically impossible for students to talk to each other. Instead, "At all times, students are engaged in meaningful educative activity within a secure environment" (ibid.). Ironically, SchoolNet's original objective of connecting students for interactive learning projects is recast as a safety risk, and the corporate surveillance that occurs in the background is normalized.

There are times, however, when hiding a marketing program in an online educational activity may backfire. When Zip4Tweens (formerly known as Cool-2B-Real) was first created, it appeared to be a girl-power site designed to teach girls about good nutrition and a healthy body image. Children were told, "We're here to help you have fun—and build a strong mind and body," and the Parents Section reassured adults, "The zip4tweens.com Web site is designed to help tween girls (about 8 to 12 years old) see the value of eating smart and being physically active. Content and activities on the site can also help them feel good about themselves and confident in what they can accomplish both physically and mentally" (Steeves 2006, 176). Children were encouraged to use the chat room and play educational games to learn about healthy eating.

What was less apparent was the fact that the site was the brainchild of the Cattlemen's Beef Board, the National Cattlemen's Association and Circle 1 Network, a company that specializes in online marketing to children. So as girls chatted about "popularity, dating, and more" and played games like "Burger Boggle" and "Grillin' and Chillin'" or visited "the party zone to make invitations for [their] next burger birthday bash," they were surrounded by marketing messages about beef (Steeves 2006, 176).

The site attracted a fair amount of controversy (see, for example, Vagnoni 2006), and eventually its corporate ownership was no longer hidden in the fine print. However, the games involving images of burgers remain, and the vast majority of eating advice and recipes on the site continues to showcase beef. The apparent conflict of interest between the stated goal of the site to educate children about healthy eating and the Cattlemen's vested interest in convincing girls that vegetarianism is not part of a "balanced" diet has been resolved by positioning the site as an act of altruism. Expert testimonials tell users:

> Yes, this Web site is sponsored by America's Beef Producers. . . . Beef provides many nutrients, including zinc, iron and protein, which are important to growth, brain development and physical performance. These are nutrients often deficient in children's diets. You may ask why beef producers in the U.S. would invest their hard-earned funds to develop such a Web site—The answer is that America's beef producers think that helping kids during this important part of their development is the right thing to do. (Zip4Tweens 2008)

Recasting edutainment as a public service is a growing trend (Molnar and Boninger 2007), but it appears to do little to mitigate the desire on the part of the corporations who create educational sites to steer children's interactions and normalize corporate surveillance. For example, Webkinz promotes itself as a "safe, educational and fun online community" (Webkinz 2008c), where children play with virtual stuffed animals. However, throughout the site, learning is reconstituted as participating in commerce. The kids must earn KinzCash in order to buy their pets food, toys, furniture, and medicine, and they earn this cash by playing "educational" games or taking quizzes based on "age appropriate, curriculum-based questions" (Webkinz 2008b). The site suggests that it provides the added benefit of teaching children about finance: "by earning KinzCash, your child learns how to save and spend money" (Webkinz 2008d). Accordingly, the site typifies Langer's critique of childhood—and by extension education—as "a cultural space constituted by consumerism" (Langer 2004, 251–277).

Moreover, the corporation monitors the children throughout their play and collects information from and about them. But, like World Maths Day, the site deproblematizes this surveillance by treating privacy as a safety issue that is mitigated by making sure children cannot interact with each other: "There is no way for a user to type what they want, nor ask or say anything inappropriate to any other user. We control everything the users are able to say. We have designed our chat menu of choices of sentences and phrases to put safety first" (Webkinz 2008b). Ironically, the site maintains that it "helps to teach children about responsibility and . . . getting along with others" (Webkinz 2008d)—even though children are not allowed to interact in any meaningful sense. It also encourages children to tattle on others who act or speak "in an inappropriate manner" and promises to ban children who "do not behave appropriately" (Webkinz 2008a). This not only normalizes the role of the corporation as educator and protector; it also co-opts the child into a system of surveillance that presents other people as untrustworthy sources of risk.

The democratic implications of this kind of socialization are made more readily apparent in corporate educational "interventions" on social networking sites. *Seventeen* magazine, for example, created a Facebook group called the *Seventeen* Body Peace Project to encourage girls to adopt better body images. The site tells girls there's a "war going on over our bodies," but the problem is not the prevalence of media images of impossibly thin models in magazines like *Seventeen*. The girls are the ones at fault: "We're the ones who won't stop beating ourselves up. It's time to call a truce!" Girls are encouraged to sign a petition agreeing to "quiet that negative little voice in my head when it starts to say mean things about my body . . . [and] remind myself that what you see isn't always what you get on TV and in ads" (Body Peace Project 2008). To help them in their new-found commitment, they can peruse statistics that indicate that the vast majority (91 percent) of girls have body issue problems, or send any questions they have about body image to *Seventeen's* body peace expert, Jess Weiner.

This type of educational intervention achieves a number of things. It responsibilizes girls and, in doing so, deflects responsibility away from a marketing industry that bombards girls with negative messages about their bodies. It also redirects the impulse to organize around a political or social issue in a way that privatizes democratic action and privileges the corporate perspective. It can achieve these objectives because a networked environment opens up previously inaccessible social spaces to corporate surveillance and manipulation.

The clearest example of this dynamic is the Facebook group *Feed a Child with Just a Click!* (Feed a Child with Just a Click 2008). The site contains a disturbing image of a starving African child over the header "PLEASE CARE PLEASE CLICK." Young people are told that, if they click on the links on the site and invite their friends to join the group and click as well, "MONEY'S DONATED FREE TOWARDS CHARITY! HELP SAVE THE WORLD." The links lead to advertisements, and every time someone views the ads, the advertisers make a small donation to the World Food Programme. The site concludes, "Billions are made from the Internet because people Clicked. It's about time a fraction of this money went to Charity!!" Once again, any responsibility for world hunger is deflected from an industry that promotes rampant and unsustainable consumption, and the democratic desire to help others in need is reconstituted as participating in the consumer economy.

Especially as the lines between corporations, schools, and children's social spaces continue to blur, it is crucial that policy makers and educators begin to address the profound consequences of wiring the classroom. Since the introduction of SchoolNet in 1994, Canadian school networks have been characterized by overt surveillance on the part of school authorities and covert surveillance on the part of corporations who seek to commodify the classroom and inject commercial messages into learning. Both trends work against the continuing democratic importance of education as a "crucial site where students gain a public voice and come to grips with their own power as individual and social agents"(Giroux 2002, 4) If networked education is going to fulfill its promise, the privatization of the classroom computer must be problematized and resisted.

ACKNOWLEDGMENTS

The author would like to thank the Social Sciences and Humanities Research Council of Canada for their generous support of the research from which this article derives.

NOTES

1. Including Grassroots, which provided financial support for the development of learning materials by Canadian teachers and students.
2. American jurisprudence provides some protection for online student speech

(see Caplan 2003). Although Canadian courts have recognized that students have constitutionally protected rights to privacy and free expression, a lower standard applies when questions safety and order are involved (Peavoy 2004), and criminal restrictions on hate speech have been held to be constitutional (*R. v. Keegstra*).

3. Under s. 301 of the *Criminal Code of Canada*, this is an indictable offence and therefore similar to a felony in the American context.

4. 3P Learning is partially owned by 9MSN, an Australian subsidiary of Microsoft. In 2008, 3P Learning extended the World Maths Day contest to individual children, extending its reach into the homeschooling and tutoring markets.

REFERENCES

Adams, A.T. 2000. The status of school discipline and violence. *Annals of the American Academy of Political and Social Science* 567 (1): 140–156.

Alphonso, Caroline. 2007. Schools want to ban my cellphone!?! *Globe and Mail.* February 3, Technology Section.

Austen, Ian. 2006. Telling tales out of school, on YouTube. *New York Times.* November 27.

Body Peace Project. 2008. http://www.facebook.com/group.php?gid=6338868252 (accessed July 7, 2008).

Canadian Broadcasting Corporation. 1999. Alberta town reeling after school shooting. *CBCNews.* April 28. http://www.cbc.ca/canada/story/1999/04/29/tabor_shoot990429.html (accessed July 4, 2008).

———. 2005. Private school punishes 6 over Nazi website. *CBCNews.* May 2. http://www.cbc.ca/canada/story/2005/05/02/students-website050502.html (accessed July 4, 2008).

———. 2006. Quebec school bans cellphones after YouTube video. *CBCNews.* November 24. http://www.cbc.ca/canada/ottawa/story/2006/11/24/you-tube.html (accessed July 4, 2008).

Canadian Teachers Federation. 2006. Commercialism in Canadian schools: Who's calling the shots? Ottawa.

Caplan, Aaron H. 2003. Public school discipline for creating uncensored anonymous Internet forums. *Willamette Law Review* 39 (2003): 115.

Cornell, D. G. 2003. Guidelines for responding to student threats of violence. *Journal of Education Administration* 41(6): 705–719.

Criminal Code of Canada, R.S.C. 1985, c. C-46.

Davis, Andrew. 2001. Do children have privacy rights in the classroom? *Studies in Philosophy and Education* 20:252.

Estrin, Michael. 2007. Getting ads to the right eyeballs. *iMedia Connections.* April 20. http://www.imediaconnection.com/content/14559.asp (accessed July 4, 2008).

Fabos, Bettina. 2004. *Wrong turn of the information superhighway: Education and the commercialization of the Internet.* New York: Teachers College Press.

Feed a child with just a click! 2008. *Facebook.* http://www.facebook.com/group.php?gid=6324544002 (accessed July 7, 2008).

Giroux, Henry. 2002. Neoliberalism, corporate culture, and the promise of higher education: The University as a democratic public space. *Harvard Educational Review* 72 (4): 4.

Giroux, Henry. (2003). Racial injustice and disposable youth in an age of zero tolerance. *Qualitative Studies in Education* 16(4): 553.

Graham, Rob. 2006. *Fishing from a barrel: Using behavioral targeting to reach the right people with the right ads at the right time.* Boscawen, NH: Learningcraft Press.

Hastings, M. 2005. Empower the children. *Marketing Magazine.* September 26.

Hope, Andrew. 2005. Panopticism, play and resistance of surveillance: Case studies of the observation of student Internet use in UK schools. *British Journal of Sociology of Education* 26 (3): 359–373.

Industry Canada. 1994. *Building a more innovative economy.* Ottawa: Industry Canada.

Keenan, T. 2005. Some schools really do get it. [Quoted in Shade and Dechief 2005.] Originally published in *ComputerWorld* 16 (2000).

Kerr, Margaret, and Hakan Stattin. 2000. What parents know, how they know it, and several forms of adolescent adjustment: Further support for a reinterpretation of monitoring. *Developmental Psychology* 36 (3): 366–380.

KPMG Consulting LP. 2000. Evaluation of the SchoolNet1 initiative: Final report. http://www.schoolnet.ca/home/e/docments/SN_evaluationE.pdf (accessed July 7, 2008).

Kupchick, Aaron, and Torin Monahan. 2006. The new American school: Preparation for post-industrial discipline. *British Journal of Sociology of Education* 27 (5): 617–631.

Lajeunesse, Claude. 2008. *Towards empowerment, respect and accountability: Report and recommendations on the impact of the Internet and related technologies on English public schools in Quebec.* Montreal: Quebec English School Boards Association.

Langer, Beryl. 2004. The business of branded enchantment: Ambivalence and disjuncture in the global children's cultural industry. *Journal of Consumer Culture* 4 (2): 251–277.

Lawson, Tony, and Chris Comber. 2000. Censorship, the Internet and schools: A new moral panic? *Curriculum Journal* 11 (2): 282.

Lofaro, Tony. 2007. Unanimous decision means pair will have to re-apply for next year. *Ottawa Citizen.* March 28.

Mappin, David. 1995. Canada's SchoolNet initiative. *Education Technology Research and Development* 43 (2): 94.

Media Awareness Network. 2000. *Canada's children in a wired world: The parents' view.* Ottawa: Media Awareness Network.

———. 2005a. *Young Canadians in a wired world, phase II: Focus groups.* Ottawa: Media Awareness Network.

———. 2005b. *Young Canadians in a wired world, phase II: Students survey.* Ottawa: Media Awareness Network, 2005.

Moll, Marita. 2001. Pianos vs. politics: Sustaining public education in the age of globalization. In *E-commerce vs. e-commons: Communications in the public interest,* ed. Marita Moll and Leslie Regan Shade. Ottawa: Canadian Centre for Policy.

Molnar, Alex, and Faith Boninger. 2007. Adrift: Schools in a total marketing environment: The tenth annual report on schoolhouse commercialism trends: 2006–2007. Commercialism in Education Research Unit.

Morris, E. W. 2005. "Tuck in that shirt!" Race, class, gender and discipline in an urban school. *Sociological Perspectives* 48 (1): 25–48.

Ottawa-Carleton District School Board. 2008. Acceptable use of computers and Internet/intranet technology agreement form. PR.622.IT.

Peavoy, Devon. 2004. Banning books, burning bridges: Recognizing student freedom of expression rights in Canadian classrooms. *Dalhousie Journal of Legal Studies* 13:125–155.

R. v. Keegstra. [1990] 3 S.C.R. 697.

Saltman, Kenneth J., and David A. Gabbard, eds. 2003. *Education as enforcement: The militarization and corporatization of schools.* New York: RoutledgeFalmer.

SchoolNet. 2004. *Management response: Evaluation of SchoolNet program.* Industry Canada. http://www.ic.gc.ca/epic/site/ic1.nsf/vwapj/EvaluationSchoolnetMgmtResponse. pdf/$file/EvaluationSchoolnetMgmtResponse.pdf (accessed July 7, 2008).

Seventeen. Body Peace Project. http://www.facebook.com/group.php?gid=6338868252 (accessed July 7, 2008).

Shade, Leslie Regan, and Diane Yvonne Dechief. 2005. Canada's SchoolNet: Wiring up schools? In *Global perspectives on e-learning,* ed. Alison A. Carr-Chellman. Thousand Oaks, CA: Sage.

Shaw, G. 1998. SchoolNet program turns out techno-entrepreneurs. *St. Catherine's Standard.* October 23, Section C9.

Steeves, Valerie. 2005. *Young Canadians in a wired world, phase II: Trends and recommendations.* Ottawa: Media Awareness Network.

———. 2006. It's not child's play: The online invasion of children's privacy. *University of Ottawa Law and Technology Journal* 3 (1): 176.

Vagnoni, Nick. 2006. No more Cool-2B-Real. *Slashfood.* June 15. http://www.slashfood. com/2006/06/15/no-more-cool-2b-real/ (accessed July 7, 2008).

Warwick, L. 1995. Students roam the world on the Internet. *Montreal Gazette.* August 12, section G2.

Webkinz. 2008a. Curious about clubhouse chat? http://www.webkinz.com/us_en/ pa_clubhouse.html (accessed July 7, 2008).

———. 2008b. For parents. Frequently asked questions. http://www.webkinz.com/ us_en/faq_parents.html (accessed July 7, 2008).

———. 2008c. Take a tour. http://www.webkinz.com/us_en/ (accessed July 7, 2008).

———. 2008d. WebKinz world and learning. http://www.webkinz.com/us_en/ pa_webkinz_learning.html (accessed July 7, 2008).

World Maths Day. n.d. Privacy policy. http://static.3plearning.com/wmd/wmd08_ privacypolicy.pdf

World Maths Day. 2008. http://www.worldmathsday.com/ (accessed July 7, 2008).

Zip4Tweens. 2008. What the experts say. http://www.zip4tweens.com/parents/experts. html (accessed July 7, 2008).

CHAPTER 6

"School Ownership Is the Goal"

MILITARY RECRUITING, PUBLIC SCHOOLS, AND FRONTS OF WAR

Tyler Wall

THE ACTIVE SEARCH FOR CIVILIAN BODIES, especially youthful bodies, to transform them into military bodies is a relentless military venture. Finding bodies for war is one aspect of a larger process of societal militarization, which can be understood as "the contradictory and tense social process in which civil society organizes itself for the production of violence" (Geyer quoted in Sherry 1995, xi). Hence, militarization can be a logistical process in that it makes mass organized violence possible while blurring civilian and military spheres by aligning other institutions with military goals (Lutz 2002a). Militarization is also a cultural process that structures the ways in which social agents make sense of the world through both material and discursive means (ibid.). Militarizing processes are highly contested and frequently relate to the social constructions of gender, sexuality, race and ethnicity, and socioeconomic status (Enloe 2000; Lutz 2002a). Thus, it may be more accurate to speak of multiple "militarizations" than of one singular and static militarization process (Gusterson 2007).

Secondary education is but one field that military agents routinely engage to shape through military logics. Military "manpower" agents, or military recruiters, are a small, albeit important, piece of societal militarization. The U.S. Army perceives all social spaces as potential "operating environments" in which to win the "hearts and minds" of citizens; however, "none have as much impact on recruiting than schools" (U.S. Army 2006, 3–5). In 1973, the military "manpower" structure switched to the All-Volunteer Force (AVF), which situated military recruiters as the practical gatekeepers of military membership (Ayers 2007). More recently, the presence of military recruiters in U.S. public schools has received increased attention as a result of the No Child Left Behind Act (NCLB) and the expansion of the war on terrorism.

NCLB mandates that public schools receiving federal funding provide military recruiters with personal information about each high school student, such as names, addresses and telephone numbers. Some people, such as anti-militarization activists, "counterrecruiters," school administrators, and parents have taken note that students can opt out of this provision by signing a form stating that they wish not to have their personal information released to military recruiters, but few people are aware of this provision. In May 2005, the Department of Defense (DoD) announced that it was in the process of creating a computerized database, which is nothing short of a surveillance system, storing the personal information of students who are sixteen to eighteen years of age as well as all college students. As of 2005, there were twelve million names on the list. The students who do in fact opt out are included on an opt-out list to ensure that military recruiters won't contact them (Lipka 2005). So, whether they are opting out or not, the contact information of U.S. youth is archived in a Pentagon database. This raises obvious issues about privacy violation; however, by solely focusing on NCLB's invasive provisions—although rightfully bringing attention to the harmful possibilities of the act and highlighting the most recent attempt of military access to youth—other forms of militarized control can all too easily be lost sight of.

Schools are extremely important in the practices of U.S. war preparation: they geographically corral youthful bodies for military recruiters to locate easily, communicate with, and eventually enlist. As Lt. Col. Dan Daoust stated in a media interview, "There's no substitute for that one-on-one communication of actually talking to a soldier that's wearing that uniform. It would be great if we had all the resources in the world to be able to go out throughout all the neighborhoods and contact them in their homes, but they simply don't. The easiest way to make contact with them is when they are all in one location" (Merrow 2004).

This important but mundane spatial role of schools for military recruitment is seen especially in the context of my research site, which can be described as an overwhelmingly white, predominantly middle- and working-class rural county in the midwestern United States. For present purposes I will refer to it as Countryside County. The local military recruiters I have talked with conceptualize their own recruiting responsibilities in relation to the handful of public high schools in the county, which each serve no more than 550 students. That is, the recruiter's geographic assignment is solely informed by the location of schools. Without the school's physical existence, recruiting in this particular rural area would be significantly more difficult.

Small rural communities rarely have large, open commercial spaces, such as shopping malls, where military recruiters can seek out potential recruits, and Countryside County is no different. Hence, the schools of Countryside County are "basically the center of the community," as one local school official told me. Therefore, to find a military recruiter in this rural geography, I would first advise one to set out for the public schools, and then perhaps to the "official" recruiting office. Public schools, in this context, must also be understood as military "recruiting stations" (Giroux 2004, 36).

Although the U.S. military does not publish data concerning the home-towns of military recruits (Bishop 2003), it is believed that large proportions of U.S. military personnel currently deployed in Iraq and Afghanistan come from or reside in small rural towns (O'Hare and Bishop 2006; Tannock 2005). Stuart Tannock observes that "whites tend to be well represented in combat positions in the military," and "small, rural towns are overrepresented in the military as a whole" (2005, 167). Similarly, military veterans live predominantly in rural and small-town areas, particularly in southern and midwestern regions, according to the 2000 U.S. Census. This rural/military nexus has contributed to a higher death rate of small-town soldiers in Iraq and Afghanistan compared with soldiers coming from urban areas (O'Hare and Bishop 2006).[1] Tom Englehardt (2007) calls these small-town soldiers "the forgotten American dead," since it is often forgotten that many of the U.S. war dead in Iraq and Afghanistan come from rural and small-town areas. This rural/military nexus has developed at least partly because small-town and rural areas have been adversely affected by uneven economic development. In addition, many people in small towns have historically prided themselves on possessing an "authentic" patriotism that is intimately tied to military logics (Cowen 2007; O'Leary 1999), and many current recruitment ads are saturated with rural imagery such as corn fields, tractors, barns, and wholesome white "farm boy" soldiers.

The issues discussed in this chapter should be seen in the context of an ongoing ethnographic study I am conducting on the relations between militarization, military presences, and everyday life in Countryside County. Following Lutz's (2006) advice that scholars should listen intently to the voices of people who act within and are acted upon by the U.S. national security state, my fieldwork consists largely of semistructured interviews with a variety of rural Countryside County residents, ranging from "civilian" to "military" actors. Several questions inform my research: "Where can military presences be found and not found in the landscape?"; "How and in what forms do these military presences manifest themselves?"; "How do local actors make sense of these military presences?" The responses to these questions quickly made it clear to me that public schools are one important space where military presences play an important role in Countryside County. For this chapter, I draw upon interviews with citizen-soldiers, a handful of military recruiters, and various school personnel such as teachers and administrators. Throughout the chapter I quote extensively from these interviews, which I conducted in Countryside County between mid-2007 and the end of 2008. I also engage the official discourses of recruiting as outlined in the U.S. Army's School Recruiting Program Handbook (SRP) and Recruiter Handbook.

I argue that military recruitment practices in schools aim to create a militarized control network that seeks to transform not only youthful students into soldiers, but also to shape and influence *all* school bodies, although notably disenfranchised youth, specifically rural, white, working poor male youths, are most directly caught in the local Countryside recruiting web.[2] This militarized control network can be understood as a network of surveillance in that surveillance is not merely about observational practices but also entails the collecting of information with the potential to exploit this information for purposes of social control (Monahan and Wall 2006). In this sense, military recruitment in schools should be seen as similar to police presences and the placement of surveillance cameras in public schools. In the final section, I suggest that military recruitment implicates, albeit in mundane ways, not only "home front" lives but also the valuable lives of seemingly distant "battlefronts," although the violent relations of military recruitment are usually "re-worked" (Scarry 1985) and "misrecognized" (Scheper-Hughes and Bourgois 2004) as something devoid of violence.

In no way do I claim that my observations and the analysis provided here present the whole picture of military recruiting. My goal is one of problematization, or a critical questioning of the banality of militarizing practices, achieved in this case by offering a counternarrative that challenges the seemingly "harmless" role of military recruiting in public education.

NETWORKS, TALK, AND PLUMP CHICKENS

Military recruiters are conceptualized by the U.S. military in various ways: as similar to elite soldiers in a war zone, as networked "ground" sensors, as public relations experts, as community leaders, as experts on the local "Future Soldier" market, and as counselors to potential recruits, the newly enlisted, and concerned parents and loved ones. Taken together the U.S. military views recruiters as occupying, penetrating, and shaping agents of space who produce social relations and elicit and leverage information solely for military objectives. Establishing a military recruiting presence in public education is ultimately about "shaping" school space and human relations in service of military objectives through physical presence and social interaction. Military recruiters, according to the army's School Recruiting Program handbook, strive for "total market penetration" (U.S. Army 2004, 2) and "to ensure an Army presence in all secondary schools. *School ownership is the goal*" (ibid., 1; emphasis added). To achieve this militarized "ownership," recruiters seem to have a great deal of flexibility because "[n]obody is really over your shoulder watching what you do. You know, it's a leadership position," as one recruiter informed me.

Militaries are always seeking the support of citizens who are not formally tied to the military (Enloe 2000). A recruiter's success in school recruiting largely depends on his or her ability to gain the trust and credibility of not only students but also administrators, teachers, counselors, parents, and friends. Military recruiting is networking. As one recruiter told me, "I think if you have a good network then people will come to you whenever they want to join." A different recruiter stated, "It's almost like an Amway network. You go out and you meet people out on the streets. You know who your VIPs are in the towns and things like that. You meet them, talk to them . . . you advertise, it's marketing." For the recruiter, the means are building militarized "networks," while the ends are a "met mission" (Ensign 2004), or achieving enlistment quotas. Indeed, as one recruiter told me: "It is numerical. It's all about the numbers." This recruiting goal of transforming the bodies of students into numerical quotas potentially leads to recruiter stress: "It's kind of like how good of a person you are is based on how good your performance is. They say you can go from a hero to zero in thirty days. It's that monthly mission . . . and there is a lot of pressure to make it." That quote is a reminder that individual recruiters are themselves located within multiple scales of power.

Meeting recruitment quotas and establishing supportive networks can be challenging: not all people may be enthusiastic about recruiter encounters. One recruiter said he is well aware that some civilians, especially potential recruits and their parents, view recruiters as untrustworthy. Interestingly, a personal friend of a recruiter told me, "Shit, recruiters will tell you anything. I have to keep my eye on him." According to the army's recruiter handbook, military recruiters strive to turn home-front enemies into friends through aggressive but flexible strategic and tactical operations within a particular "market" that should be understood "through the prism of the principles of war" (U.S. Army 2006, 1-5). The conflation of both market and battlefield metaphors in military recruiting discourse is a frequent occurrence.

Gaining the consent of parents is integral to a recruiter's "success," and one recruiter conceptualized parents as being a "challenge." A school official affirmatively comments, "Any time there's a war going on, when we have recruiters into the school, the parents are more reluctant to allow their kids to hear the good things about the military because ultimately they're trying to get bodies to go overseas."[3] A mother told me that military recruiting practices in public schools are similar to child molesters preying on small children. This metaphor of preying has also been observed among some high school student's perceptions of recruiters (Bigelow 2005), although it must be said that the recruiters I have met in my research in no way seem like predators but rather like people with welcoming and friendly personalities who wholeheartedly see themselves and their jobs as moral and just.

The SRP handbook states that if a school official rejects a recruiter's idea, the recruiter should try to accomplish his or her goal through other means: "Never react negatively to a school's refusal to do something you've asked. Look for another way to achieve your mission" (U.S. Army 2004, 2). However, the recruiters I have talked with claimed that overall the public schools in Countryside County were very open to school recruiting. Only one recruiter I interviewed claimed that a school was mildly apprehensive about his presence, but the recruiter admitted that he had contact with only one school counselor. In addition, this school still allows him to set up a few "lunch displays" a semester, but more encompassing access is limited. This particular school, according to the recruiter, is "depriving the kids" of hearing about the positive dimensions of military service. One school official did acknowledge a "tricky balance" between recruiting and public education:

> I'm not opposed to recruiters coming to schools; I think that that's ok. But I have been in situations where the recruiters were almost to the point of harassment of kids. And so I've kind of tempered my thoughts about them coming. . . . Because they do tend to, some of them, I shouldn't say they do . . . but there have been some recruiters who are extremely pushy, if you will. And you know, some kids say "no I'm not interested." You know, they [recruiters] don't take no for an answer.[4]

The official who made the statement about the "tricky balance," although somewhat dubious of military recruiters occupying school space, remained convinced that this practice is necessary for national security and that military life should be seen as a positive career choice for many students. In fact, he ultimately framed his concern of recruiter "harassment" of youth as more of a military concern than a concern for education in that recruiter aggressiveness could negatively influence student perceptions of the military: prospective student recruits might be turned off to the allure of martial life. Indeed, although some might question the legitimacy of recruiters, to my knowledge there are no organized campaigns against military recruiting in Countryside County.

Military recruiters, at least in theory, see all youthful bodies as potential military bodies. For instance, the recruiter handbook encourages local recruiters to seek out and influence not only high school students but also "students at every level of education," including "seventh and eighth graders" so that they might "emulate and fearlessly approach" recruiters to discuss the military (U.S. Army 2006, 3–6). The handbook goes on: "Remember, first to contact, first to contract . . . that doesn't mean just seniors or grads; it means having the Army perceived as a positive career choice as soon as young people begin to think about the future. If you wait until they're seniors, it's probably too late" (ibid., 3). The mother who equated recruiting with "preying" also stated that her seventh grader came home from school with military recruiting memorabilia, told her that he had talked to a recruiter, and that he "was going to join the army" when he became eligible. His mother was angered at both the recruiter's advances and her child's subsequent statement about enlisting in the military, while her husband was more encouraging to the adolescent.

The military desire for total sway over social relations was expressed to me most clearly by a recruiter: "I believe that everyone could be positively affected and benefit from the National Guard. I mean everyone out there. I don't care if you are the richest kid in the community or, you know, the smartest kid getting scholarships for college or you know . . . anybody in the community. Anybody and everybody." However, the successful lassoing of "anybody and everybody" with the goal of pulling them into a formal military community is a completely different thing in practice: "And the rich kids that I dealt with. . . . they were a harder sale. I mean, the kids that were too popular were a harder sale. You know they just thought they were too good for it." Another recruiter described the kids who usually find the Indiana National Guard a possible career choice as kids that are "eighteen to mid-twenties, mostly males, and most of 'em has holes in their shoes."

Indeed, a common critique of military recruiting practices is that recruiters seek out the urban poor and other disenfranchised populations with more frequency and intensity than privileged communities, and this is also the case in rural areas like Countryside County. Declining unemployment rates and increases in civilian sector jobs can be seen as a threat to the home-front "mission" of military recruiters. In this sense, the structural violence of economies serves as a militarizing process and recruiting tool. As a result of the end of conscription and the force of the neoliberal economy, the military became an institution for upward socioeconomic mobility, creating a situation where "the working class and lower middle class disproportionately staff the U.S. military today" (Tannock 2005, 167). The AVF assists citizens in their quest for the American dream by providing welfare services within a larger civilian context bent on stripping away social welfare. The result is that the military has come to serve as the "patriotic home of the deserving poor" (Cowen 2006, 177). In general, this seems to be the case in Countryside County.

A schoolteacher expressed disappointment that not enough students, especially the underprivileged, look to the military as a way to "get out" of the poor rural areas because they are either "uneducated as to what it can do for them and how rewarding a career it could be" or because of teenage fear of "getting shot at" in a military conflict. Because of this, this particular teacher takes it upon herself to encourage youth to enlist. That is, she takes the task of recruiting upon herself:

> We have recruiters in here all the time and there are kids always going up to them and you know, talking to them and discussing with them. I think it is a great thing. Even me in the classroom . . . I even encourage the military because I see so many of my kids [working poor white kids] who will do nothing and that could be an avenue for them . . .

In an attempt to "shape," "own," or "penetrate" a school and its human agents, a recruiter strategically situates him- or herself to become privy to information that can be used for tactical advantage. In my fieldwork observations, the most blatant intelligence-gathering practice that borders on "school ownership" is that of a military recruiter substitute teaching free of charge at a local high school. From the school's perspective, not having to pay the fifty dollar substitute fee each time the recruiter substitutes across an entire school calendar is a small but helpful financial relief for a budget already struggling to make ends meet. A parent informed me that the recruiter/substitute teacher, while teaching a science class, replaced the chemistry "periodical" chart hanging above the chalkboard with a military recruiting poster. Each week on "Military Monday" this recruiter visits the physical education class and takes the students through military-style physical training, or "PT," and has them run lengthy distances in military formation while singing cadences the whole way. According to the substitute/recruiter, "all the teachers were impressed" with the enthusiasm and discipline the youth displayed toward military drilling and marching.

This same recruiter has given special presentations on Iraq's "geography and culture" and "land navigation" to geography classes while also visiting other classrooms to promote the military, sometimes entertaining students by having them eat military MREs (meals ready to eat). The recruiter claims that "every student there knows my name" and says, in a somewhat joking manner about this particular school and another school where he enjoys similar access, "I could literally walk into any of those schools anytime I want and do whatever I want. I think Rural High is going to put me in the yearbook." Indeed, it is this generally enthusiastic embrace of military recruiters that allowed one local recruiter to state that he "can't ask for a better selection of high schools." It is important to keep in mind that this military/school nexus has developed not through some inevitable fate, but through the "deliberate decisions," specifically "decisions of commission and omission," of both civilian and military actors (Enloe 2000, 293) who are not solely "machines of logic and interest" (ibid., 289).

"Intelligence" is also frequently collected through the "shaping operations" of "lunch displays" where recruiters hand out military memorabilia
like key chains, posters and T-shirts during lunchtime, mingle in the hallways
with students, give classroom presentations, and attend various extracurricular
events. One recruiter reported that a successful tactic of seeking out potential
recruits and establishing "leads" is visiting local fairs, festivals, and school
sporting events:

> Going to school events, school football games and basketball games,
> things like that. Walk around just like with a polo shirt that says "National
> Guard" . . . people talk to you. "Hey did you know that such and such is
> thinking about joining?" Bam! Now we go and talk to 'em. It's amazing
> what you get out of little sporting events [laughs].

Recruiters must find ways to obtain access to youth but must also
convince young students not only to welcome the recruiter's advances but
also to actively aid in the recruiting process. Hence, social networks are
militarized when a student, although not the actual recruiter, transforms
him- or herself into a military public relations expert by telling the "army
story" to a friend. This successful technique was referenced when talking
to recruiters and former students who eventually became "citizen-soldiers,"
most while still in high school. One recruiter discussed his own method of
creating a credible relationship with one popular student, or what he called
the "plump chicken" among a particular group:

> The biggest thing I tried to do was get that plump chicken. You
> know . . . an influencer. You know . . . my success was, was kind of like . . . if
> you recruited that kid that nobody wanted to be around or nobody liked,
> you probably weren't going to get anybody else in. If you recruited a
> popular kid, a smart kid, an athletic kid, you know, a scholar-athlete or
> leader . . . you know, those are the kids that people, that other kids want
> to be like, suddenly a trend started, "Hey, this kid's cool and he's joining
> the Guard so that must mean the Guard's cool so it's cool now."

One National Guard soldier, who enlisted while in high school partly for
college financial assistance, which he says he has yet to "take advantage of,"
told me that at first he was extremely reluctant to join; it was the influence
of his classmates, or what we might now refer to as "plump chickens," and
the local recruiter that convinced him he was making the right decision.
This particular teenager worked at a local fast food joint in the evenings. The
recruiter sent newly enlisted high school friends to the restaurant to convince
the reluctant youth to enlist. The soldier stated,

He'd send them in for me, you know, trying to get me to join. I would hide from 'em and you know, "I'm not here."... They all came walking in one night and I am outside changing the board. You know they didn't even see me and they turned around and left. You know, they [his co-workers] told me over the headset and said "Hey, they came in here trying to talk to you trying to get you to join." This maybe had been the twentieth or thirtieth time they did; they tried getting me to join.

Indeed, my discussions with several local small-town soldiers confirm the success of the "plump chicken" technique, as one soldier commented: "I got a lot of my buddies to join.... I enlisted when I was a junior. So through my junior and senior year I bet I talked ten or twelve guys into joining with me." Military recruiters actively attempt to militarize friendships and other mutual social relations by transforming interpersonal unions among friends or acquaintances into martial social relations.

While talking to potential future soldiers and attempting to shape their decisions, recruiters express multiple selling discourses, from individualistic to nationalistic, such as adventure and world travel, finding direction in one's life, friendship, college tuition, sign-on bonuses, and serving and protecting one's country and state. I noticed this clearly at one recruiting event intended for school-aged youth; the event, called the "Guard Experience," took place off school grounds at the local recruiting station. After playing on an obstacle course and eating free pizza, students sat and listened to recruiters and new recruits who had already attended basic training tell them about the positive dimensions of military service. Throughout the two hours, military personnel loudly queried: "Are there any warriors here?"

Successful recruiting is flexible, depending on the targeted recruits' own personal, cultural, and economic particularities. As one recruiter stated, "When you talk to somebody, you need to find out ... 'Why do you want to join?' 'What are your values?' 'How can we help you?' That type of thing." One recruiter discussed this tailor-made approach:

I try to find his motivator. You know, I am a salesman. I mean whenever someone comes in and tells me their interested in the military first thing I'm gonna do is find out why they are interested in the military. I am gonna ask a lot of open-ended questions. You know, the more they talk to me the better off it is. Because you know what, this kid maybe coming in here is interested in the military for job experience, or he may wanna you know, get into law enforcement or be an EMT.... The first thing I would do is ask a lot of questions.... And then that gives me ... a good selling point and two, I can actually help this kid with where he wants to go in life.

The preceding examples show how seemingly simple conversations can elicit vital information that can be deployed for tactical leverage. In this sense, recruiter/civilian relations are militarized: the very micro-substance of a verbal exchange can be leveraged for military advantage. Recruiting, then, is collecting military intelligence concerning people's dreams and aspirations, personal histories of fortunate and unfortunate circumstances, and social relationships, with the hope of exploiting them for military purposes. On-the-ground recruiting in a rural context can exploit pastoral particularities for tactical advantage, as when a recruiter draws upon the rural hunting and gun culture in his interactions with male youth:

A kid from Countryside County, you know [chuckles], he would come in and I would say, "Hey let's ah, first of all, are you afraid of the woods?" Well, no kid from Countryside County is gonna say they're afraid. "Are you afraid of weapons?" Ah, if he says he is then he's just you know, there is no kid from Countryside County that's afraid of weapons or he's not gonna say he is.

The recruiter went on to explain how he would then show the recruit various weapons stored in the local armory. This particular recruiting tactic is playing on a version of masculinity that Gibson (1994) calls "warrior dreams," and it is specifically tapping a rural/military/masculinity relation (see Woodward 1998 and 2000). Indeed, military recruiting is intimately tied to diverse notions of gender, especially manliness (Enloe 2000). The recruiter claimed this technique of showing potential future soldiers the hardware of military violence not only served the purpose of making the military appealing to the recruit but also, he claimed, provided "transparency" in that the recruiter was acknowledging the potential for violence that comes along with military life.

One recruiter stated that another "challenge" of his job is "the person that's thinking 'Hey I am automatically going on deployment, I'm gonna get shot at, die, whatever.'" This recruiter counsels fearful recruits that, "[s]tatistics prove that . . . it's less likely that anything [will] happen over there than right here, on the street out in front of your house." However true this might be, this apparent disregard and disarticulation, which effectively disconnects military membership from an organized violence binding the bodies of recruits with the bodies of enemy others, is implied by many of the school personnel I have conversed with and is one rhetorical tactic that warrants critical scrutiny.

RECRUITING FOR VIOLENCE

Taking a cue from the youth and parents who might associate military service with bodily violence, military recruiting must be understood in context of an "examination of what the military is actually doing" (Bigelow 2005; Tannock 2005). By the military's own admission, organized violence is undeniably included in the military's job description; therefore, U.S. military recruiting must be seen in relation to the fact that the state is "massively involved in ordering the killing, training others to kill, and threatening to kill" (Lutz 2002b, 291). Therefore, a critical consideration of military recruiting must underline the important fact, albeit all too easily forgotten or obscured, that war is ultimately about "out-injuring" enemy bodies, although this fact of injuring is always being "re-worked" to appear as something other than injuring (Scarry 1985). This section concludes the chapter by suggesting connections between the seemingly peaceful recruiting of "home front" youth with the violent subjugation of seemingly distant, "foreign" bodies and territories.

The process of reworking helps produce a "misrecognition" (Scheper-Hughes and Bourgois 2004) of military recruiting as a practice removed from the act of injuring by deploying a variety of individualistic images such as free college tuition, cash sign-on bonuses, world travel, becoming a "man" and "warrior," and developing self-esteem, to name a few, as well as nationalist/patriotic narratives of obediently serving an innocent, civilizing, enlightened country. Thus militarization "in its everyday forms . . . scarcely looks life threatening" (Enloe 2000, 3). Yet a recruiter's presence can also instill a "banal terrorism," whereby his or her body is "emblematic of a muscular state" while producing a mundane and subtle reminder of "terrorism in our midst" (Katz 2007, 353). Therefore, military recruiting often produces a commonsensical moral logic, whereby citizens recognize only certain forms of violence as violence, and consequently only certain manifestations of human suffering as suffering.

Although racialized minorities in the United States, especially African Americans, are disproportionately targeted and represented in the military (Tannock 2005), whites still make up the majority of military "manpower" (67 percent), although their representation is smaller in proportion to their civilian representation (71 percent) (U.S. Government Accountability Office, 2005). Nonwhite military membership is at approximately 33 percent. As Tannock (2005) notes, however, class inequality across racial categories is one major continuity in military service. Cowen (2007) offers the concept of "military workfare" where working poor and racialized citizens must risk their lives (and I would add to potentially kill human life) in order to achieve a basic standard of living. Therefore, military workfare is a highly racialized project that helps to sustain and fuel racial inequality at home and abroad (ibid.). This is especially observed when considering that significant numbers of U.S. military soldiers are lower-middle-class and working-poor whites, while the subjects of U.S.–directed state violence are historically and currently nonwhite populations. Current military activities must be situated within both the "colonial present" (Gregory 2004) and colonial past where racialized and gendered violences are the rule, not the exception, although these violences are all too often discursively reworked with sentiments of freedom, civilization, and human rights.

This has been made apparent by my conversations with working-class white male soldiers from small-towns in Countryside County. Many of them joined up while still in high school only to soon deploy to Iraq for over a year. Many of these soldiers convey a racialized subjectivity, or a "practical Orientalism" (Herzfeld 2005; Haldrup et al. 2006) toward Iraqi "Others." As Olund states, "We can't seem to do without race in defining our enemies" (2007, 64). These racializations never just reside "over there," however, but contribute to the negative constructions of racialized, home-front Others following the soldiers arrival "home." Consequently, the military recruiting of youthful bodies, at least in the U.S. context, should be linked with what Mills (1997) has called the "global racial contract," although a focus on racialization, despite being highlighted here, is only one piece of the puzzle; notions of femininity, masculinity, and patriarchy are equally important (Enloe 2004).

Military recruiting is a practice of relating to others, to both home-front and battlefront populations. It is imperative to see the destructive capacities embedded in so-called peaceful landscapes: since home-front practices such as military recruiting often "function as unquestioned 'givens,' they enjoy a unique near-immunity to enactments of moral reproach" (Cuomo 1996, 42). In this sense, Cuomo's explication of how "war is not just an event" but is rather an everyday "presence" (31) is fitting in that it blurs the categories of peace with war, military with civilian, life with death. Making the connections visible and known between so-called peaceful geographies and the violent "war zones," that is, identifying a "continuum of violence" allows us to see that "[t]here is no primary impulse out of which mass violence and genocide are born, it is ingrained in the common sense of everyday social life. . . . The preparations for mass killing can be found in social sentiments and institutions from the family, to schools, churches, hospitals, and the military" (Scheper-Hughes and Bourgois 2004, 21–22).

The presence of military recruiters in public education is just one example of how public schools and military institutions join forces to produce normalizing practices of social control of home-front populations while actively contributing to injuring and control of battlefront populations. This is done by a variety of means, but I have highlighted how recruiters use what a recruiting handbook calls "tactical savvy," such as social networking, logics of flexibility, leveraging friendship, and exploiting mundane social interaction, for military objectives. The simple fact that schools spatially concentrate youthful bodies allows military recruiters to recruit boys and girls, men and women, and transform them into the foot soldiers or at the very least trusting supporters of the U.S. national security state.

NOTES

1. Similar small-town military participation was relevant in the Vietnam conflict (Appy 1993). Gill (1997) has discussed a rural/military nexus in the context of Bolivia.
2. See Perez (2006) on the role of Junior Reserve Officer Training Corps, gender, and the recruiting of disenfranchised urban youth.
3. My fieldwork has elicited mixed views on the local impact of current conflicts on local National Guard recruiting. One recruiter claimed that the "war" makes recruiting more challenging, while others said that although the consciousness of conflict is an issue, local recruiting quotas (two enlistments a month) have not been adversely affected. In fact, they claimed current conflicts may have helped local recruitment.
4. One teacher also expressed criticism of recruiting tactics and reported that she had her students complete writing projects about the role of recruiters in their lives.

REFERENCES

Appy, Christian. 1993. *Working-class war: American combat soldiers and Vietnam*. Chapel Hill and London: University of North Carolina Press.

Ayers, William. 2007. Hearts and minds: Military recruitment and the high school battlefield. *Mr. Zine*. http://mrzine.monthlyreview.org/ayers011105.html.

Bigelow, Bill. 2005. The recruitment minefield. *Rethinking schools online*. http://www.rethinkingschools.org/archive/19_03/recr193.shtml.

Bishop, Bill. 2003. Who's gone to war. *Washington Post*. November 16.

Cowen, Deborah E. 2006. "Fighting for "freedom": The end of conscription in the United States and the neoliberal project of citizenship." *Citizenship Studies* 10 (2): 167–183.

———. 2007. National soldiers and the war on cities. *Theory & Event* 10 (2). http://muse.jhu.edu.ezproxy1.lib.asu.edu/journals/theory_and_event/v010/10.2cowen.html.

Cuomo, Chris J. 1996. War is not just an event: Reflections on the significance of everyday violence. *Hypatia* 11 (4): 30–45.

Englehardt, Tom. 2007. The forgotten American dead. *The Nation*. January. http://www.thenation.com/blogs/notion?pid=161392 (accessed April 2, 2009).

Enloe, Cynthia. 2000. *Maneuvers: The International politics of militarizing women's lives*. Berkeley and Los Angeles: University of California Press.

———. 2004. *The curious feminist: Searching for women in a new age of empire*. Berkeley and Los Angeles: University of California Press.

Ensign, Tod. 2004. *America's military today: The challenge of militarism*. New York and London: New Press.

Gibson, William James. 1994. *Warrior dreams: Manhood and violence in post-Vietnam America*. New York: Hill and Wang.

Gill, Lesley. 1997. Creating citizens, making men: The military and masculinity in Bolivia. *Cultural Anthropology* 12 (4): 527–550.

Giroux, Henry. 2004. *The terror of neoliberalism: Authoritarianism and the eclipse of democracy*. Boulder, CO: Paradigm.

Gregory, Derek. 2004. *The colonial present*. Malden, MA, Oxford, UK, and Victoria, Australia: Blackwell.

Gusterson, Hugh. 2007. Anthropology and militarism. *Annual Review of Anthropology* 36:155–175.

Haldrup, Michael, Lasse Koefoed, and Kirsten Simonsen. 2006. Practical Orientalism: Bodies, everyday life, and the construction of otherness. *Geografiska Annaler. Series B. Human Geography* 88 (2): 173–184.

Herzfeld, Michael. 2005. *Cultural intimacy: Social poetics in the nation-state*. New York and London: Routledge.

Katz, Cindi. 2007. Banal terrorism: Spatial fetishism and everyday insecurity. In *Violent geographies: fear, terror, and political violence*, ed. Derek Gregory and Allan Pred, 349–361. New York and London: Routledge.

Lipka, Sara. 2005. Pentagon system to gather student data raises privacy fears. *Chronicle of Higher Education* 51 (44): A30.

Lutz, Catherine. 1999. Ethnography at the war century's end. *Journal of Contemporary Ethnography* 28(6): 610–619.

———. 2002a. Making war at home in the United States: Militarization and the current crisis. *American Anthropologist* 104 (3): 723–735.

———. 2002b. The wars less known. *South Atlantic Quarterly* 101 (2): 285–296.

———. 2006. Empire is in the details. *American Ethnologist* 33 (4): 593–611.

Merrow, John. 2004. *Jim Lehrer News Hour*. March 27, 2008. www.pbs.org/newshour/bb/military/july-dec04/recruit_12–13.html.

Mills, Charles W. 1997. *The racial contract*. Ithaca, NY, and London: Cornell University Press.

Monahan, Torin, and Tyler Wall. 2006. Somatic surveillance: Corporeal control through information networks. *Surveillance & Society* 4 (3): 154–173.

O'Hare, William, and Bill Bishop. 2006. U.S. rural soldiers account for a disproportionately high share of casualties in Iraq and Afghanistan. Carsey Institute, University of New Hampshire, fact sheet no. 3, Fall. http://www.carseyinstitute.unh.edu/documents/RuralDead_fact_revised.pdf

O'Leary, Cecilia. 1999. *To die for: The paradox of American patriotism*. Princeton, NJ: Princeton University Press.

Olund, Eric N. 2007. Cosmopolitanism's collateral damage: The state-organized racial violence of World War I and the war on terror. In *Violent geographies: Fear, terror, and political violence*, ed. Derek Gregory and Allan Pred, 55–75. New York and London: Routledge.

Perez, Gina M. 2006. How a scholarship girl becomes a soldier: The militarization of Latina/o youth in Chicago public schools. *Identities: Global Studies in Culture and Power* 13:53–72.

Scarry, Elaine. 1985. *The body in pain: The making and unmaking of the world*. Oxford: Oxford University Press.

Scheper-Hughes, Nancy, and Philippe Bourgois. 2004. Introduction: Making sense of violence. In *Violence in War and Peace*, ed. Nancy Scheper-Hughes and Philippe Bourgois, 1–31. Malden, MA, Oxford, UK, and Victoria, Australia: Blackwell Publishing.

Sherry, Michael. 1995. *In the shadow of war: The United States since the 1930s*. New Haven: CT: Yale University Press.

Tannock, Stuart. 2005. Is "opting out" really an answer? Schools, militarism, and the counter-recruitment movement in post–September 11 United States at war. *Social Justice* 32 (3): 163–178.

U.S. Army. 2004. School recruiting program handbook. *USAREC Pamphlet 350–13*. http://www.usarec.army.mil/im/formpub/REC_PUBS/p350_13.pdf.

———. 2006. The recruiter handbook. *USAREC Manual 3–01*. http://www.usarec.army.mil/im/formpub/rec_pubs/man3_01.pdf.

U.S. Government Accountability Office. 2005. *Military personnel: Reporting additional servicemember demographics could enhance congressional oversight. GAO-05–952.* http://www.gao.gov/new.items/d05952.pdf. Washington, D.C.: U.S. Government Accountability Office.

Woodward, Rachel. 1998. "It's a man's life!": Soldiers, masculinity, and the countryside. *Gender, Place and Culture* 5 (3): 277–300.

———. 2000. Warrior heroes and little green men: Soldiers, military training, and the construction of rural masculinities. *Rural Sociology* 65:640–657.

PART THREE

Security Cultures

Preparing for the Worst

CHAPTER 7

Reading, Writing, and Readiness

Richard A. Matthew

IN 1999, THE DEPARTMENT OF JUSTICE issued a report entitled *The Appropriate and Effective Use of Security Technologies in U.S. Schools*. The author of the report, Mary Green, identifies a large number of threats that "can be reduced with appropriate surveillance technology such as cameras, sensors, [and] microdots" (Green 1999, 21). Even schools that have not yet experienced violence, thefts, and other problems should consider increased surveillance—and other measures. "Many school buildings in the United States," the author notes, "have been constructed to achieve an inviting and open-to-the-community feeling, with multiple buildings, big windows, multiple entrances and exits, and many opportunities for privacy. Needless to say, these layouts are not conducive to many current requirements to address security needs" (15). Green further warns: "If a school is perceived as unsafe . . . then 'undesirables' will come in, and the school will actually become unsafe" (21). It is time, the report makes clear, for America's schools to accept the need for surveillance technology, security-optimizing architecture, and higher levels of staff scrutiny.

In the past decade, incidents such as those occurring at Columbine (1999), Beslan (2004), and Virginia Tech (2007) have reminded America of the vulnerability of schools and triggered much debate over the pros and cons of different approaches to increasing school security. In the post-Columbine world, the era of fire drills, bomb shelters and innocence is distant and unrecoverable. But is more intrusive surveillance and garrison architecture the solution to contemporary threats to schools? Is this approach effective? Does it lend itself to misuse? Is it culturally acceptable?

In the days after 9/11, many Americans indicated a willingness to accept a reduction in personal privacy and freedom in exchange for higher levels of surveillance-based security, but within a year this willingness began to erode as questions arose about effectiveness, abuse, and cultural fit. More recent polls suggest that while many Americans may be struggling to define an acceptable balance between freedom and privacy on one hand and surveillance and security on the other, few feel the former should be freely traded for the latter (Matthew et al. 2008).

Although Americans value privacy and freedom as much as they value security and are uncomfortable sacrificing one for the other, high-tech surveillance may be gaining acceptance among those charged with school safety. A 2006 *USA Today* article, for example, reports that "the U.S. Justice Department recently chose Raptor [a surveillance system used by over 2000 schools in over 200 districts] as a pilot program for schools nationwide" (2).

Not all school safety guides stress surveillance. In 2007, the U.S. Department of Education released the document *Practical Information on Crisis Planning: A Guide for Schools and Communities*. In the section on prevention, where one might expect a discussion of surveillance, the emphasis is on leadership, controlling access, and planning, and it is left to schools themselves to determine whether surveillance technology is desirable. The authors of this guide note that "the research on what works in school-based crisis planning is in its infancy," and stress the importance of tailoring plans to the context at hand (U.S. Department of Education 2007a, 1–4). While support for surveillance is muted in the guide, there is no questioning of the need for more comprehensive top-down safety measures in American schools, and no discussion at all of their relationship to the mission of schools.

Against that background, this chapter explores two questions:

1. On what empirical and normative bases should we accept the assertion that schools require more elaborate security systems, including intrusive surveillance technology, architectural changes and background checks? My hypothesis is that the same interactive forces that are transforming the broader security landscape at national and global levels—rapid technology innovation and diffusion, the empowerment of individuals and groups, global environmental change, and the expansion and deepening of capitalism—are affecting threats and vulnerabilities at the school level, but that a careful analysis of these changes is not driving the steps that are actually being taken in response to new challenges.

2. Given the need for a new generation of security measures, how can they be identified and how can and should they be integrated into the mission of education? My hypothesis here is that many measures being taken encourage passivity, consumption, and dependence, whereas a different set of measures could foster community, responsibility, and the acquisition of skills and knowledge that would cultivate

a generation of confident risk managers and first responders through building resilience and capability that would have immediate and long-term positive effects at the local, state and national levels.

THE CHANGING SECURITY ENVIRONMENT

On September 1, 2004, armed rebels took 1,100 children and adults hostage in a school in Beslan, Russia. A three-day standoff ended in a chaotic gun battle that left 186 children and 148 adults dead. C. J. Chivers described the scene at the end of the third day.

> The place was a horror. Each element of the siege—from the capture of the children to the enforced conditions of their captivity among the bombs to the murders of their fathers and teachers in the literature classroom to the explosions that ripped apart people by the score—had been a descent deeper into cruelty, violence, and near-paralyzing fear. Now they had reached the worst. Women stood at windows, screaming and waving white cloths. Bullets struck the walls. Dust and smoke hung in the air. Glass covered the floor, much of it splattered with blood. The room stunk of gunpowder, rotting food, and sweat. Terrorists raced through the haze, bearded, whooping, firing, and yelling instructions. Larisa had her son, Zaurbek, by the hand, and apprehended their new conditions; Madina had the two children she had brought from the weight room. She did not know their names. They rushed around a corner near the dish-washing room, where at least twenty other hostages were massed tight. Two girls were trying to squeeze themselves into a massive soup pot. Dead women and children were strewn on the kitchen tiles. The Kudziyeva family took a place on the floor. (2007, 10)

The magnitude of this event shocked the world, and as details of the events emerged, the high costs of inadequate preparedness became disturbingly clear. Although there is much controversy over the broad trends in global terrorism, the attacks in Beslan and elsewhere have persuaded many analysts that terrorists have trespassed moral thresholds, and thus significantly changed the global security landscape (Delpeche 2007). Indeed, terrorists have become for many observers the human face of a new security environment in which everyone is a potential victim of both accidental and nefarious transnational activities, and everyone is a potential first responder. In this context, many argue that schools need to look anew at safety.

The focus on terrorism as the epitome of a new generation of security challenges has substantial academic support. For example, for the past two decades influential scholars such as James Rosenau (1990) and

Thomas Homer-Dixon (2006) have been arguing that a diacritical feature of the world today is the enormous capacity technology has made available to small groups—capacity that can be used for both good (Bill Gates's global health initiative) or malevolent (catastrophic terrorism) ends. But terrorism is scarcely the only threat schools face, and while it may be analytically captivating and have great symbolic value, it remains a low-probability event from a statistical perspective. In contrast, another element of contemporary security discourse, environmental disasters, is having a far wider impact on schools and students (Fagan 2008; Homer-Dixon 1999; Intergovernmental Panel on Climate Change 2007; Kaplan 1994; Myers 1993).

For example, reporting in the wake of the earthquake that killed thousands, including hundreds of children in poorly constructed schools, in Sichuan province on May 12, 2008, the science journalist Andrew Revkin wrote:

> In recent years, there have been deadly school collapses after earthquakes in Italy, Algeria, Morocco and Turkey. Most notably, in Pakistan on Oct. 8, 2005, at least 17,000 children died as more than 7,000 schools collapsed after a powerful jolt shook a mountainous region near the Indian border. Similar risks, and delays in reducing them, exist in countries rich and poor from the Americas across Europe and Asia. In 2006, Brian Tucker, an earthquake specialist who runs a private group, GeoHazards International, presented a study on schools to the Economic Cooperation Organization, a group of 10 countries in Europe and Asia. The analysis found that 180 million people, including 40 million school-age children, faced "an earthquake risk equal to that of northern Pakistan." (2008)

Terrorist attacks and natural disasters are not new, but from the perspective of many analysts their frequency and intensity are increasing as a result of a number of variables that are dramatically reshaping the global context of human activity and interaction (Intergovernmental Panel on Climate Change 2007; hereafter IPCC). There is no single and definitive list of these variables, but the recent work of Thomas Homer-Dixon provides a good starting point for discussion. In his 2006 study, *The Upside of Down: Catastrophe, Creativity, and the Renewal of Civilization*, he identifies five "tectonic stresses" that are rendering the world less secure and more vulnerable to violence and breakdown:

- Energy stress resulting from a general imperative for growth that is now at odds with the declining availability of cheap and easily acces-sible oil—humankind's major energy source
- Economic stress, a complex problem that has much to do with income inequality
- Demographic stress, as populations grow rapidly in areas like the

megacities of the developing world that are hard-pressed to provide them with what they need to survive and flourish

- Environmental stress, the focus of Homer-Dixon's earlier work, which worsens as we continue to degrade forests, fisheries, and other natural resources
- Climate stress, the result of greenhouse gas emissions that alter the composition of the atmosphere in ways that have dramatic, alarming, and often unpredictable impacts across the planet

On their own these stresses are bad. When they interact—which they frequently do—they are worse. Complicating matters further, they are sensitive to two "multiplier" variables:

- The globe-spanning technologies that amplify their destructive potential by deepening and expanding social connectivity
- The small groups and individuals that wield unprecedented technological power that can be exercised for malevolent ends

The highly influential UCLA scholar Jared Diamond offers a historical perspective that supports Homer-Dixon's analysis. In his 2005 book, *Collapse: How Societies Choose to Fail or Succeed*, Diamond explores the environmental and geographical factors that make some societies more prone to collapse than others. In the same genre of looming disaster, another historian, Brian Fagan (2008), focuses on climate change and creates an alarming vision of where the world is heading. Of course, not everyone examining the set of trends Homer-Dixon analyzes reaches the same conclusions, and a number of authors (Simon 1996; Lomberg 2001; Zakaria 2008; Friedman 2007) have argued that human innovation buttressed by many positive trends in areas such as economic growth, literacy gains, and political empowerment will generate the ingenuity needed to solve the challenges the more pessimistic writers describe (against this see Homer-Dixon 2000). But while these authors are remarkably different in terms of their predictions—a century of peace and flourishing versus a century of breakdown and violence—they do not disagree that humankind is facing new security challenges, driven in large measure by unprecedented environmental and social—especially demographic—pressures.

In this context of new forms of social and ecological vulnerability, technology functions to destroy or diminish historical barriers while also giving people the means to change things—through extraction, production, and disposal systems—on a planetary scale. For centuries the United States was largely insulated from invaders of all kinds by its geography. Two oceans, a cold northern neighbor, and the isthmus of Central America provided very effective natural barriers from the rest of the world. But the dynamics of technology and the imperatives of economic growth have changed this situation. For example, microbial invaders from the tropics have established themselves in the country as a result of population flows and global warming. In 1993, Louis V. Kirchhoff identified the emergence of American trypanosomiasis and related this new disease to the fact that "[s]ince the mid-1970s, large numbers of immigrants have entered the United States from regions where Chagas' disease [trypanosomiasis] is common, especially Central America. Epidemiologic evidence suggests that many of these people are infected with T. cruzi" (639).

Unfortunately observations such as this do far more than merely announce a scientific finding of significance for public health. They also divest a complex process—immigration—of history and context and suggest a stark and misleading association with a threat. This remarkably common rhetoric—which wraps science in opinion and in many other settings has severely compromised our capacity to address challenges such as HIV/AIDS—creates an opening for simplistic policy positions—such as the argument that dramatically reducing immigration will dramatically reduce transboundary threats. But all of these transboundary threats are generated by large-scale processes of capital expansion, technological innovation and diffusion, and climate change; policy needs to be shaped by an understanding of these forces, which is a considerably more difficult but also more just and effective way of approaching problems such as the spread of tropical disease curtains. As Shirley Gregory writes, linking the disease threat to the broad and complex process of climate change:

> Dengue, a disease previously found mostly in the tropics and sub-tropics, could become a growing threat to the United States, medical experts worry. Many scientists are putting the blame on climate change. As average temperatures around the world continue to rise, diseases once limited by cool nighttime and winter temperatures will be able to spread into new, warmer territories. That's especially the case with so-called vector-borne diseases, which are spread by pests like mosquitoes. (2008, 1)

As natural borders have eroded under the pressures of technological infiltration and economic migration, the human capacity to affect things on a macro scale has developed. Perhaps the paradigm case of this is climate change, the unintended outcome of fossil fuel use that has altered the amount of carbon in the atmosphere enough to change the temperature of the planet.

According to *World in Transition: Climate Change as a Security Risk*, a report by the German Advisory Council on Global Change, "Climate change will overstretch many societies' adaptive capacities within the coming decades" (German Advisory Council on Global Change 2008, 1). The report identifies a set of "conflict constellations" (ibid., 2) related to climate change:

- Degradation of fresh water in areas that "lack the political and institutional framework necessary for the adaptation of water and crisis management systems. This could overstretch existing conflict resolution mechanisms, ultimately leading to destabilization and violence" (ibid.).
- Decline in food production that could lead to "regional food crises and further undermine the economic performance of weak and unstable states, thereby encouraging or exacerbating destabilization, the collapse of social systems, and violent conflicts" (ibid., 3).
- Increase in storm and flood disasters, undermining crisis management systems and triggering out-migration and other social problems.

The basic point, which is echoed in a flood of scholarship, is that anthropogenic climate change is having, and for many decades will continue to have, mixed—and often very negative—effects around the world (Intergovernmental Panel on Climate Change 2007; Matthew 2008).

In summary, there is broad consensus that the security challenges of the twenty-first century are unique in at least three ways. First, technology and demographic change in the context of sustained economic growth have made it possible for people to have a significant impact at the planetary level on both earth and social systems. The energy use of China and United States—two countries that combined have a quarter of the world's population—clearly affects the climate of the entire planet: over 190 countries with a total population of 6.6 billion people, as well as perhaps 100 million other species.) The longer droughts, changes in precipitation patterns, and severe weather events associated with climate change introduce new diseases, disrupt agricultural economies, and create new and often unmet demands for natural resources around the world.

Second, this combination of driving forces also has enabled the creation of dense global networks that have significantly increased our connectedness (Barabasi 2003). A disease originating in one country can travel via air to any other country in a matter of hours; the outbreak of SARS in 2002–2003 is one example of this. Panicked international currency trading can quickly overwhelm a country's ability to manage its national currency; the case of the Thai baht in 1997 exemplifies this. So even if an event is not global in scale and impact, its effects can travel quickly through transportation, communication, information, and other networks to affect distant and remote social and environmental systems.

Third, technology has created enormous power at the micro level that can be used for both good and bad ends. Scientists all over the world can collaborate in real time on analyzing climate data or decoding a new infectious agent through the Internet. But individuals are also able to launch computer viruses into cyberspace; cleanup measures cost over twenty billion dollars worldwide each year, capital that creates jobs but does not produce wealth and is thus an additional cost of doing business. A small group of poorly funded nongovernmental organizations based in different countries worked successfully in the 1990s toward a global ban on antipersonnel landmines—a goal that many government officials believed to be impossible at that time (Matthew et al. 2004). In sharp contrast, according to one estimate, the 9/11 terrorist attacks, organized by a handful of extremists, cost as little as $500,000 to stage and imposed hundreds of billions—and possibly trillions—of dollars of costs on the United States and the rest of the world.

An important feature of analyses of new threats—and one that is often ignored in the familiar claim in popular culture and political rhetoric that "no one is safe"—is the argument that vulnerability to new threats is heavily biased toward the poor—as was the case for the previous generation of threats. Suffering from micronutrient deficiencies, the poor are more sensitive to viruses and bacteria. Forced to eke out livings on marginal lands, they live in the front lines of drought, earthquakes, and floods. Living hand to mouth they are hard-pressed to adjust to changes in their environment and likely therefore to be displaced, fall ill, lose their livelihoods, or go hungry (Barnet and Adger 2007; CNA Corporation 2007; Diamond 2005; Homer-Dixon 2000; Intergovernmental Panel on Climate Change 2007; Kaplan 1994; Matthew 2008; Sachs 2005 United Nations Development Programme 1994).

Schools in the New Security Environment

There is broad agreement that while traditional security threats like war, state-sponsored violence, and poverty remain, many of the security threats of today are unique—such as computer viruses and climate change———or dramatically amplified—such as transnational terrorism and antibiotic-resistant viruses (Reddy 2007). In consequence, we have witnessed more than a decade of innovative research and debate around "rethinking security." This has generated a vocabulary ("human security," "environmental security") that aims to articulate the key features of a new security paradigm. But this intense activity has not generated consensus on two issues. First, is our overall security situation improving or worsening? Some people perceive that the synergetic combination of climate change, economic instability, and transnational crime, and terrorism is overwhelming governance institutions and much—perhaps all—of the world is headed for catastrophe. But others see broad grounds for optimism as an increasingly educated and global civil society mobilizes, constructs new norms and aspirations, and experiments with new technologies and new institutions. All we can say with confidence is that today poverty correlates strongly with vulnerability to new security threats.

Second, whatever the trends, what should we do today? Do we give greater freedom to the market, or introduce more regulation to reshape the arena in which the market must function? Do we invest heavily in climate change mitigation, or in climate-change adaptation? In a world of agile and powerful transnational networks, do we try to improve the filtering capacity of our borders so we can keep undesirable elements out, or do we allow them to erode on the grounds that the benefits of openness vastly outweigh the risks? Do we work through multilateral processes on these issues, or do we focus more on self-reliance and self-sufficiency? Do we strive to protect and empower the poor, or do we do whatever we have to do to isolate and contain them?

These are difficult questions, and it is not surprising that we struggle to answer them. There is consensus on one point, however: the new security threats affect every sector of society, including education. While the poor are more vulnerable today than the rich, no one is immune from extreme weather, market collapses, acts of terrorism, or infectious agents, and no one is sure how deeply or how quickly these threats will intrude into communities of wealth and privilege. It seems reasonable to assume that ensuring the safety of children in schools is a priority in every society. So what does meeting this goal entail in a world of new threats, great uncertainty, and significant disagreement?

Of course perennial problems such as head lice, bullying, and fires continue to plague schools, even as new ones such as climate change and obesity gain momentum and attention. But on the familiar side of the equation, there is some good news: according to a set of 2007 reports issued by the U.S. Department of Education's National Center for Education Statistics, there are very clear and positive trends for many of these perennial issues. For example,

> From July 1, 2005, through June 30, 2006, there were 14 homicides and 3 suicides of school-age youth (ages 5–18) at school. Combined, this number translates into 1 homicide or suicide of a school-age youth at school per 3.2 million students enrolled during the 2005–06 school year. The most recent data available for the total number of homicides of school-age youth are from the 2004–05 school year, during which there were 1,534 homicides. In the 2004 calendar year, there were 1,471 suicides of school-age youth. In each school year, youth were over 50 times more likely to be murdered and were over 150 times more likely to commit suicide when they were away from school than at school. (U.S. Department of Education 2007b, 1)

During the period under review, there was a sharp decline in the percentage of students who were the victims of attempted and completed thefts, violent crimes, and serious violent crimes at school as well as in the percentage of teachers who were threatened or attacked each year. Yet in spite of these numbers, students do not feel safer today than in the past:

> In 2005, approximately 6 percent of students ages 12–18 reported that they were afraid of attack or harm at school, and 5 percent reported that they were afraid of attack or harm away from school. There was no measurable change between 2003 and 2005 in the percentage of students reporting fear of attack or harm at or away from school. Consistent with findings from 1999 and 2001, students in 2005 were more likely to report being afraid of an attack at school than away from school. The percentage of students who reported that they were afraid of being attacked at school (including on the way to and from school) decreased from 12 to 6 percent between 1995 and 2001; however, no measurable difference was detected between 2001 and 2005. Similarly, there was no change in the percentage of students who feared such an attack away from school between 1999 and 2005. (Ibid.)

A number of studies argue that we live today in what Ulrich Beck (1992) and Anthony Giddens (1999) call a "risk society"—a society in which we have a heightened sense of being surrounded by risk. Many authors are concerned that this perception is not grounded in any reasonable or empirically defensible assessment of threat and vulnerability; instead, it is a sensibility carefully cultivated by people who stand to profit from those investments that are prompted by high levels of generalized fear (Klein 2007; Matthew 2006; Mueller 2006).

But profiteers are not the only people who describe a world on the edge of disaster. As noted in the preceding section, prominent journalists and scholars, after sifting through reams of data, have also crafted frightening visions of the world we inhabit and the future that lies before us. For example, in his widely cited 1994 piece, "The Coming Anarchy," Robert Kaplan writes:

> It is time to understand the environment for what it is: the national security issue of the early twenty-first century. The political and strategic impact of surging populations, spreading disease, deforestation and soil erosion, water depletion, air pollution, and, possibly, rising sea levels in critical, overcrowded regions like the Nile Delta and Bangladesh—developments that will prompt mass migrations and, in turn, incite group conflicts—will be the core foreign policy challenge from which most others will ultimately emanate. (Kaplan 1994, 3)

Matthew Connolly and Paul Kennedy picked up this line of argument in another widely read essay, "Must It Be the Rest Against the West?": "We are heading into the twenty-first century in a world consisting for the most part of a relatively small number of rich, satiated, demographically stagnant societies and a large number of poverty-stricken, resource-depleted nations whose populations are doubling every twenty-five years or less" (Connolly and Kennedy 1994). Ironically, in a culture of permanent crisis, the voices of scholars like Homer-Dixon, who lays considerable blame for our predicament on the excesses of capitalism and the unwillingness of government to accept the magnitude of the threats we face, blend rather well with those of a George W. Bush arguing that massive—and often secretive—investments in the Global War on Terror (GWOT) are justified.

In other words, are students afraid they may be attacked or harmed at school because they have been bombarded with dire—but unsupported—pronouncements and flooded with frightening Columbine-type imagery, behind both of which lurk capitalists seeking to profit by selling safety systems that are not truly needed? Or are they afraid because they see a growing gap between the measures being taken to protect them and the array of threats gathering mass all around them?

Having spent the last fifteen years studying climate change, resource scarcity, and other forms of environmental stress in conflict and post-conflict zones in East Africa and South Asia, I am personally persuaded that many of the threats we currently face are complex, severe and worsening (Matthew 2008). I believe that the potential for catastrophe on unprecedented scales is very real. The challenge, from my perspective, is to continue to evaluate these risks and ensure that risk management practices are designed in the general interests of society as opposed to the particular interests of its politicians and vendors.

In this new security context, school safety is complicated because schools are important to society in many ways. They are simultaneously the most alarming sites of violent events and catastrophes, the staging areas for community preparation and response activities, and the training grounds for the next generation of more or less prepared and resilient adults. They are beacons of light when society succeeds in providing security, and flower-strewn memorials when it fails.

This leads to the question: are more invasive surveillance systems and garrison architecture—the measures discussed at the beginning of this chapter and widely promoted within the U.S. Department of Education as well as the private sector—likely to improve school safety? Of course, these technologies may not be desirable for other reasons, but if they appreciably improve the safety of students, then critiques will have a lot of work to do to discredit them. If not, then ancillary concerns simply add weight to criticism.

As noted earlier in this chapter, satisfactory evaluations of new school safety measures are not yet available, so we will have to approach this issue from a somewhat theoretical vantage. The organization Safe Kids Worldwide is a valuable resource with which to begin. According to its U.S. branch: "In general, children are primarily at risk of unintentional injury-related death from: motor vehicle injuries, which include children as occupants, pedestrians and bicyclists; drowning; fire and burns; airway obstruction injury (including suffocation and choking); unintentional firearm injuries; falls; and poisoning." Moreover, "the vast majority of unintentional injury-related deaths among children occur in the evening hours, when children are most likely to be out of school and unsupervised." According to Safe Kids, schools are indeed the safest places for children to be. Moreover, whether at home, at school or elsewhere, "Unintentional injuries disproportionately affect poor children and result in more fatalities among these children than among children with greater economic resources." Not surprisingly, "Black and Native American children have disproportionately high death and injury rates, primarily due to higher levels of poverty and lower levels of education, employment and income." Based on this data, one might reasonably conclude that U.S. schools are very safe and that the best overall approaches to reducing the current rates of severe injuries and deaths experienced by school-age children would include poverty reduction, supervised after school care, and universal health care (Safe Kids USA Web site).

Data on perennial threats are unambiguous: vulnerability is clearly and principally linked to socioeconomic status. Schools, of course, cannot be expected to solve these large-scale societal problems of inequality and marginalization, which place poor children more directly in the pathways of harm than others. By educating the poor, schools may be building bridges out of poverty, but this process has been slow and uneven. So the question becomes, what can be done? In answering this question, it is not at all clear that investments in surveillance systems and architectural reform would reduce vulnerability to many of the threats that currently cause injury and death to children. Schools in middle- and upper-class neighborhoods are already largely insulated from these problems, so such investments could be wasteful, channeling resources away from more critical needs. Schools with these problems—with the type of threats that might be described as criminal acts—are disproportionately located in areas of poverty where these problems are endemic. Surveillance and architectural reform might further the role of schools as safe havens in these neighborhoods, but they might not, and they probably would have little impact on the overall probability of a school-age child experiencing violence or death.

What about other threats such as exposure to pollutants or to the microbes, fires, and heat waves associated with climate change? What about health problems like childhood obesity? Here we can theorize that the poor currently have heightened vulnerability to these threats as well; whether their impact on middle- and upper-class schoolchildren will grow is not known, but there are compelling reasons to believe that this growth is likely to happen. So, again, what is the best response for a school?

It is easy to see that good hydration and nutritious diets, requiring the application of sunscreen, monitoring air quality, encouraging social distancing, and facilitating personal hygiene are all the sort of measures that a school might implement to good effect. It is much less obvious how increased surveillance or garrison architecture would be of help on these issues.

This leaves one further threat domain—that situation in which the school is the specific target of hyperviolence or terrorism. Shooters and terrorists are rare, but their impact is enormous, and there are clearly steps that can be taken to reduce what is already a small risk. Improved control of access to the school and a safe and systematic process for collecting and analyzing suspicious-circumstance reports are among the low-cost, high-impact measures that all schools ought to contemplate.

Schools are safe places but they do face a range of threats, some of which may be growing, perhaps dramatically. It is not clear, however, that increased surveillance or garrison architecture—two high-cost measures—would significantly reduce most of these threats. The marginal benefits they might confer need therefore to be assessed on a case-by-case basis against other ways in which security dollars could be spent, and the possible and likely negative effects of those ways. These latter include encouraging a culture of apathy, dependence, and distrust; motivating people to innovate resistance and evasion tactics; and generating data that can be misused. Where surveillance is stepped up, for example, it seems inevitable that administrators will suddenly find themselves in compromising positions on YouTube, victims of unforeseen—and unforeseeable—countersurveillance activities.

CONCLUSIONS: PROTECT AND EMPOWER

I agree that protecting schoolchildren should be a national priority and I believe that some schools are today dealing with a much higher level of risk than others, an unfair and unwise situation rooted in socioeconomic disparities. I also believe that all schools may soon find themselves facing an alarming array of new and very serious threats. Under these conditions, surveillance systems and architectural changes may be of value, but they are not obviously or universally of value. Their utility needs to be assessed case by case, as schools go through the process of developing their mandated safety plans.

No matter what schools do, schoolchildren will face dangers both on and off school premises, and later as adults they will also face dangers, some of which will cause harm and death. Sadly, protection sometimes fails. There-fore, another key feature of school safety has to do with response capacity or empowerment. In this regard, schools could do much more than they currently do.

There is a very simple explanation for why everyone—at any age—should have first-response training. Everyone could find themselves facing a direct threat or arriving first at the scene of an accident or disaster, and the decisions made at that point in time will likely determine the extent of the human and other costs.

There are three reasons why schools are an obvious setting for this training. First, at any point during most days of the year a significant portion of a society is in school or on school premises in some capacity. Schools are therefore common sites for everything from bomb threats to disease transmission to flooding. Many students will thus find themselves directly threatened or first on the scene of an accident or disaster. In these cases, professionals may not arrive for minutes—or even hours. Although schools are likely to be among the first recipients of emergency-response resources, a large-scale disaster such as an earthquake could exhaust resources very quickly, leaving schools largely on their own. Second, at times of emergency schools are often a critical resource to the communities in which they are located—they immediately become shelters, staging areas, and distribution points. Third, training in schools can be universal, thereby establishing national standards, and it can have long-term benefits to society. Of course, this raises thorny questions about the educational mission of schools—do we want to nurture creativity, critical thinking, and problem solving, or do we want to prepare students to be competent at standardized testing? I will not pursue this issue here but I can see no basis for arguing that these are basically goals that can be met through the same training processes.

In any case, like most countries, the United States has a national standard for certification in emergency response training (CERT). Through the CERT program, trainees learn standard procedures for evacuation and lockdown, first aid, integrating into an accident scene, and handing off to professionals when they arrive. The training is straightforward and can be mastered by people of all ages. Integrating this type of training into school curricula would increase national capacity, instill confidence, encourage civic responsibility, and promote self-reliance.

This empowerment strategy ought to be a minimal requirement. Schools could do much more than they currently do to prepare students for success in the multicultural, high-speed, interconnected world they inhabit; help them understand the environmental, health, transportation, and other threats they face; and provide them with opportunities to experiment with adaptation and mitigation strategies. In this regard, architectural changes could be of tremendous value in transforming schools into living laboratories of healthy green space, food cultivation, energy self-sufficiency, waste management, water efficiency, low-cost heating and cooling, and sustainable material use. In such environments students would be safer, and they would learn processes and skills that would make the nation and the world safer.

REFERENCES

Barabasi, Albert-Laszlo. 2003. *Linked: How everything is connected to everything else and what it means*. New York: Plume.

Barnet, Jon, and Neil Adger. 2007. Climate change, human security and violent conflict. *Political Geography* 26:639–655.

Beck, Ulrich. 1992. *Risk society: Towards a new modernity*. New Delhi: Sage.

Brem, Stefan, Richard Matthew, and Ken Rutherford, eds. 2003. *Reframing the agenda: Middle powers and world politics*. New York: Praeger.

Chivers, C. J. 2007. "The School." *Esquire.* http://www.esquire.com/features/ESQ0606BESLAN_140 (accessed July 3, 2008).

CNA Corporation. 2007. National security and the threat of climate change. http://securityandclimate.cna.org/report.

CNN. 1998. Fearing copycats paper keeps Oregon shooting off front page. http://www.cnn.com/US/9805/22/school.shooting.page.one (accessed June 3, 2005).

Connolly, Matthew and Paul Kennedy. December 1994. 'Must it be the rest against the West?' *Atlantic Monthly* 274 (6): 61–84. http://www.theatlantic.com/politics/immigrat/kennf.htm, 8 (accessed July 3, 2008).

Delpeche, Therese. 2007. *Savage century: Back to barbarism*. Washington: Carnegie.

Diamond, Jared. 2005. *Collapse: How societies choose to fail or succeed*. New York: Viking.

Fagan, Brian. 2008. *The great warming: Climate change and the rise and fall of civilizations*. London: Bloomsbury Press.

Friedman, Thomas. 2007. *The world is flat 3.0: A brief history of the twenty-first century*. New York: Picador.

German Advisory Council on Global Change. 2008. *World in transition: climate change as a security risk*. London: Earthscan. http://www.wbgu.de/wbgu_jg2007_engl.html.

Giddens, Anthony. 1999. 'Risk and responsibility.' *Modern Law Review* 62 (1): 1–10.

Green, Mary. 1999. *The appropriate and effective use of security technologies in U.S. schools*. Washington, DC: U.S. Department of Justice. http://www.ncjrs.gov/school/178265.pdf (accessed July 3, 2008).

Gregory, Shirley. 2008. Tropical disease dengue could impact United States. http://www.associatedcontent.com/article/528335/tropical_disease_dengue_could_impact.html?cat=5 (accessed July 3, 2008).

Homer-Dixon, Thomas. 1999. *Environment, scarcity and violence*. Princeton, NJ: Princeton University Press.

———. 2000. *The ingenuity gap*. New York: Alfred A. Knopf.

———. 2006. *The upside of down: Catastrophe, creativity, and the renewal of civilization*. Washington, DC: Island Press.

Infoplease. 2005. A timeline of recent school shootings world wide, 2005. http://www.infoplease.com/ipa/A0777958.html (accessed May 26, 2005).

Intergovernmental Panel on Climate Change. 2007. *Working Group II report: Climate change impacts, adaptation, and vulnerability.* http://www.ipcc.ch/.

Kaplan, Robert. 1994. The coming anarchy: How scarcity, crime, overpopulation, tribalism, and disease are rapidly destroying the social fabric of our planet. February. http://theatlantic.com/politics/foreign/anarchy.htm.

Kirchhoff, Louis V. 1993. American trypanosomiasis (Chagas' disease)—A tropical disease now in the United States. *New England Journal of Medicine.* August 26: 639–644. http://content.nejm.org/cgi/content/full/329/9/639 (accessed July 3, 2008).

Klein, Naomi. 2007. *The shock doctrine: The rise of disaster capitalism.* New York: Henry Holt.

Lomberg, Bjorn. 2001. *The skeptical environmentalist: Measuring the real state of the world.* Cambridge: Cambridge University Press.

Macfarlane, S. Neil, and Yuen Foong Khong. 2006. *Human security and the UN: A critical history.* Bloomington: Indiana University Press.

Mack, Andrew, ed. 2008. Human security brief 2007. http://www.humansecuritybrief. org/HSRP_Brief_2007.pdf (accessed July 3, 2008).

Matthew, Richard. 2006. "Bioterrorism and national security: Peripheral threats, core vulnerabilities." In *Making Threats: Biofears and Environmental Anxieties,* ed. Elizabeth Hartmann and Banu Sumerian, 237–246. New York: Rowman & Littlefield.

———. 2008. "Challenges for human and international security: Resource scarcity." *Coping with Crisis, Working Paper Series.* New York: International Peace Institute.

Mueller, John. 2006. *Overblown: How politicians and the terrorism industry inflate national security threats and why we believe them.* New York: Free Press.

Myers, Norman. 1993. *Ultimate security: The environmental basis of political stability.* New York: Norton.

Paris, Roland. 2001. Human security: Paradigm shift or hot air? *International Security* 26 (Fall): 87–102.

Paulson, Steven K. 1999. Agents creating models of Columbine. *Daily Camera.* http:// www.boulderclassifieds.com/shooting/07bcolum.html (accessed June 3, 2005).

Reddy, Vinay. 2007. Antibiotics, bacteria and (usually not) viruses. http://www.drreddy. com/antibx.html.

Revkin, Andrew C. 2008. China earthquake brings faulty school design to the fore. *International Herald Tribune.* May 14. http://www.iht.com/articles/2008/05/14/ asia/schools.php (accessed July 8, 2008).

Rosenau, James N. 1990. *Turbulence in world politics: A theory of change and continuity.* Princeton, NJ: Princeton University Press.

Sachs, Jeffrey. 2005. Climate change and war. http://www.tompaine.com/print/ climate_change_and_war. php (accessed March 11, 2005).

Safe Kids USA. Injury facts: Child injuries. http://www.usa.safekids.org/tier3_ cd.cfm?folder_id=540&content_item_id=1030.

Scholte, Jan Aarte. 2000. *Globalization: A critical introduction.* New York: St. Martin's.

Simon, Julian. 1996. *The ultimate resource 2.* Princeton, NJ: Princeton University Press.

Stout, Martha. 2007. *The paranoia switch.* New York: Farrar, Straus and Giroux.

Toppo, Greg. 2006. High-tech school security is on the rise. *USA Today.* October 9. http://www.usatoday.com/news/education/2006-10-09-school-security-x.htm.

UNDP. 1994. *Human development report 1994.* Oxford: Oxford University Press.

U.S. Department of Education. 2007a. Practical information on crisis planning: A

guide for schools and communities. http://www.ed.gov/admins/lead/safety/emer-
gencyplan/crisisplanning.pdf.

———. 2007b. Institute of Education Sciences, National Center for Education Statistics.
Fast facts. http://nces.ed.gov/fastfacts/display.asp?id=49.

Wilson, Edward O. 1992. *Diversity of life*. Cambridge, MA: Harvard University Press.

World Commission on Environment and Development. 1987. *Our common future*.
Oxford: Oxford University Press.

Zakaria, Fareed. 2008. *The post-American world*. New York: Norton.

CHAPTER 8

Risky Youth and the
Psychology of Surveillance

THE CRISIS OF THE SCHOOL SHOOTER

Tyson Lewis

DRAWING ON THE WORK OF SOCIOLOGIST Ulrich Beck, Nanette Davis has argued that "surplus-risk" has come to define American adolescents (1999, xiii). Surplus risk is an excessive form of risk above and beyond the normal trials and tribulations that define adolescence. Davis's list of social risks include the uncertainty of an unstable economy, the inability of schools and social institutions to provide individuals with the information and skills needed to make rational choices, the replacement of community bonds with market logics and consumerist identities, and the growing inability to assess benefits from social participation beyond self-interest. For youth, these risks translate into lifestyles that involve the rampant consumption of media violence, drug use, economic glass ceilings, and a pervasive loss of a sense of purpose and/or meaning to one's life. All in all, postmodern cultural logics, a technological-industrial worldview, and the destabilizing effects of global capitalism work together to create the social conditions leading to these excessive risk factors in the lives of young boys and girls. As Benjamin Frymer (2005) has argued, the broad-reaching implications of the risk society do not solely affect the disadvantaged. Rather, middle-class children in white suburban and rural areas are also deeply integrated into a culture of fragmented identity, media spectacle, and one-dimensional consumerism that leads to a pervasive ethos of depression, rage, detachment, and suicide (also see Spina 2000).

Perhaps the limit case of this pervasive youth crisis is the proverbial school shooter phenomenon. While youth violence in schools is nothing new, the recent string of hyperviolence is noteworthy on two accounts. First, the stage for displaying iconic images of male youth violence shifted decisively from largely African American and Latino urban centers to white, rural, and suburban "safe" neighborhoods as well as prestigious institutions of higher learning (Bowman 2001). Second, this violence is on a mass scale, displaying a startling callousness and indifference to the victims. Take for instance the case of Barry Loukaitis. One day in 1996, he walked into his algebra class at Frontier Middle School east of Seattle and shot a popular boy who had harassed him. Standing over the dying boy, Barry—without cynicism or irony—proclaimed, "This sure beats algebra, doesn't it?" He then turned and fired at two other students and his teacher, killing her while she still held an eraser in her hand. After being arrested for the brutal murders, Barry was taken to a prison cell where, exhausted from the adrenalin rush, he promptly took a nap before interrogation. When asked why he had continued to kill after his intended target had died, Barry had no motive. "I don't know," he said, "I guess my reflex took over."

In this chapter, I will position the violence of the school shooter in relation to the broader forces and relations of production that condition both subjective and material risks. In order to accomplish this task, I have to extend the understanding of the nature of "risk" in two respects. First, I will frame the notion of the risk society in relation to key shifts in our under-standing of normality. I will then argue that the violence of school shootings is the net result of the unstable psychic life of power in young men as it is constructed in a postindustrial, postmodern cultural logic of surveillance and security. Certainly, excessive male rage is, according to Douglas Kellner (2008), multidimensional, yet I would like to argue that in the last instance, it is the peculiar problem of enjoyment that forms the psychological bedrock of male aggression in a flexible, risky, and permissive society such as the United States. In conclusion, I suggest an alternative notion of health and safety beyond the pathologies of surveillance and risky youth.

DISCOURSES AND PRACTICES OF NORMALITY IN SCHOOLS

In this section I outline the relationship between power, discourses and practices of normality, and the overall surveillance logic of capitalism. My goal is to create a new theoretical framework for understanding how global trends affect the psychological dispositions of youth. Because of the high correlation between school shootings and white, male, middle-class students, I have chosen to focus exclusively on this population.

Counter to the more or less widely held conception of power as negative and repressive, Michel Foucault argues for the opposite view: power as purely productive. "We must cease once and for all to describe the effects of power in negative terms: it 'excludes,' it 'represses,' it 'censors,' it 'abstracts,' it 'masks,' it 'conceals.' In fact, power produces; it produces reality; it produces domains of objects and rituals of truth. The individual and the knowledge that may be gained of him belong to this production" (1979, 194). Here Foucault rejects the repressive hypothesis often applied to analyses of Victorian culture (most famously Freud's analysis of the unconscious) that subjectivity is repressed by certain forms of power. Rather, in Foucault's genealogical project, subjectivity is thoroughly historicized as the product of a certain regime of power and the various discourses, institutions, and practices through which this power is mobilized. There is nothing alienated or repressed in Foucault's counterhistory, simply the production of new bodies, new pleasures, new technologies of policing, new perversions, and new discourses. To quote Foucault: "My objective . . . has been to create a history of the different modes by which, in our culture, human beings are made subjects" (1984, 417).

Yet as Jurgen Link (2004) states, this thesis overreaches its historical specificity and generalizes a much more recent shift in relation to the discourse of normality as the "realization" of biopower. For Link, the Victorian period *was* repressive in a more or less classically Marxian or Freudian sense, leading to alienation and/or melancholic attachment to a lost object cause. Here normality as a unique product of the modern, western science of statistical analysis operates through what Link describes as protonormalistic discourses and practices of control. The protonormalistic is concerned with the demarcation of borders between normality and abnormality. Biopower in this sense locates the body in relation to normality, standardization, and burgeoning industrial profitability through the practice of a ban over and against the unhealthy, the feebleminded, and the abnormal. According to Link, "Individuals must be frequently 'normalized' against their will and wishes along established guidelines—in the French sense of *normalises*, that is 'standardized'" (2004, 27).

Link perceives a decisive shift in the concept and practice of normality around the end of World War II, a time that witnessed the rise of what he terms "flexible-normalistic" measures. As opposed to the protonormalistic, flexible models function in terms of the subject's ability to normalize him- or herself without external compulsion. It is not so much concerned with the construction and maintenance of strict boundaries between the normal and the abnormal. Rather, a continuum is constructed and a fragile equilibrium is sought. This model of flexible-normalistic discourse is thus tolerant of deviance and is highly inclusive. Such a notion is closer to Foucault's original model of power proposed in *History of Sexuality Volume I*, but has been relocated in the much more immediate present.

I would add to Link's important insights that the shift in normality is itself conditioned by a more foundational movement within capitalism toward a flexible economy. Late capitalism—characterized by free trade, easy relocation of industries across national borders in pursuit of lower labor costs, increase in business mergers, rampant privatization of formerly public institutions, a widening of social and economic inequality beyond anything seen previously in the capitalist era, and the replacement of full-time jobs with temporary work—demands a flexible and mobile theory of normality. Biopower, as the distribution of bodies in relation to normality, moves from a much more striated, fixed, and permanent concept of protonormalistic (Taylorism) to flexible-normalistic discourses needed by global capitalism (Toyotaism). Stated in relation to Gilles Deleuze and Félix Guattari (2000), we could argue that the break that Link has located in the domain of normality is itself a result of the two central movements of capitalism: territorialization and deterritorialization. The protonormalistic is the territorialization of the body through external compulsion and training (the physical apparatus of the panopticon, the rationalized structure of the factory, the objective gaze of the educator and/or foreman), but the flexible-normalistic practices of late capitalism are a deterritorialization of such control, relying heavily on internal modes of self-regulation in relation to an ever-changing landscape of social relations. Link's comments could also be positioned within Michael Hardt and Antonio Negri's description of biopower within the global system of empire. Drawing on Deleuze and Guattari, Hardt and Negri (2000) argue that the age of empire no longer creates boundaries predicated on inside and outside dichotomies but rather manages diversity through a networked form of sovereignty immanent to production and consumption.

While Link's emphasis on the flexible is important, we must historicize his claims in light of both the 1999 Columbine shootings and in relation to 9/11 and the war on terror. After both incidences, the flexible-normalistic society, wherein agents managed the fragile equilibrium of normality and abnormality through their abilities to calculate and thus control risk factors in their daily lives, once again saw a return to a protonormalistic model. Rejecting lenient disciplinary measures, post-Columbine high schools witnessed a surprising reversal from flexible normality back to protonormality. This trend was not so much a quantitative reversal as it was an intensification of a latent trend that began in the 1980s. As Philip Wexler describes, the restorationist agenda in schooling (aligned with the rise in neoconservative political control of education) fought to restore authority and moral clarity to schooling. This movement was, according to Wexler, a "reaction against the torn social fabric of the Vietnam era, but more deeply against the liberal humanism that was seen as responsible for the permissiveness *malaise*, cultural decadence and social disorder resulting from the decline of traditional institutional moral authority" (1992, 13). Such a trend merely intensified and solidified after Columbine, accelerating a return to protonormality against the permissiveness of the risk society—a permissiveness that itself led to the very chaos which risk management attempted to but ultimately failed to contain.

In the aftermath of the school shooting, districts across the United States began to implement a plethora of new surveillance measures, including the use of cameras in the halls and night-vision cameras in parking lots, bomb-sniffing dogs, random locker checks, armed police guards, crime analysts, metal detectors, transparent backpacks, and computerized student ID cards (Pressly and Chojnacki 1999; Firestone 1999; Beaupre and Southwell 1999). Fifteen to 30 percent of post-Columbine high schools suddenly had metal detectors installed, and there were security cameras in half of primary and secondary schools.

The increasing interest in school security led to an unforeseen boom in the security technologies industry. Firms that at one time had very little interest in the school market were seeing school security deals account for upward of 20 percent of their sales. Denver-based security engineering firm Digatron Inc. teamed up with Lorinx Information Systems to produce the DigaNET security system. Originally, this security system was supposed to be implemented in airports and in the U.S. Capitol, but since Columbine, the company has also produced a new model specifically geared toward the unique concerns of school security. Perhaps the company that profited the most from the Columbine shootings, however, was Garrett Metal Detectors. Since Columbine, schools became the company's largest clients. Jim Dordrei, the vice president of marketing for Garrett at the time of the shootings, stated that school orders quickly surpassed those of prisons and airports (Bazemore 1999). Dordrei stated, "We never dreamed there would be a market in schools. Now it's our largest-selling segment of our business—twenty to twenty-five percent of our business—and I project that our sales to schools will probably double in the next year" (ibid.). In the same article, Dordrei is reported to have said, "Three or four years ago, we would hear parents saying, 'We do not want metal detectors. It looks like a prison,' now they are demanding that schools provide a safe environment," which translates into protonormalistic measures of prevention and prohibition in the form of surveillance equipment in hallways.

Besides adding new hardware, schools also fostered closer relationships to the police. In Omaha, Nebraska, Elkhorn High School installed a new surveillance system that allowed police to monitor the school directly from the police department. Similarly, in 2002 Glenbard South High School in Illinois inaugurated a security system that allowed police access to surveillance imagery through a Web connection (Rosik 2002). And in Tewksbury Memorial High School in Massachusetts, the Columbine massacre led school administrators to invest in a new kind of security camera that was linked to a nearby police station (Kirchofer 2001). This new camera system is a discreet black ball six inches wide developed by Eastern Video Systems Inc. in North Andover, Massachusetts. Even though the price tag is steep (especially for working-class rural school districts), the sky seemed to be the limit for security spending after Columbine. James J. Falls, an Eastern Video Systems manager, reported that more and more schools were interested in this technology, regardless of the cost (ibid.).

The Cleveland Municipal School District is an excellent example of post-Columbine surveillance amplification. After Columbine, the district increased its safety and security budget from $12.5 million to $21.3 million. That is a 70 percent increase in money spent on security measures (Townsend 2001). This money was used to install cameras in 122 schools. Two more mobile X-ray systems for backpack searches were also purchased, upping the total to four such units. Furthermore, the number of armed security officers increased. Pottsgrove High School in Pottstown, Pennsylvania, is an even more extreme case of protonormalization. In 2001, Pottsgrove students were no longer allowed to drive to school for fear of hidden car bombs. Soda cans and backpacks were not permitted on school grounds unless they were transparent. Security cameras were installed, hall monitors signed students in and out of bathrooms, and concerned citizens raised $10,000 for Pottsgrove to buy a bomb-sniffing dog (Cannon 2001). Both the Cleveland Municipal School District and Pottsgrove represent extreme cases of a general post-Columbine trend toward protonormalization in such forms as extreme prohibitions, external surveillance, and overt police presence.

School architecture also was transformed. Along with government facilities and businesses, schools adopted the Crime Prevention Through Environmental Design (CPTED) strategy. Columbine's new library was designed according to CPTED principles, which attempts to construct wide open, easily observable spaces with large windows to increase light and visibility. There are also multiple surveillance stations where staff can monitor the entire room from a fixed position. Bookshelves at Columbine now stand only forty-eight inches high in order to maximize visibility (Zissman 2001). In Cleveland, Ohio, the 2001 design of Avon Elementary School also incorporated CPTED security concerns directly into its blueprints. Rather than line the halls with security cameras, Avon decided to opt for a school design that would maximize school hallway visibility. In this new design, the principal is able to stand in one fixed location and see 75 percent of the building. Todd Wrobleshi of MKC Associates Inc. in Mansfield, Ohio, attempted to meet the demands of his clients by providing a point of omniscient sight so that nothing could hide from the purview of the principal's gaze. As Wrobleshi states, "[The school board] really emphasized to us that they wanted the principal to see as much territory as possible from one spot in the building" (Gonzalez 2001). Such clear lines of sight effectively eliminate the mazes of corridors in schools were students could hide. Thus school plans in the post-Columbine world of fear and terror began to look more and more like the classical panopticon, adopting the centralized architectural form as a blueprint to security. The internal regulation of flexible normality fell in the face of an overall security crisis through which a return to protonormality (via external surveillance technologies, architectural forms, and administrative procedures) was secured but with a new twist: now students and parents desired to be monitored and actively participated in their own surveillance (Loftholm 2000). If the panopticon classically produced a fear of being watched (an internal paranoia in the form of a symbolic prohibition), this return to protonormality produces a fear of not being watched. Even when alternatives to accelerated, technological, and impersonal surveillance are implemented (such as new notions of community including student-centered care groups), such efforts are essentially reified into institutional apparatuses, which in the end merely reinforce the fact that social bonds do not exist organically within school relations but are administered from above by a protonormalistic bureaucracy. Architecturally panoptic designs and adult-centered authority attempt to reinstitute a certain form of efficiency and institutional control through prohibition of student-centered autonomy, flexibility, and self-regulation.

But a question remains: what is the psychological impact of these shifts in surveillance, security, and normality? It is not simply the case that we must shift back to flexible-normalistic modes of control in schools, for both are plagued by an underlying problem. In short, both forms of normalistic surveillance in schools produce psychological effects that pathologize subjectivity. Here we have to shift our analysis from an external description of surveillance in schools to the underlying effects of such measures on the psychology of young boys. It is only through this shift that we will be able to understand how youth are conditioned by the surveillance economy of late capitalism and in turn how these youth act out against this very economy.

NORMALISTIC PSYCHOLOGY:
A QUESTION OF ENJOYMENT

Perhaps a move toward psychoanalysis will help to answer this question and give more specificity to the notion of flexible normality as a mode of normativity locked within the framework through which protonormative surveillance is reinstituted in schools. Slavoj Žižek describes the libidinal economy of the "risk society"—a concept indigenous to the formula of flexible-normality—as characterized by the waning of the symbolic law and the underlying ordering function of the Master-Signifier, which holds together the social-symbolic world. Žižek writes, "What if the disintegration of the public ('patriarchal') symbolic authority is paid for (or counterbalanced) by an even stronger disavowed 'passionate attachment' to subjection" (2000, 344). There might very well be a cost for the waning of symbolic prohibition in the form of a new set of social anxieties and paranoias. According to Žižek, without symbolic efficiency guaranteed by the symbolic law, there is a loss of symbolic trust between subjects, a loss of meaning to actions, and the rise of an "uncertainty principle" that opens up to the overall undecidability of existence. The newfound "freedom" to choose (independently of tradition) in the risk society is full of uncertainty that in turn prevents subjects from selecting the norms needed to regulate the self within an overall flexible economy. While I agree with Žižek on this point, I must add that the deterritorialization of the symbolic law (traditional laws and injunctions giving coherence and stability to the subject), which he describes in broadly Lacanian terminology, and the attending unconscious results are not universalizable. In fact, I would argue that the waning of symbolic efficacy, the rise of a flexible economy, and the shift toward hybrid identity have differential results according to gender, race, and class. The comments that follow are meant to be situated in relation to the analysis of masculine subjectivity in youth culture. It is this population in particular whose subjectivity is at stake with the flexible crisis in the paternal law that traditionally conveyed an anchoring point for their entry into the social world.

The net social results of the loss of symbolic efficiency for young boys is twofold. On one hand, there is a strange inversion whereby society becomes increasingly "psychologized"—a therapeutic society in which everyone proclaims his or her victim-hood and/or psychosis—while individuals become more and more machine-like, devoid of psychological depth. Identification with the level of the imaginary world of media simulacra comes to dominate our psychical landscapes. Thus media images have an increasingly pervasive ability to directly socialize the subject into a hypersensualized world of narcissistic desires and fears directed at and against imaginary rivals.

Here, it is important to return to the opening example of Barry Loukaitis whose shocking crimes were coupled with an even more shocking emotional and psychological emptiness. His seemingly directionless anger indicates the machinelike, one-dimensional psychology described by Žižek. Furthermore, the endless rants of boundless and polymorphous hate (Cullen1999) expressed in the diary of Columbine shooter Eric Harris—which opens with the sentence "I hate the fucking world!"—speak directly to an overarching anger at the world filtered through a narcissistic sense of thwarted entitlement, or, rather, abandonment by a sensational world of images without guarantees. While a major point of contention concerns the motives behind school shootings (such as what are they, do they even exist), Žižek would argue that clear motives are missing precisely because of the unique psychology of the risk society. The mystery behind Dylan Klebold and Eric Harris's murderous rampage in Columbine is thus no mystery at all. Directly after Columbine, there were rumors that Klebold and Harris were pinpointing African American students, Christians, and jocks. Yet there is no evidence to suggest that the shooters were motivated by racism, sexism, or other specific hatreds (Kellner 2008). The target of such violent outbursts is therefore not directed at special religious, sexual, or ethnic groups. Rather it stems from a profound resentment directed at the loss of symbolic efficiency itself, at being abandoned to the "freedoms" of a flexible, permissive, risky socio-economic world.

Here analysts of youth alienation (Giroux 1996 and 2000; Frymer 2005) have it backward. Particular segments of the youth population do not suffer from alienation but rather from what Žižek refers to as "disalienation" (2000). Missing in the flexible normality of late capitalism is the crucial relation between the imaginary (as a register of rivalry and aggressiveness, of narcissistic vulnerability) and the symbolic (as a register concerning law, meaning, motives, and traditions). In an environment of latch-key children, suburban isolation from community, the panopticism of Internet surveillance, and reality TV, the imaginary no longer connects the subject to the symbolic world of social norms, prohibitions, and traditions but instead locks the subject to a narcissistic fixation on the level of individual threats, personal conspiracies, and antagonistic rivalries. If alienation is the distance needed to have a critical comprehension of the self in relation to prohibitions, then disalienation is submergence into a narcissistic enclosure that, as we will see, involves its own forms of subjection. In relation to Link's neo-Foucauldian analysis of power, I would argue that disalienation is the psychic life of flexible normality for young boys.

On the other hand, the failure of the symbolic function induces a turn to brutality and trauma as an inherently self-destructive force. Here we confront what Žižek calls the "stupid superego death drive of enjoyment" (2000, 390) where the clarion call of flexible normality to enjoy—through rampant consumption—is supported by an obscene Master, by the injunction of the sovereign, tyrannical, imaginary father. To quote Žižek: "Far from imposing on us a firm set of standards to be obeyed unconditionally [as in protonormalistic discourse which institutes the symbolic Law], the totalitarian Master is the agency that suspends (moral punishment)—that is to say, his secret injunction is: *You may!*: the prohibitions that seem to regulate social life and guarantee a minimum of decency are ultimately worthless, just a device to keep the common people at bay, while you are allowed to kill, rape and plunder the Enemy, let yourself go and excessively enjoy, violate moral prohibitions . . . *in so far as* you follow Me" (2000, 391). Another way of framing the same injunction is through the typical postmodern call to "just be yourself." As Žižek argues, such statements lead to the "ultimate identity crisis" wherein the male subject is left "radically unsure" faced with a possible confrontation with the void exposed by the lack of symbolic fiction giving meaning to one's life: a meaning predicated on the stability and security of a patriarchal symbolic order. Those conferred with privilege are constantly reminded that they are privileged and thus have no claim to injustice within the confessional, therapeutic society. They are not allowed to be "victims" precisely because their suffering will always be less than the racial/ethnic other, the lower classes, or women. In a culture of complaint, their complaints remain invisible until they manifest themselves as overt violence. As such, they are confronted with a destabilized understanding of the self, unsure of their place in the overall symbolic order.

Thus traditional notions of normativity and alienation are called into question by flexible normality in late capitalism. For instance, classical Marxian notions of alienation imply the existence of an essence from which one is estranged, an ontological constant in the form of a species-being against which injustice can be measured. Yet such discussions of alienation crumble in the risk society, for here the self is nothing but its own infinite set of permutations that desire their own regulation and administration. Disalienation, or desublimation, is precisely a loss of alienation, an alienation from alienation itself, creating an unbearable sense of proximity to the primal father (as obscene Master) to enjoy rather than the separation instituted by the symbolic father's prohibitions. Furthermore, Foucault's analysis of disciplinary power as homogenizing and normalizing is also rendered problematic by the risk society. Here the self is not constituted in relation to a consistent norm (an inside/outside) but is composed of abnormal flows and vectors that are contextually specific and highly volatile. Thus what is most sought after in postmodern flexible normality is the management and ultimate co-optation of the idiosyncratic rather than the compartmentalization of inside/outside, same/different, self/other. To complicate matters further, the psychoanalytic reading adds another layer to Foucault's analysis of sovereignty. For Foucault, the sovereign acts to punish and to kill, yet in Žižek's reading, the sovereign as the internal/psychological Master compels us to enjoy. This obscene Master proclaims: "You will do x and y, and you will enjoy it!" This is the proper role of the sovereign injunction in a society of biopower: to make survive in a state of radical enjoyment. As such, the psychology of young men in the risk society cannot be located in either strictly Marxist notions of alienation or in Foucault's traditional theories of disciplinary versus sovereign power. The sovereign shadow existing within postmodern forms of biopower is enjoyment itself.

Yet this injunction to enjoy or to be one's self is in the end the perfect way to strip life of all enjoyment. As Alenka Zupancic argues, the postmodern hedonism of the high-risk society does not concern itself with enjoyment so must as with nihilism. For her, postmodern hedonism is directly related to resentment in such a way that the subject can be supremely awake, frantic, and hyperactive, yet psychologically dead (2003, 49, 69). In Zupancic's language, we could stage this psychological situation in terms of two nihilisms. On one hand there is active nihilism, a will to destroy. On the other hand there is passive nihilism, which acts as a defense against excitement and thus is a "will to will without willing" (ibid., 68). The properly disciplined subject, who is the efficient, productive, and docile subject of protonomalistic surveillance and discipline, does not chose between one or the other but is positioned at their mediation point, through which passive and active nihilisms supplement one another. Zupancic's examples here include decaf coffee, which offers the rush of coffee without the rush of caffeine. Thus, while Žižek emphasizes the split between the automaton of passive nihilism and the violence of active nihilism, Zupancic argues that they are properly interdependent. I would add to this discussion that in both cases, the position of in-betweenness versus disintegration is itself conditioned by the forces of the risk society (such as shifts in the economy or institutional authority), and the two nihilisms are themselves contingently related and constantly interacting in a volatile and potentially dangerous manner.

Here it is important to return to the school shooter. This enigmatic figure enables us to understand how postmodern nihilism in both of its guises offers a tragic choice for contemporary male youth: a choice between bad and worse. I must emphasize along with Jessie Klein and Lynn Chancer (2000) that extreme displays of male aggression exist within the range of "acceptable" male behavior. In other words, the flexible norm governing the social wisdom "boys will be boys" increasingly justifies overtly violent behaviors. As Klein and Chancer argue, "Hyper-male expectations tend to be made 'normal' in three specific ways: accepting a 'boys will be boys' ideology, tolerating violence, and condoning misogynist and homophobic attitudes and acts" (2000, 146). Within the increasingly flexible norm of "masculine behaviors," extremes are simply ignored—ignored, that is, until the rubber band of flexible normality is stretched too thin and ultimately breaks. Or even worse, these extremes are not really ignored but rather incorporated into the range of what it means to be a boy and thus ultimately a man and in the end celebrated through sports or war. In this sense, new credence is given to the observation by Michael Kimmel, the noted theorist of adolescent masculinity, that school shooters such as Dylan Klebold and Eric Harris are not so much abnormal as they are overconformists to a hypermasculinized display of sovereign execution. Overconformity thus links with Žižek's theory of disalienation as a state of claustrophobic approximation to the "obscene" side of the positive symbolic law: the command to enjoy. While on the surface such cases appear to be social outcasts suffering from alienation in the classical sense, they are at their core suffering from the opposite condition in relation to the obscene Master.

It is in the school shooter that the abnormal reaches its breaking point as a discursive figure and is replaced by its distant cousin: the moral monster. As

Foucault has described (2003), the abnormal is an everyday subject defined by his or her "condition." These conditions are not medical states per se nor are they to be feared as violent and destructive. The "monster" on the other hand is violent, disturbing, and often seen as a contaminated site. In flexible normality, such contamination becomes increasingly pervasive to the point where the abnormal pushes to the very limit of the monster. Thus for instance, the rise of the discourse of the monster is seen in popular publications such as *Time*, whose cover story concerning Columbine was titled "The Monsters Next Door." With the fear induced by the risk society, the monster becomes once again a pervasive discursive pattern. Hence the often heard warning that the violent actions of Klebold and Harris were the result of their alleged homosexuality. Here contamination between the sexes (the haunting of the male by the female) is associated with illness and ultimately the monstrous, the demonic, the unholy (note the Christian backlash against the Columbine shooters days after the killings). Such popular press stories simply act to mystify the more concrete and direct relation between the shooters' behaviors and hypermasculinity, thus misrecognizing the continued power and influence of the sovereign in the form of the imaginary, obscene father. Thus the monster returns in the popular imagination as the school shooter, the uncontrollable and contaminated other that is no longer an educational problematic from the outside but rather emerges from the radical inside of machismo culture itself.

In all cases, active nihilism was meant to outscream the displeasure and pain of a social system that had become cruel (urging enjoyment yet denying it at all turns), indifferent (lacking the peaceful security of a stable and effective symbolic order), and devoid of choices and meaning (animating a form of extreme nihilism). As with Nietzsche's theory of the ascetic ideal, this active nihilism "is about immersing the human soul in terrors, ice, flames, and raptures to such an extent that it is liberated from all petty displeasure, gloom, and depression" (Zupancic 2003, 47). Against the passive nihilism as a will not to will, active nihilism would prefer to will nothingness itself, to smash through the tranquilizing veil of social relations. Yet because there is no hope, no transformative moment emerging from the antiseptic, suburban, commodified lifestyle, active nihilism remains transfixed by the pain of callous violence. To outscream the intolerance of depression brought about by resentment toward the loss of enjoyment, these boys turned toward the terror, ice, and flames of cold-blooded murder as ways to enjoy the lack of enjoyment itself. Thus Luke Woodham, a teenager who killed his mother, his ex-girlfriend, and her friend, argued that "murder is gutsy and daring" (Chua-Eoan, 1997), supplanting his lost, confused, and unstable self-image with an actively nihilistic will to power. Michael Carneal, who killed the girl who was the object of his unrequited love, two other girls, and wounded five classmates in West Paducah, Kentucky, expressed similar feelings of empowerment through murder. "I was feeling proud, strong, good, and more respected," he reported after being charged with the crime (Blank 1998). In all cases, guns offered a way of actively expressing this sense of nihilism.

Before his rampage, Woodham wrote, "I do this to show society, 'Push us and we will push back. I suffered all my life. No one ever truly loved me. No one ever truly cared about me" (Hewitt 1997). Harris also wrote a similar note in his room before the Columbine shooting: "Teachers, parents, LET THIS MASSACRE BE ON YOUR SHOULDERS UNTIL THE DAY YOU DIE" (Savage 1999). While the Master-Signifier—the supplement to the symbolic law—has lost its efficiency in the flexible normality of postmodernism, this state of individual "freedoms" to transgress produces a profound anxiety directed at the new, heightened proximity to the obscene Master of enjoyment. As Žižek writes, "Far from cheerfully assuming the nonexistence of the big Other, the subject blames the Other for its failure and/or impotence, as if *the Other is guilty of the fact that it doesn't exist*" (2000, 361). The journals of the school shooters—which demonstrate a desire to be a victim even if the pervasive victimhood of postmodernism is denied them—speak to a feeling of abandonment and anger directed at the symbolic law itself as having destroyed the very possibilities for enjoyment by its injunction to enjoy, leaving nothing but the acceptance of a passive nihilism (consumerist hedonism drained of affect) or active nihilism (in the form of sadomasochistic violent outbursts). That many of the school shooters come from "well-adjusted," middle-class families might seem shocking to their neighbors, but from a psychoanalytic point of view there is really no mystery here at all. The choices offered by the risk society deprive the consumerism and security of this middle-class existence of enjoyment. The ability to supplement one nihilism with the other as in Zupancic's model slowly unravels as the risks of the risk society create ever-increasing cleavages within the subject, transforming melancholia into meaningless rage directed at an absent Other (the symbolic law that grants meaning to life). In the risk society, normality is this fragile coexistence of active and passive nihilisms as they supplement one another. This relation is one that has reached a certain impasse, resulting in the rage of the school shooter.

Beyond the Double Bind

Two options are thus presented, both of them in the end unacceptable. On one hand we have flexible normality with its attending culture of complaint, its resentment, and its collapse into the imaginary world of narcissistic indulgence in media spectacle and/or the return of the repressed violence of the obscene Master. On the other hand we have a prohibitive social order that relies on institutional surveillance and security apparatuses to maintain a protonormalistic demarcation between the normal and the abnormal, the right and the wrong. On a psychological level, flexibility means nihilism and hedonism, and protonormality means repression and melancholia (as in Freud's and Marx's original analyses of alienation). But what are alternatives to this system of perpetual back and forth, broadly orchestrated along liberal and conservative educational policy shifts?

What both sides share is the formal framework of normality as it is conceptualized by biopower to regulate subjects for the overall maintenance of the population. Yet another approach is possible here, a paradigm shift beyond the rubric of flexible versus protonormality. As Lacanian psychoanalyst Paul Verhaeghe argues, there must be a movement away from questions of the normal (and all of its statistical methodologies, averages, and industrialized utility) back to questions of individual health (2004). In flexible normality the abnormal becomes increasingly the "norm" and, for little boys, this means that the definition of acceptable behaviors becomes increasingly expansive. Thus it is okay to do x, y, and z (once thought to be taboo and prohibited). If a boy does not engage in these activities (masturbation comes to mind here, or premarital sex) then he is abnormal precisely because he is not abnormal. Hence underlying the formal freedom of flexible normality is the injunction of a secret Master: "boys will be boys" or perhaps even more appropriately "boys must enjoy being boys." In protonormalistic discourses the reverse holds true. Here if one transgresses, one is labeled a threat.

The backlash from Columbine speaks directly to this circumstance. The FBI document entitled "The School Shooter: A Threat Assessment" institutes a juridical-social diagnosis of a student based on a profile of abnormal behaviors. Here the abnormal is not endorsed as part of our collective diversity but as a deviation from a fixed notion of the normal that must be safeguarded against abnormality, which is seen as a monstrous threat. Simultaneously, the category of the abnormal expands until all students can be policed while at the same time the tolerance for abnormality decreases, producing an anxious and paradoxical state. Instead of establishing the abnormal as normal, the profile transforms the abnormal into a threat, hunts it down, pinpoints it, and proceeds to interrogate it, police it, and monitor it for the possibility of its transformation into monstrous violence (leading to a preemptive spree of suspensions for rather minor infractions in dress code and similar transgressions). Protonormality criminalizes abnormality as a social deviance. This procedure does not shed light on the psychological needs of the subject so much as on the paranoia of the self and the profound anxiety of Otherness experienced within protonormality. The only way that protonormality contains abnormality as deviance is through a militarized discourse of security, not safety. Hence the return to military surveillance solutions supported by a structurally prohibitive Master ("don't do that or you will be punished!").

For Verhaeghe, notions of socially arbitrary and politically informed norms have to be replaced by an emphasis on the psychological health of the subject, which cannot come from a third party, from a Master (the socio-juridical law or the obscene master of stupid enjoyment). This is not a purely relativist argument, and it thus resists the narcissism of the postmodern clarion call to "just be one's self," which misrecognizes that the various permutations available are nevertheless depended on the verification of a sovereign injunction. As Verhaeghe writes, "As opposed to the social-juridical realm, in the field of psychotherapy, the subject's demand is central, and the only criterion for normality or abnormality rests with the subject itself" (2004, 70). This demand cuts through to the very heart of the fantasy structuring the seemingly infinite permutations of identity that lie within a postmodern, flexible life-world. Thus we end with a simple conclusion that links psychological health with a new notion of safety beyond security or leniency: the cure to the school shooter rests in our ability not to criminalize (as in a juridical model), not to pathologize (as in a psychological model), not to standardize (as in an industrial model), not to legitimize (as in a flexible, postmodern sense) but rather to listen closely in order to hear the desire to regain psychological health against the permissiveness of flexible normality and the prohibitions of protonormality. Here enjoyment is not a command from an obscene Master or a prohibition instituted by the law; rather, it is permitted, and the subject is able to make a choice concerning this enjoyment beyond bad or worse. This means that educators have to reconceptualize joy itself outside the deadlock of control, surveillance, and capitalism. If, according to the philosopher Spinoza, joy is an increase in the power to think, to act, and to dare to take risks, then we must ask what forms of pedagogy offer training in a joyful life. In conclusion, I would like to offer a provocative answer to this question: only an education for transformative social, economic, and political equality offers the collective joy necessary to combat the deadlock of nihilism and the foreclosure of enjoyment for risky youth.

REFERENCES

Bazemore, J. 1999. Safety schools: Principals buying high-tech security equipment. *Chicago Sun-Times*. April 29, 34.

Beaupre, B., and D. Southwell. 1999,. Local students will find new security precautions. *Chicago Sun-Times*. August 17, 16.

Blank, Jonah. 1998. The kid no one noticed. *U.S. News & World Report*. October 4. http://www.usnews.com/usnews/news/articles/981012/archive_004919_3.htm (accessed February 1, 2002).

Bowman, D. H. 2001. School safety lessons learned: Urban districts report progress. *Education Week on the Web*. May 30. www.edweek.org (accessed February 1, 2002).

Cannon, A. 2001. The latest school daze. *U.S. News and World Report*. March 26, 25.

Chua-Eoan, Howard. 1997. Mississippi gothic. *Time*. October 20. http://www.time. com/time/magazine/article/0,9171,987224–2,00.html (accessed February 1, 2002).

Cullen, Dave 1999. Inside the Columbine high investigation. *Salon.com*. September 23.

Davis, N. 1999. *Youth crisis: Growing up in the risk society*. London: Praeger.

Deleuze, G., and F. Guattari 2000. *A thousand plateaus*. Minneapolis: University of Minnesota Press.

Firestone, D. 1999. Getting ready for school: Safety measures take high priority after Columbine. Cleveland *Plain Dealer*. August 13, 1A.

Frymer, B. 2005. Freire, alienation, and contemporary youth: Toward a pedagogy of everyday life. *Interactions: UCLA Journal of Education and Information Studies* 1 (2).

Foucault, M. 1979. *Discipline and punish: The birth of the prison*. New York: Vintage.

———. 1980. *Power/knowledge*. New York: Pantheon Books.

———. 1984. Why study power? The question of the subject. In *Art after modernism*, ed. B. Wallis, 417–424. New York: New Museum of Contemporary Art.

———. 1990. *History of sexuality: An introduction*. New York: Vintage Books.

———. 2003. *Abnormal*. New York: Picador.

Giroux, H. 1996. *Fugitive cultures: Race, violence, and youth*. New York: Routledge.

———. 2000. *Stealing innocence: Youth, corporate power, and the politics of culture*. New York: St. Martin's Press.

Gonzales, J. 2001. Safety now a part of school design: Security cameras, building layout can all help monitor students. *Cleveland Plain Dealer*. March 18. 7B.

Hardt, M., and A. Negri. 2000. *Empire*. Cambridge, MA: Harvard University Press.

Hewitt, Bill. 1997. The avenger. *People*. November 3. http://www.people.com/people/ archive/article/0,,20123633,00.html (accessed February 1, 2002).

Jameson, F. 1995. *Postmodernism or, the cultural logic of late capitalism*. Durham, NC: Duke University Press.

Kellner, D. 2008. *Guys and guns amok: Domestic terrorism and school shootings from the Oklahoma City bombing to the Virginia Tech massacre*. Boulder, CO: Paradigm Press.

Kirchofer, T. 2001. High school, high security: Tewksbury students live post-Columbine life on video. *Boston Herald*. December 3.

Klein, J., and L. Chancer. 2000. Masculinity matters: The omission of gender from high-profile school violence cases. In *Smoke and mirrors: The hidden context of violence in schools and society*, ed. U. Spina, 129–175. Lanham, MD: Rowman & Littlefield.

Link, J. 2004. From the "power of the norm" to "flexible normalism": Considerations after Foucault. *Cultural Critique* 57:14–32.

Loftholm, N. 2000. Sleuthbot takes state science-fair honors. *Denver Post*. April 18.

Pressley, D., and J. Chojnacki. 1999. Mass. schools boost security for new year. *Boston Herald*. August 15.

Rosik, D. 2002. Cameras would give police eyes in schools. *Chicago Sun-Times*. May 2, 10.

Savage, Martin. 1999. Diary reveals Colorado massacre was planned for year. *CNN. com*. April 24. http://www.cnn.com/US/9904/24/school.shooting.04/ (accessed February 1, 2002).

Spina, S. U. 2000. Introduction: Violence in schools: Expanding the dialogue. In *Smoke and mirrors: The hidden context of violence in schools and society*, ed. S. U. Spina, 1–39. Lanham, MD: Rowman & Littlefield.

Townsend, A. 2001. Stepping up safety at school: Cleveland spending $20 million for security. *Cleveland Plain Dealer*. November 19, B1.

Verhaeghe, P. 2004. *On being normal and other disorders: A manual for clinical psychodiagnostics*. New York: Other Press.

Wexler, P. 1992. *Becoming somebody: Toward a social psychology of school*. London: Falmer Press.

Zissman, M. A. 2001. Securing the future: Security gets top priority on new facility. *Building Design and Construction*. September 1, 48.

Žižek, S. 2000. *The ticklish subject: The absent center of political ontology*. London: Verso.

Zupancic, A. 2003. *The shortest shadow: Nietzsche's philosophy of the two*. Cambridge, MA: MIT Press.

PART FOUR

Accountability Regimes

*Tests, Standards, and
Audits as Surveillance*

CHAPTER 9

"Politics by Other Means"

EDUCATION ACCOUNTABILITY
AND THE SURVEILLANCE STATE

Pauline Lipman

STUART HALL FAMOUSLY NOTED THAT "Education might be thought of as the pursuit of politics 'by other means'[;] . . . it is not therefore by chance or in error that every major change in the education structure needs to be understood as being intimately connected to a shift in power" (quoted in Grace 1984, 37). In this chapter, I address the questions, in what sense is education, as Hall suggests, "politics by other means" in the post–9/11 context, and what is at stake? To appreciate what is at stake, I begin by situating education policies within the present social conjuncture: neoliberalism, the crisis of neoliberal legitimacy, and the U.S. drive for world domination. My analysis of education policy is based on an examination of current U.S. education accountability policies and my own data on education accountability and market-style reforms in Chicago, a city that is in the forefront of these policies nationally (Lipman 2004; Lipman and Haines 2007). Here, I focus particularly on the ways in which these policies are implicated in the construction of state coercion and surveillance. Following from this analysis, I argue that a turn toward an equitable education that promotes critical thought and democratic public action is urgent and tied to our collective future.

EDUCATION POLICIES AS CULTURAL POLITICS

Drawing on Michel Foucault, Stephen Ball argues that policies can be understood as discourses—values, practices, ways of talking and acting—that shape consciousness. Discourses "systematically form the objects of which they speak" (1994, 21). Power works through educational practices, social interactions, and the normative language of schooling to construct social identities, social relations, and dominant modes of thought. Policy discourses also "exercise power through a production of 'truth' and 'knowledge'" (ibid., 21). The authority to frame debates on social issues limits the range of options available, and this can be more important than the specific policy choices themselves (Kumashiro 2008; Lankshear 1998). For example, imposition of the economic logic of neoliberalism has been facilitated by the power of neoliberal discourses to reorganize consciousness and shape the public conversation by substituting the vocabulary of self-interest and individual responsibility for the collective good and by rearticulating equity to standards and choice in the market (Apple 2001). Thus, the potency of education accountability and corporate-driven education policy is as much about shaping how we think and who we become as it is about dictating policies.

Education as Surveillance and Punishment

The revolution in information technology has made possible a dramatic expansion of data gathering on individuals and organizations for profit and for government surveillance. From compiling data on consumers for marketing and investment strategies, to monitoring every keystroke on a computer, to video cameras in public places and face-recognition software at airports, we are living in the ultimate panopticon. Yet surveillance in the name of national security won new legitimacy in the aftermath of 9/11 and the "war on terror." The new license in the United States to spy on individuals and organizations, search and seize records and personal belongings without a warrant, wiretap and monitor e-mail communications, and detain and interrogate people indefinitely without trial or legal representation is now internationally notorious yet paralleled by similar policies in the United Kingdom, Spain, and elsewhere. The USA Patriot Act, Guantanamo detentions, "rendition" of terror suspects to other countries for torture, suspension of habeas corpus, and other government initiatives institutionalized a state apparatus that can intrude into every aspect of people's lives and punish without legal recourse those singled out by the government. The chilling of dissent with protest pens to contain demonstrators and preemptive police sweeps of antiwar protesters, violent police attacks on peaceful political gatherings such as at the 2007 Los Angeles immigrant rights demonstration, and mass deportations and/or incarceration of undocumented immigrants without legal recourse all point to the use of police state tactics to curtail democracy.

If education is "politics by other means," we might consider how accountability policies are implicated in the construction of a climate that takes surveillance as necessary and makes democracy expendable. Under Chicago's accountability system, rolled out nationally through No Child Left Behind (NCLB), failure is made highly visible while the state intrudes into the lives of teachers and students through intensified regulation and monitoring

(Macrine 2003); this includes holding them accountable to standardized tests, classroom inspections, scripted curricula, and punishment—putting schools on probation, retaining students for failing standardized tests, closing schools, and evaluating teachers based on their students' test scores. These very public and widely accepted practices help to legitimate surveillance and punishment as a normalized state practice. In my studies of public elementary schools in Chicago (Lipman 2004), I found that teachers experienced accountability as a system of intense monitoring and punishment. They worked under the omnipresent eyes of district supervisors and subcontracted outside "experts" who visited classrooms unannounced and checked what was written on the chalkboard, displayed on the walls, and recorded in teachers' grade books. In some schools teachers were scrutinized for their adherence to a scripted curriculum and test preparation.

By measuring and sorting students, teachers, and schools and holding them publicly accountable for results on standardized tests, the state brings those who are "failing" more closely under the gaze of power (Ball 1994). These schools and students are overwhelmingly African Americana and Latino. Racialized surveillance and punishment have become routine, but using tests to identify and root out "failure" and normalizing the surveillance of these "deviants" establishes the basis for scrutinizing and inspecting everyone. As accountability has turned into the dominant discourse, surveillance has come to be accepted as a necessary and inevitable part of the way all schools function to some degree. The annual ritual of the publication of standardized test results and NCLB's index of failing schools is now "normal."

In the schools I studied, this authoritarian system of state monitoring bred powerlessness. Although fear and intimidation were especially salient at the lowest-scoring schools I studied, to different degrees in all the schools there was a culture of coercion that stifled oppositional voices as people felt pressured to bow to the authority of policies instigated by the "central office." A teacher described this culture:

> And then, I have wanted so badly to rally parents, to talk with and inform them, but knowing that what would most likely happen is that the administrator would find a reason to fire me. You have to do something pretty awful to get fired from the Chicago Public Schools . . . and I have a feeling that someday, I might have been accused of having done something pretty awful in order to get rid of me. (Personal communication to author, May 1, 2000)

She was not alone. It is well known among Chicago public school educators that the best practice is to avoid any controversy that could bring scrutiny from school administrators or district authorities. In short, accountability as a system of surveillance and coercion breeds fear and suppression of dissent and teaches people to silence themselves.

Techniques of Silencing and Suppression of Critical Thought

In 1995, Paul Vallas, the CEO of Chicago Public Schools, berated critics of newly installed accountability policies as defenders "of the failed policies of the past." Appropriating the language of equity, he framed the issue as a simple choice: accountability and centralized regulation of schools or continue the injustices of social promotion, low expectations, and low achievement (Lipman 2004). By speaking to real problems and presenting accountability as the only alternative, official policy became a "discourse of containment" (Popen 2002), stifling debate and claiming sole authority to speak for Chicago's schoolchildren. As Ball points out, discourses are "about what can be said, and thought, but also about who can speak, when, where and with what authority" (1990, 17).

In this framework, to oppose education accountability and the redirection of schooling to economic competitiveness is to oppose improvement. This is part of the neoliberal version of reality: there is no alternative to the primacy of the market and neoliberal social policies and goals. To varying degrees, in the schools I studied, there was accommodation to the existing educational order as an immutable reality that no one contested. For example, a first-grade teacher described why she gave the high-stakes standardized test to her first-graders even though it was optional until third grade: "I don't mind taking the Iowa test because you might as well get them used to it." The focus on test preparation had become taken for granted.

The effects do not stop at the school door: "A discourse of containment—of what can be said and by whom—produces a culture of containment and epistemic privilege" (Popen 2002, 386). It does not require much imagination to connect the silencing technologies of the regime of school accountability with the post-9/11 culture of containment and epistemic privilege that has delimited public discussion about the root causes of 9/11 and any mention of the U.S. terrorist role in the world. Indeed, the "discourse of inevitability" (Hursh 2001) that frames dominant U.S. education policy is part of a larger discourse of containment that normalizes what is as the only possible form of social organization. It reinforces a politics in which the war on terror, the security state, and invasion and occupation of other nations are presented as the only possible paths to a safer world. Stephen Gill summarizes the political implications: "[T]he operation of the neo-liberal myth of progress in modernist capitalism is intended to implicitly engender a fatalism that denies the construction of alternatives to the prevailing order, and thus, negates the idea that history is made by collective human action" (2003, 130).

In the wake of 9/11, there was a rare opportunity to reexamine the U.S. role in the world. A new interest in world affairs created an opening for critical analysis, especially in classrooms where students of all ages asked, "Why do they hate us?" It is precisely this sort of social–historical analysis that is undermined by educational processes driven by standardized education, right answers to decontextualized standardized tests, high stakes accountability, and economic competitiveness as the legitimate goal of public education. A whole generation of students knows no other kind of education than that dominated by policies that structure out "the possibility for discussing student learning in terms of cognitive and intellectual development, in terms of growth, in terms of social awareness and social conscience, in terms of social and emotional development" (McNeil 2000, 202). I do not want to overstate the significance of critical thought in U.S. schools prior to high-stakes accountability, but standardized tests, scripted instruction, standardized curricula, and the proliferation of corporate-run charter schools are further restricting the space for engagement in critical and ethical examinations of knowledge just when we need it most. This is both built into changes in curriculum and embedded in social practices.

One technique of stifling critical thought is literalism, a claim to epistemic authority that defines truth as ahistorical, authentic, and absolute and therefore closed to debate. Literalists controlled the meaning of September 11 by drawing on the rhetorical power of absolutes (Popen 2002, 390)—"good vs. evil," "American vs. anti-American." "In this world of emergency time, politics assumes a purity that posits only one right answer, one side to choose" (Giroux 2003a, xvi). "You are either with us or against us." Although this way of thinking could be attributed to Christian fundamentalism in the White House, it was cultivated and valorized by seemingly nonideological literalist social practices that teach us to think in simplistic binaries and that reinforce the epistemic authority of those who claim the power to name what is true and correct.

The pedagogy of standardized tests is just such a literalist discourse. Real learning involves investigation, dialogue, and examination of multiple perspectives. But the construction of high-stakes tests around one right answer, the reconstitution of the curriculum around predesigned standards, scripts, and that which is tested, and substitution of test preparation materials for texts rule out contextualized knowledge and critical analysis. There is little space for students and teachers to propose complex and competing interpretations, contextualize knowledge, or challenge the authority of official knowledge. NCLB is built around simplistic binaries that sort students, teachers, schools, and school systems into "failing" and "successful." The complexity of schools as spaces for human development and intellectual, ethical, and political engagement is reduced to a "cut score." The certitude with which people and schools are officially sorted into categories of good and bad and punished or rewarded accordingly reinforces moral absolutes and normalizes and encourages public acts of denunciation and punishment. These practices cannot be separated from an ideological framework that singles out and names individuals and organizations as potential terrorists and demarcates countries as "partners" versus the "axis of evil" (see Giroux 2003a).

The construction and consumption of images of "good education" based on labels of "successful" versus "failing" works to discipline students and teachers to a set of educational practices that obscure the complexity and sociocultural and historically situated nature of actual teaching and learning, while privileging how the school looks on standardized measures over what is really going on there (Vinson and Ross 2003). By so doing, schools become another arena for the production of images to condense and demarcate complex realities. There are examples of this everywhere in Chicago's public schools: teachers whose students score the highest on standardized tests are celebrated regardless of what is actually going on in their classrooms, and teaching is reduced to test preparation. Such a system robs education of any meaning or purpose, reducing it to the production of images at all costs, including recruiting or rejecting students based on test scores (as some charter schools are doing), focusing instruction on those with the greatest potential to raise the school's scores (educational triage), and condemning public schools as failures which can be fixed by privatizing them. This is part of a larger ideological process that undermines contextual analysis and nuanced judgment. Yet this is exactly the sort of analysis and judgment we need in the face of racial profiling and draconian measures that allow individuals and organizations to be cast as enemies based on superficial criteria.

Undermining Social Solidarity and Collective Action

Since 9/11, the state increasingly claimed sole authority to define and police the public interest while encouraging suspicion and mistrust among us. A new round of racial profiling of Muslims and people of Middle Eastern descent was cultivated on the fertile ground of racism and justified by supposed threats to "our way of life." People were convinced to trade civil liberties for the promise of protection from dangerous others in our midst. The new security state solution continues to play to people's real fears in a world made insecure by economic and political policies that have robbed countries and regions of their resources and self-determination and produced economic and social instability in the United States. But the ascendance of the security state as a commonsense solution was also grounded in the erosion of social solidarities over the past twenty years. As neoliberal policy privatized the public sphere, including education, and shifted responsibility for social problems onto individuals, it undermined the ethic of social responsibility and collective action forged by labor and social movements in previous decades. Education accountability and school privatization exemplify the lived experience of shattered solidarities. From the magnified consequences of individual failure, to competition over test scores, to an elaborate hierarchy of surveillance and blame, to the competition for students in market driven charter schools, neoliberal policies pit people against each other and promote individual interests against collective action. A circular culture of blame and competition pits administrators against teachers, teachers against students and parents, parents against teachers, and parents against each other.

The intensification of racism is predictable. Teachers report that in some schools disaggregating test scores by race, as required by NCLB, leads to blaming African American, Latino, and some immigrant students for bringing down the school's scores. In the context of systemic racism, I found that racially disaggregated test scores in a school that supposedly "worked" for the majority of white students reinforced the belief that those for whom the school was not "working" (especially African American males) had something wrong with them and led to a focus on methods to improve these deficient individuals (Lipman 2004).

Accountability has opened the door to charter schools as an alternative to "failed' public schools (Lipman and Haines 2007), and school communities are fractured into individual consumers in the education market. This is especially the case in communities where failing schools are concentrated. Collective action for the welfare of children is supplanted by the cutthroat logic of the market, where "good" schools are obtained by the most savvy, attractive, and persistent consumers (see Whitty, Power, and Halpin 1998). We should not underestimate the ideological implications of these experiences in which people learn to shun solidarity, seek individual rewards, and cast individual blame. In this sense, school accountability and mechanisms that promote competition for resources contribute to a larger ideological shift that erodes our capacity to act together for the common good.

This has important implications for the growth of the security state. The neoliberal state is weak in the provision of social goods and social welfare, but the erosion of the public sphere promotes reliance on a strong state in matters of security. An example is the increase in school surveillance and policing as a response to school violence, as opposed to community-based solutions. Especially since 9/11, policies that weaken social solidarities make the public more vulnerable to the authoritarian state for security against "terrorism" and the draconian measures it institutes in the name of "national security."

Challenges to the Politics of Silencing

Henry Giroux (2003b) argues that we are witnessing the end of any notion of education as a public space in which to critically engage ideas

and prepare students for thoughtful democratic participation. This is true for
the dominant discourse and the constraints of accountability and education
for economic competitiveness, yet educators and parents have also mounted
resistance. While some have left teaching as a profession, others are proactively
evading these policies, challenging them, or actively developing liberatory
educational practices and agendas. On one hand, the coercion, demoraliza-
tion, and evisceration of ethical education goals furthers the privatization
agenda by pushing teachers out of public schools and into charter schools
where they hope to have more autonomy (Lipman 2008). Although most are
corporate charter outfits, some are community or teacher-led schools with
a social justice mission. On the other hand, there are examples of educators
and parents across the spectrum challenging the constraints and misuses of
high stakes accountability within public systems (Hursh 2008) and a new
public critique of the failures and even assumptions of NCLB as reflected in
the 2008 national political campaign (see http://www.fairtest.org/). Perhaps
most significantly, NCLB is partly responsible for the emergence of a nascent
countertrend—organizations and networks of critical, liberatory educators, and
schools explicitly focused on the development of critical social consciousness
and agency.[1]

NEOLIBERALISM, RESISTANCE, AND U.S. DRIVE FOR EMPIRE

What is at stake with these education policies and the countertrend
they have helped to spawn can only be fully understood in relation to the
global situation and the specific role of the United States. Drawing on the
work of Harvey (2004), Gill (2003), and others, we can describe the present
situation as the conjuncture of neoliberalism and global resistance and the U.S.
unilateralist drive for global domination. The complex relationship of these
economic and territorial processes is beyond the scope of this short chapter
(see Bello 2003; Harvey 2004; Tabb 2003). The political aspect I focus on
here is the strategic shift from the politics of hegemony toward the politics
of supremacy as a form of rule. This shift is central to an understanding of
the implications of coercive education policies.

The Crisis of Neoliberal Legitimacy

The relative stability of the post–World War II Keynesian welfare state
period in the United States and Western Europe was characterized by the
political hegemony of capitalism as an economic and social system. This
hegemony was rooted in the social compact between capital and labor. In the
United States, labor traded increased wages, benefits, and consumer power in
exchange for support for imperialism abroad and the capitalist order at home
(Ranny 2004). Following Gramsci (1971), Gill explains that in periods of

hegemonic rule, "the coercive face of power recedes and the consensual face becomes more prominent" (2003, 84) as the ruling class persuades other classes to accept its leadership and core values. Although capitalism was politically undermined by the social movements of the 1960s, in the United States and the United Kingdom the welfare state period came to an end in the mid-1970s with the worldwide structural crisis of capitalism and a shift to the neoliberal strategy of economic deregulation, gutting social welfare and cutting wages, and marketization of everything from cultural and intellectual production, to biological life, to social goods such as education, health care, and public infrastructure. This strategy of a new regime of "accumulation by dispossession" (Harvey 2004) is at the heart of global neoliberal economic and social policy and its crisis of legitimacy.

Neoliberal policies and practices have produced increasing impoverishment, social dislocation, destruction of traditional ways of life, devastation of whole countries, possibly irreversible environmental degradation, intensified exploitation, and unfathomable disparities of wealth and poverty within and among nations, including the United States (for example, Bello 2001; Jomo and Baudot 2007). After more than three decades, the effects are undermining neoliberal claims of progress and social betterment (Gill 2003). In the United States, while a handful have amassed enormous wealth and a small stratum of professional knowledge workers at the headquarters of globalization have benefited, the majority are working longer hours for less pay and fewer social benefits and suffering from lack of health care, quality education, increased housing costs, homelessness, and massive consumer debt. (See Extreme Inequality Working Group for comprehensive data at http://extremeinequality.org/.) A vast army of immigrants displaced by globalized capitalism fills low-wage service and manufacturing jobs. At the same time, many African Americans have become a superfluous population to be banished to urban and suburban Bantustans and criminalized and controlled by the penal state (Brown 2003; Parenti 1999), as evidenced by the magnitude of African American incarceration.

Internationally, the promise of market-driven economics began to unravel with the late 1990s meltdown of neoliberal economic policies; Argentina is a prime example. Today popular opposition to neoliberal policy has brought to power anti-neoliberal governments across Latin America, and resistance to neoliberal economic arrangements has forced stalemates of the World Trade Organization (WTO) and other neoliberal regional trade agreements. Most significantly, neoliberal economic and social policy has spawned a diverse global social movement of farmers, workers, environmentalists, human rights activists, feminists, indigenous peoples, and intellectual and cultural workers that increasingly defines itself in opposition to capitalist relations of production, imperialism, and war. They are concretely and ideologically challenging the claim that there is no alternative to neoliberal social policy and the primacy of the market.

In the United States, job insecurity, lack of health care, the mortgage and credit crises exploding in 2007, escalating food and fuel prices, and deep fractures in the growth potential of the neoliberal economy are all signs of neoliberal capitalism in crisis. Even before 2000, there were signs that the neoliberal strategy was weakening from within, its volatility exposed by the collapse of Enron and the Asian financial crisis of the late 1990s (Harvey 2005). In short, international resistance, growing inequalities and social immiseration, and the internal weaknesses of finance capital itself signal a crisis of the "globalist project" (Bello 2003).

From Hegemony to Supremacy

Stephen Gill (2003) argues that the state's response to the structural crisis of capitalism and neoliberal policy is a shift from the politics of consent to the politics of supremacy—power without consensus. Power is organized around a supremacist bloc with the states of the major Western economic powers, transnational capital, and a stratum of privileged workers at its core. This transnational bloc uses the coercive institutional pressures of global financial institutions, such as the International Monetary Fund and WTO, to impose the dominance of the market and the logic of capital globally. When necessary, institutional coercion is backed up by political and military force, primarily from the United States but also from Western Europe and Canada. Equally, coercion is increasingly a domestic strategy of Western "democratic" states as reflected in anti-immigrant and antiterror crackdowns in Western Europe and authorization of detention without legal process in the United Kingdom. But the epicenter is the United States. After September 11, 2001, the U.S. government set in motion a material and ideological process that threatens democracy, civil liberties, and movements for economic and social justice. The legal basis has been laid, and significant steps taken, to erase fundamental civil liberties, vastly increase government surveillance of individuals and organizations, curtail protest, and persecute and incarcerate people without legal recourse. In short, we are living through a process of establishing the ideological and material conditions for what the generally mainstream United Steel Workers Union called "a police state" after witnessing the police violence and denial of rights at demonstrations against the Free Trade Act of the Americas (FTAA) in Miami in 2003 (United Steel Workers of America 2003).

Supremacist rule is inherently unstable because it lacks the consent of the vast majority (Gramsci 1971). It maintains power, but it lacks legitimacy and thus must increasingly resort to force to maintain its rule. Gill suggests that the contradictions that are created by new patterns of neoliberal accumulation

"may cause governments to engage increasingly in coercive processes of intensified surveillance—as well as discipline, punishment and incarceration—to
sustain order in society" (2003, 182). Wacquant points out that the regulation
of the working classes by what Pierre Bourdieu calls "the left hand" of the
State, symbolized by education, public health care, social security and social
housing is being superseded—in the United States—or supplemented—in
Western Europe—by regulation through its "right hand," that is, the police,
courts, and prison system (Wacquant 2001, 1).

Of course, this is not to say that hegemony is dead, as exemplified by
school curricula of official knowledge and the corporate media's manufacture
of consent to the "new world order." But the point is to recognize in education and other social spheres the implications of a politics of supremacy
that is supplanting, as well as operating hand in hand with, the production
of compliant, self-regulating individuals and dominant ideology of freedom
and economic opportunity. Indeed, coercion and surveillance are justified by
the language of democracy and individual rights. Educational practices that
promote social discipline through the autonomous, self-regulating individual
are being supplemented or replaced by practices that coerce, threaten, and
reduce possibilities for critical and independent thought.

U.S. Drive for Empire

The neoconservatives who ascended to power in the George W. Bush
administration attempted to impose U.S domination of the neoliberal world
order. Their project was a new U.S. imperialism (Harvey 2004; Tabb 2003)
based on unilateral and preemptive military force. For them, September 11 was
a fortuitous opportunity and pretext to politically reconfigure the Middle East
and regain faltering dominance of the world economy by controlling Middle
East oil resources (Chomsky 2003; Harvey 2004). Wars for domination abroad
also require military-like discipline at home (Harvey 2004). Restriction of
civil liberties and legalized surveillance are necessary tools to contain potential
resistance to the social and economic consequences of militarism as a strategy
as well as to neoliberal policy. Again, 9/11 provided a rationale to build up a
coercive state apparatus. Harvey puts it succinctly: "[T]he U.S. has given up
on hegemony through consent and resorts more and more to domination
through coercion" (2004, 201). The stakes in this contest are perhaps higher
than at any time in human history. South African antiapartheid leader and
scholar Neville Alexander argues compellingly that either capitalism will be
eliminated or the world will be plunged into barbarism (Alexander 2003).

Social policies that regulate and surveil, coerce, and disrupt social solidarities are tactics in this contest. These are political and ideological dimensions of
neoliberal education policy that go beyond its role in capital accumulation. I
am not arguing that education accountability was designed to serve a politics

of supremacy. I am arguing that it takes on new ideological implications in the context of state coercion that is not simply driven by the ideology of the "right" but also by the logic of power at a time when neoliberalism is losing legitimacy. Although the new national security climate was fueled by a discourse of fear and jingoistic appeals to patriotism, it is buttressed ideologically and materially by social practices that regiment, coerce, and further undermine collective action and critical and complex thought. In this context, dominant education policies take on new political dimensions.

RACIALIZED DISCIPLINE AS IDEOLOGICAL GROUND FOR POLITICAL REPRESSION AND EMPIRE

The politics of coercion is built on the intersection of geopolitical political agendas and the ideology and practice of racism. Racism is the ideological fault line through which the legitimation of police state tactics and imperialist wars takes hold. The containment and control of dangerous others through the "prison-industrial complex" (Parenti 1999), the penalization of poverty (Wacquant 2001), and the persecution and detention of immigrants and citizens as terrorists are all highly racialized. The ideology of white supremacy has nurtured support for U.S. imperialist wars and invasions from Puerto Rico and the Philippines to Vietnam, Grenada, Haiti, and now the Middle East. Bringing democracy to Iraq is another (white) Western civilizing project.

We should also recall that previous periods of political repression were made acceptable by targeting those defined as not "white" or as aliens (for example, immigrant trade unionists and Socialists persecuted in the 1919 Palmer raids, Japanese interned during World War II, the targets of the anti-communist witch hunt of the 1950s, and the FBI's COINTELPRO operations against the Black Panthers, American Indian Movement, and other people of color in the 1960s and 1970s). "[T]he coupling of nationalism with imperialism cannot be accomplished without resort to racism" (Harvey 2004, 197).

The current climate of scapegoating, suspicion, fear, and intimidation also relies on demarcating "dangerous others" who are not "white," Christian, Western, or "American" from the rest of "us." It is this racialization of the enemy that perhaps helps to explain why large sections of the U.S. public continue to believe the false link between Iraq and those supposedly responsible for 9/11 as if they were an undifferentiated Middle Eastern mass.

Education policies that target, discipline, and criminalize people of color help reproduce the ideological basis for a racialized nationalism and imperialism. This ideological agenda intersects with the economic imperative to further stratify education for a highly stratified labor force and to institute education policies that discipline African American and Latino youth (Lipman 2003). It is in the context of these economic, ideological, and political logics that education accountability makes sense as a form of racialized social discipline.

In Chicago, the schools subject to the strictest regulation and control, the students that are retained, and the communities stigmatized by low test scores are African American and Latino (Lipman 2004). In these schools, accountability is experienced as public humiliation and punishment as individuals are blamed for historical and present failures of an education system grounded in race and class inequality and injustices. The process of testing, sorting, and displaying failure becomes a spectacle of the dysfunction of African American and Latino students, schools, and communities. It demonstrates for the entire world to see that these are the people who need monitoring and correction. Punishing teachers, students, and parents and employing the vocabulary of the prison system—probation, retention, and supervision—accountability is another vehicle for the "criminalization of social policy" (Giroux 2003b, 39) and the production of a "culture of punishment and incarceration" (ibid., 41). Education policies that demonstrate supposed deficiencies of youth of color and justify their regulation are another facet of the criminalization of these youth and their communities. They help legitimate racial profiling and regulation of people of color as official policy.

A Moment of Danger and Opportunity: Implications for Educators

I have argued that accountability policies discipline students and teachers alike. The policies produce a coercive climate in which teachers and school administrators learn not to speak up against practices many privately abhor. They sort students and schools based on the superficial images constructed out of test scores and promote simplistic binary thinking. They create a culture of fear, competition, and individual blame that erodes social solidarities. The authoritarianism of these policies is publicly directed to students of color and their schools and communities, defining them as deficient and in need of regulation. The supposed efficacy of education accountability legitimates surveillance and coercion as public policy. Learning inside accountability practices apprentices students to the compliant dispositions, uncritical habits of thought, and a culture of blame and suspicion that support tolerance for systematic government surveillance and political repression, racial profiling, and jingoistic appeals to patriotism and war. In other words, schools become part of the fabric of coercion as a social process.

Contradictions between the rhetoric of democracy and opportunity and the reality of curtailed rights and economic polarization and war have opened up a pedagogical space, however. September 11 changed the political landscape and made the U.S. role in the world an immediate topic. The disparity between massive military spending and the need for educational resources, jobs, housing, and health care lays bare the U.S. government's social and economic priorities and challenges the legitimacy of capitalism itself. The disheartening effects of school accountability policies on teaching and learning have opened cracks in their legitimacy, with calls for the revamping or scrapping of NCLB coming from school reform organizations, educators, parents, and elected officials. Opposition to the war in Iraq, emerging recognition of potentially cataclysmic climate change, and anxiety about the unfolding economic meltdown in the United States and other Western capitalist countries signals a shift in mood since the heyday of neoconservative triumphalism following 9/11. The election of Barack Obama to the presidency in 2008 signaled a bubbling recognition that something fundamental must change in government policy and the way the state governs. It is in these fissures of neoliberal and neoconservative domestic and foreign policy and lived experience that teachers can help students think critically about their lives and our collective future.

We are living in a dangerous historical moment, a period that calls upon us to recognize and act on the connections between education policy and global politics. Global capitalism, preemptive war, the security state and the abdication of democracy have been presented as the only option. Public education can be a space in which educators make the present situation and its connection to everyday life a curriculum of critical thought and action. More than twenty years ago, Henry Giroux (1988) argued that teachers should be transformative intellectuals who make the pedagogical more political and the political more pedagogical. That charge is more pressing than ever.

NOTE

1. These include the Education for Liberation Network, Teacher Activist Groups, Association of Rasa Educators, national and local social justice education conferences, and local teacher activist organizations in New York, Chicago, San Francisco, St. Louis, Milwaukee, Oregon, and elsewhere.

REFERENCES

Alexander, N. 2003. New meanings for pan-Africanism in the age of globalization. Fourth Annual Franz Fanon Distinguished Lecture, Center for Culture and History of Black Diaspora, DePaul University, Chicago. October.

Apple, M. W. 2001. *Educating the "right" way*. New York: Routledge.

Ball, S. J. 1990. *Politics and policy making in education*. London: Routledge.

———. 1994. *Education reform: A critical and post-structural approach*. Buckingham, UK: Open University Press.

———., ed. 2001. *The future in the balance: Essays on globalization and resistance*. Oakland, CA: Food First Books.

———., ed. 2003. Crisis of the globalist project and the new economics of George

Bush. Paper presented at the McPlante Conference, Berlin, Germany. July. http://www.zmag.org/content/print_article.cfm?itemID+3920&sect (accessed August 8, 2003).

Brown, E. 2003. Freedom for some, discipline for "others." In *Education as enforcement*, ed. K. L. Saltman and D. Gabbard, 127–151. New York: Routledge.

Chomsky, N. 2003. Confronting the empire. http:/www.zmag.org/content/print_article.cfm?itemID=2938&sectionID=40 (accessed July 5, 2003).

Gill, S. 2003. *Power and resistance in the new world order.* New York: Palgrave Macmillan.

Giroux, H. 1988. *Teachers as intellectuals: Toward a critical pedagogy of learning.* South Hadley, MA: Bergin & Garvey.

———. 2003a. Democracy, schooling and the culture of fear after September 11. In *Education as enforcement*, ed. K. L. Saltman and D. Gabbard, ix–xxiv. New York: Routledge.

———. 2003b. *Public spaces, private lives: Democracy beyond 9.11.* Lanham, MD: Rowman & Littlefield.

Grace, G. 1984. Urban education: Policy science or critical scholarship. In *Education and the city: Theory, history and contemporary practice*, ed. G. Grace, 3–59. London: Routledge & Kegan Paul.

Gramsci, A. 1971. Selections from the prison notebooks. New York: International Publishers.

Harvey, D. 2004. *The new imperialism.* Oxford, UK: Oxford University Press.

———. 2005. *A brief history of neoliberalism.* Oxford, UK: Oxford University Press.

Hursh, D. 2001. Neoliberalism and the control of teachers, students, and learning. *Cultural Logic, 4* (1). http://eserver.org/clogic/41/41.html (accessed December 12, 2001).

———. (2008). *High stakes testing and the decline of teaching and learning.* Lanham: Rowman & Littlefield.

Jomo K. S., with J. Baudot, eds. 2007. *Flat world, big gaps.* New York: Zed books and United Nations.

Kumashiro, K. K. 2008. *The seduction of common sense.* New York: Teachers College Press.

Lankshear, C. 1998. Meanings of literacy in contemporary education reform proposals. *Educational Theory* 48 (3): 351–372.

Lipman, P. 2003. Chicago school policy: Regulating Black and Latino youth in the global city. *Race, Ethnicity and Education* 6 (4), 331–355.

———. 2004. *High stakes education: Inequality, globalization, and urban school reform.* New York: Routledge.

———. 2008. Paradoxes of teaching in neoliberal times. In *Changing Teacher Professionalism: International trends, challenges and ways forward*, ed. S. Gewirtz, P. Mahony, I. Hextall, and A. Cribb, 67–80. London: Routledge.

Lipman, P., and N. Haines. 2007. From education accountability to privatization and African American exclusion—Chicago Public Schools' 'Renaissance 2010.' *Educational Policy* 21 (3): 471–502.

Macrine, S. L. 2003. Imprisoning minds. In *Education as enforcement, ed.* K. L. Saltman and D. Gabbard, 203–211. New York: Routledge.

McNeil, L. M. 2000. *Contradictions of school reform: Educational costs of standardized testing.* New York: Routledge.

Mészáros, I. 2003. Militarism and the coming wars. *Monthly Review* 55 (2): 17–24.

Parenti, C. 1999. *Lockdown America: Police and prisons in the age of crisis.* London: Verso.

Popen, S. 2002. Democratic pedagogy and the discourse of containment. *Anthropology & Education Quarterly* 33 (3): 283–294.

Ranny, D. 2004. *Global decisions, local collisions: Urban life in the new world order.* Philadelphia: Temple University Press.

Tabb, W. K. 2003. The two wings of the eagle. *Monthly Review* 55 (3): 76–82.

United Steel Workers of America. 2003. USWA calls for congressional investigation into police state assaults in Miami. Press release. November 24.

Vinson, K. D., and E. W. Ross. 2003. Controlling images. In *Education as enforcement,* ed. K. L. Saltman and D. Gabbard, 241–257. New York: Routledge.

Wacquant, L. 2001. The penalization of poverty and the rise of neoliberalism. *European Journal of Criminal Policy and Research* 9 (4): 401–412.

Whitty, G., S. Power, and D. Halpin. 1998. *Devolution and choice in education: The school, the state and the market.* Buckingham, UK: Open University Press.

CHAPTER 10

The Measure of Success

EDUCATION, MARKETS,
AND AN AUDIT CULTURE

Michael W. Apple

IN A NUMBER OF VOLUMES over the past decade, I have
critically analyzed the processes of "conservative modernization"—the
complicated alliance behind the wave after wave of educational reforms that
have centered around neoliberal commitments to the market and a supposedly
weak state, neoconservative emphases on stronger control over curricula and
values, and "new managerial" proposals to install rigorous forms of accountability in schooling at all levels (Apple 2000; Apple 2003; Apple 2006). The
first set of reforms has not demonstrated much improvement in education
and has marked a dangerous shift in our very idea of democracy—always a
contested concept (Foner 1998)—from "thick" collective forms to "thin"
consumer-driven and overly individualistic forms. The second misconstrues
and then basically ignores the intense debates over whose knowledge should
be taught in schools and universities and establishes a false consensus on what
is supposedly common in U.S. culture (see Apple 1996 and 2004, Levine
1996, and Binder 2002). The third takes the position that "only that which
is measurable is important" and through a variety of surveillance mechanisms
has threatened some of the most creative and critical practices that have been
developed through concerted efforts in some of the most difficult settings
(McNeil 2000; Lipman 2004; Apple and Beane 2007; Shor 1992; Aronowitz
2000). Unfortunately, all too many of the actual effects of this assemblage of
reforms have either been negligible or negative, or they have been largely
rhetorical (Apple 2006; Smith et al. 2003). This is unfortunate, especially
given all of the work that well-intentioned educators have devoted to some
of these efforts. But reality must be faced if we are to go beyond what is
currently fashionable.

The odd combination of marketization on the one hand and centralization of control on the other is not occurring only in education; nor is it going on only in the United States. This is a worldwide phenomenon, something that is very visible as I sit here writing this at my second "home," the University of London Institute of Education. And while there are very real, and often successful, efforts to counter it (Apple et al. 2003), this has not meant that the basic assumptions that lie behind neoliberal, neoconservative, and new managerial forms have not had a major impact on our institutions throughout society and even on our commonsense.

In many nations there have been attempts, often more than a little successful, to restructure state institutions (Jessop 2002). Among the major aims of such restructuring were to ensure that the state served business interests, to have the state's internal operations model those used in business, and to "take politics out of public institutions," that is to reduce the possibility that government institutions would be subject to political pressure from the electorate and from progressive social movements (Leys 2003). Chubb and Moe's (1990) arguments about voucher plans that place educational institutions on a market mirror this latter point, for example.[1]

This last point, removing politics from government institutions, is based on a less than accurate understanding not only of the state but of the market as well. While most economics textbooks may give the impression that markets are impersonal and impartial, they are instead highly political as well as inherently unstable. To this, other points need to be added. To guarantee their survival, firms must seek ways of breaking out of the boundaries that are set by state regulation. Increasingly, this has meant that the boundaries established to divide nonmarket parts of our lives must be pushed so that these spheres can be opened to commodification and profit making. As Leys reminds us, this is a crucially important issue. "It threatens the destruction of non-market spheres of life on which social solidarity and active democracy have always depended" (Leys 2003, 4).

It is not an easy process to transform parts of our lives and institutions that were not totally integrated into market relations so that they are part of a market. To do this, at least four significant things must be worked on (Leys 2003).

1. The services or goods that are to be focused upon must be reconfig-
   ured so that they can indeed be bought and sold.
2. People who received these things from the state must be convinced
   to want to buy them, often through techniques of coercion and
   exclusion.
3. The working conditions and outlook of the employees who work
   in this sector must be transformed from a model based on collec-

tive understandings and providing service to "the public" on the one hand to working to produce profits for owners and investors and subject to market discipline on the other. Surveillance and discipline of workers is used to enforce compliance to obtain this objective.

4. When business moves into what were previously nonmarket fields, as much as possible their risks must be underwritten by the state.

Under these kinds of pressures, standardized and competitive labor processes begin to dominate the lives of the newly marketized workers. But this is not all. A good deal of labor is shifted to the consumer. She or he now must do much of the work of getting information, sorting through the advertising and claims, and making sense of what is often a thoroughly confusing welter of data and "products."[2] In the process as well, there is a very strong tendency for needs and values that were originally generated out of collective deliberations, struggles, and compromises, and which led to the creation of state services, to be marginalized and ultimately abandoned (Apple 2000; Leys 2003, 4). Once again, in Leys's words, "The facts suggest that market-driven politics can lead to a remarkably rapid erosion of democratically-determined collective values and institutions" (ibid.).

These arguments may seem abstract, but they speak to significant and concrete changes in our daily lives in and out of education. For more than two decades, we have witnessed coordinated and determined efforts to reconstruct not only a "liberal" market economy but also a "liberal" market society and culture. This distinction is important. In Habermas's (1971) words, the attempt is to have the "system" totally colonize the "life-world." As many aspects of our lives as possible, including the state and civil society, must be merged into the economy and economic logics. Although there will always be counter-hegemonic tendencies (Jessop 2002; Apple 2006; Apple et al. 2003), our daily interactions—and even our dreams and desires—must ultimately be governed by market "realities" and relations. In this scenario—and it is increasingly not only a scenario, but also a reality—a society and a culture are not to be based on trust and shared values. Rather, all aspects of that society are to be grounded in and face "the most extreme possible exposure to market forces, with internal markets, profit centers, audits, and 'bottom lines' penetrating the whole of life from hospitals to play-groups" (Leys 2003, 35–36). As Margaret Thatcher once famously put it, the task is not to just change the economy, but to change the soul.

Interestingly, because of the focus on measurable results and central control over important decisions, the federal government's power has actually been sharply enhanced. The Bush administration's legislation concerning No Child Left Behind—by which schools labeled as "failing" on standardized tests are to be subject to market competition and central sanctions—becomes

a good example of this at the level of elementary and secondary schools.[3]
As this current volume makes clear, practices of measurement and control
are ultimately forms of surveillance, the likes of which are reshaping all
public institutions undergoing conservative modernization. This has been
accompanied by a loss of local democracy. At the same time, the role of the
state in dealing with the destructive rapaciousness produced by "economically
rational" decisions has been sharply reduced (Leys 2003, 42; see also Katz
2001 and Shipler 2004).

As many people have recognized, behind all educational proposals are
visions of a just society and a good student. The neoliberal reforms I have been
discussing construct this in a particular way. While the defining characteristic
of neoliberalism is largely based on the central tenets of classical liberalism, in
particular classic economic liberalism, there are crucial differences between
classical liberalism and neoliberalism. These differences are absolutely essential
in understanding the politics of education and the transformations education
is currently undergoing. Mark Olssen clearly details these differences in the
following passage. It is worth quoting in its entirety.

> Whereas classical liberalism represents a negative conception of state
> power in that the individual was to be taken as an object to be freed
> from the interventions of the state, neo-liberalism has come to represent
> a positive conception of the state's role in creating the appropriate market
> by providing the conditions, laws and institutions necessary for its opera-
> tion. In classical liberalism, the individual is characterized as having an
> autonomous human nature and can practice freedom. In neo-liberalism
> the state seeks to create an individual who is an enterprising and competi-
> tive entrepreneur. In the classical model the theoretical aim of the state
> was to limit and minimize its role based on postulates which included
> universal egoism (the self-interested individual); invisible hand theory
> which dictated that the interests of the individual were also the interests of
> the society as a whole; and the political maxim of laissez-faire. In the shift
> from classical liberalism to neo-liberalism, then, there is a further element
> added, for such a shift involves a change in subject position from "homo
> economicus," who naturally behaves out of self-interest and is relatively
> detached from the state, to "manipulatable man," who is created by the
> state and who is continually encouraged to be perpetually responsive.
> It is not that the conception of the self-interested subject is replaced or
> done away with by the new ideals of "neo-liberalism," but that in an
> age of universal welfare, the perceived possibilities of slothful indolence
> create necessities for new forms of vigilance, surveillance, "performance
> appraisal" and of forms of control generally. In this model the state has
> taken it upon itself to keep us all up to the mark. The state will see to

it that each one makes a "continual enterprise of ourselves" . . . in what seems to be a process of "governing without governing." (1996, 340)

Increasingly, those who are unable or unlikely to become competitive entrepreneurs are criminalized, whether they be poor minority students encountering police officers at school or homeless people encroaching upon—or being encroached upon by—places of commerce. New modalities of control are exercised upon such "failed neoliberal citizens" (see Monahan and Torres, introduction to this volume).

In attempting to understand this, in *Educating the "Right" Way* I demonstrated the power of Olssen's point that neoliberalism requires the constant production of evidence that you are doing things "efficiently" and in the "correct" way by examining the effects on the ground of the suturing together of the seemingly contradictory tendencies of neoliberal and neoconservative discourses and practices, for this is exactly what is happening at all levels of education, including higher education (Apple 2006). There is also the active surveillance of people through the documents and databases they produce. And this is occurring at the same time as the state itself becomes increasingly subject to commercialization. This situation has given rise to what might best be called an *audit culture*. To get a sense of the widespread nature of such practices, it is useful here to quote from Leys, one of the most perceptive analysts of this growth:

> [There is a] proliferation of auditing, i.e., the use of business derived concepts of independent supervision to measure and evaluate performance by public agencies and public employees, from civil servants and school teachers to university [faculty] and doctors: environmental audit, value for money audit, management audit, forensic audit, data audit, intellectual property audit, medical audit, teaching audit and technology audit emerged and, to varying degrees of institutional stability and acceptance, very few people have been left untouched by these developments. (2003, 70)

The widespread nature of these evaluative and measurement pressures, surveillance enabled by them, and their ability to become parts of our commonsense crowd out other conceptions of effectiveness and democracy.

In place of a society of citizens with the democratic power to ensure effectiveness and proper use of collective resources, and relying in large measure on trust in the public sector, there emerged a society of "auditees," anxiously preparing for audits and inspections. A punitive culture of "league tables" developed (purporting to show the relative efficiency and inefficiency of universities or schools or hospitals). Inspection agencies were charged with "naming and shaming" "failing" individual teachers, schools, social work departments, and so on; private firms were invited to take over and run "failing" institutions. (Ibid.)

The ultimate result of a fundamentally surveillant audit culture of this kind is not the promised decentralization that plays such a significant role rhetorically in most neoliberal self-understandings, but what seems to be a massive recentralization and what is best seen as a process of de-democratization (ibid., 71). Making the state more "business friendly" and importing business models directly into the core functions of the state such as hospitals and education—in combination with a rigorous and unforgiving ideology of individual accountability—these are the hallmarks of life today (ibid., 73). Once again, the growth of for-profit ventures such as Edison Schools in the United States, the increasing standardization and technicalization of content within teacher education programs so that social reflexivity and critical understanding are nearly evacuated from courses (Liston and Zeichner 1991; Apple 2006; Johnson et al. 2007), the constant pressure to "perform" according to imposed and often reductive standards in our institutions of higher education, the routine monitoring and disciplining of those who fail to perform as dictated, and similar kinds of things are the footprints that these constantly escalating pressures have left on the terrain of education.

A key to all of this is the devaluing of public goods and services. It takes long-term and creative ideological work, but people must be made to see anything that is public as "bad" and anything that is private as "good." And anyone who works in these public institutions must be seen as inefficient and in need of the sobering facts of competition so that they work longer and harder (Clarke and Newman 1997). When the people who work in public institutions fight back and argue for more respectful treatment and for a greater realization that simplistic solutions do not deal with the complexities that they face every day in the real world of schools, universities, and communities, they are labeled as recalcitrant and selfish and as uncaring. Sometimes, as in the case of former U.S. Secretary of Education Rod Page's public comments to what he thought was a sympathetic audience, they are even called "terrorists." And these "recalcitrant, selfish, and uncaring" employees—teachers, academics, administrators, social workers, and almost all other public employees—can then have their labor externally controlled and intensified by people who criticize them mercilessly and control major corporations while these same businesses are shedding their own social responsibilities by paying few or no taxes.

I noted earlier that it is not just the labor of state employees that is radically altered; so too is the labor of "consumers." When services such as hospitals and schools are commodified, a good deal of the work that was formerly done by state employees is shifted onto those using the service. Examples of labor being shifted to the "consumer" include online banking, airline ticketing and check-in, supermarket self-checkouts, and similar things. Each of these is advertised as enhancing "choice" and each comes with a system of incentives and disincentives. Thus, one can get airline miles for checking in on one's computer. Or, as some banks are now doing, an extra charge is imposed if you want to see a real live bank teller rather than using an ATM machine (which itself often now has an extra charge for using it).

The effects of such changes may be hidden, but that does not make them any less real. Some of these are clearly economic: the closing of bank branches; the laying off of large numbers of workers, including in elementary, middle, and secondary schools and in higher education; the intensification of the workload of the fewer workers who remain. Some are hidden in their effects on consumers: exporting all of the work and the necessary commitment of time onto those people who are now purchasing the service; searching for information that was once given by the government; doing one's banking and airline work oneself; bagging and checking out at supermarkets.[4] The classed and raced specificities of this are crucial, since the ability to do such electronic searching and education for example is dependent on the availability of computers and, especially, time to engage in such actions. It requires resources—both temporal and financial, to say nothing of emotional—that are differentially distributed.

This all may seem trivial. But when each "trivial" instance is added up, the massiveness of the transformation in which labor is transferred to the consumer is striking. For it to be successful, our commonsense must be changed so that we see the world only as individual consumers and we see ourselves as surrounded by a world in which everything is potentially a commodity for sale. To speak more theoretically, the subject position on offer is the deraced, declassed, and degendered "possessive individual," an economically rational actor who is constructed by and constructs a reality in which democracy is no longer a political concept but is reduced to an economic one (Ball 1994; Apple 2006).

Mark Fowler, Ronald Reagan's chair of the Federal Communications Commission, once publicly stated that television is simply a toaster with pictures. A conservative media mogul in England seemed to agree when he said that there is no difference between a television program and a cigarette lighter (Leys 2003, 108). Both positions are based on an assumption that cultural form and content and the processes of distribution are indeed commodities. There are few more important mechanisms of cultural selection and distribution than schools and universities. And under this kind of logic, one might say that educational institutions are simply toasters with students. There is something deeply disturbing about this position not only in its vision of education but, profoundly, in its understanding of the lives of the people who work in such institutions and in the often underfunded, understaffed, and difficult conditions experienced there. While it would be too reductive to see educational work merely in labor process terms, the intensification that has resulted from the conditions associated with this assemblage of assumptions has become rather pronounced (Apple 1995; Apple 2000).

Of course, many of us may be apt to see such things as relatively humorous or innocuous. Aren't market-based proposals for such things as schools, universities, health care, and so much more just another supposedly more efficient way of making services available? But not only are these ideologically driven "reforms" *not* all that efficient (Apple 2006; Lipman 2004), the process of privatization is strikingly different from public ownership and control. For example, in order to market something like education, it must first be transformed into a commodity, a "product." The product is then there to serve different ends. Thus, rather than schooling being aimed at creating critically democratic citizenship as its ultimate goal (although we should never romanticize an Edenic past when this was actually the case; schooling has always been a site of struggle over what its functions would actually be, with the working class and many women and people of color being constructed as "not quite citizens"), the entire process can slowly become aimed instead at the generation of profit for shareholders or a site whose hidden purpose is to document the efficiency of newly empowered managerial forms within the reconstituted state (Leys 2003, 211–212).[5]

The fact that such things as the for-profit Edison Schools in the United States have not generated the significant profits that their investors had dreamed of means that the process of commodification is at least partly being rejected. For many people in all walks of life, the idea of "selling" our schools and our children is somehow disturbing, as the continuing controversy over Channel One, the for-profit television station with advertising now being broadcast in 43 percent of all public and private middle and secondary schools in the United States, amply demonstrates (Apple 2000). These intuitions reveal that in our everyday lives there remains a sense that something is very wrong with our current and still too uncritical fascination with markets and audits. However, this optimism needs to be immediately balanced by the immense growth of for-profit on-line universities such as the University of Phoenix, an institution that exemplifies the transformation of education into a salable commodity.

David Marquand summarizes the worrisome tendencies I have been describing in the following way:

> The public domain of citizenship and service should be safeguarded from incursions by the market domain of buying and selling. . . . The goods of the public domain–health care, crime prevention, and education—should not be treated as commodities or proxy commodities. The language of buyer and seller, producer and consumer, does not belong in the public domain; nor do the relationships which that language implies. Doctors and nurses do not "sell" medical services; students are not "customers" of their teachers; policemen and policewomen do not "produce" public order. The attempt to force these relationships into a market model undermines the service ethic, degrades the institutions that embody it and robs the notion of common citizenship of part of its meaning. (2000, 212–213)

I agree. In my mind, public institutions are the defining features of a caring and democratic society. The market relations that are sponsored by capitalism should exist to pay for these institutions, not the other way around. Thus, markets are to be subordinate to the aim of producing a fuller and thicker participatory democratic polity and daily life (Skocpol 2003). It should be clear by now that a cynical conception of democracy that is "for sale" to voters and manipulated and marketed by political and economic elites does not adequately provide for goods such as general and higher education, objective information, media and new forms of communication that are universally accessible, well-maintained public libraries for all, public health, and universal health care. At best, markets provide these things in radically unequal ways, with class, gender, and especially race being extremely powerful markers of these inequalities (Katz 2001). If that is the case—even if the definitions of the "public" were and often still are based on the construction of gendered and raced spaces (Fraser 1989; Kelly 1993, 75–112)—the very idea of public institutions is under concerted attack.[6] These institutions need to be provided—and defended—collectively. Such things are anything but secondary. They are the defining characteristics of what it means to be a just society (Leys 2003, 220).

Unfortunately, the language of privatization, marketization, and constant evaluation has increasingly saturated public discourse. In many ways, it has become commonsense—and the critical intuitions that something may be wrong with all of this may slowly wither. In many nations where conditions are even worse, however, this has not necessarily happened, as the growth of participatory budgeting, Citizen Schools, and close relations between teacher education programs and building more socially responsive and critical curricular and pedagogical initiatives in Porto Alegre, Brazil, and elsewhere documents (Apple et al. 2003; Apple and Buras 2006). We can learn from these nations' experiences and we can relearn what it means to reconstitute the civic in our lives (Skocpol 2003). Education has a fundamental role to play in doing exactly that. But it can only do so if it is protected from those who see it as one more product to be consumed as we measure it and who interpret the intellectual and emotional labor of those who are engaged in educational work though the lenses of standardization, rationalization, and auditing.

Having said this, however, I must also note that interrupting conservative modernization requires that we have a more adequate understanding of both some fundamental dynamics and conservative madernizations's social functions and roots. I want to turn to this now.

NEW MANAGERIALISM IN CLASS TERMS

Throughout this chapter, I have been broadly describing particular kinds of tendencies that are reconstructing what counts as legitimate knowledge, legitimate education, legitimate evidence, and legitimate labor. We need to be cautious, though, about reductive analyses in understanding where these ideological movements come from. It would be too easy to simply say that these are the predictable effects of competitive globalization, of capital in crisis and its accompanying fiscal crisis of the state, or in more Foucauldian terms of the micropolitics of governmentality and normalization, although there is some truth to all of these. These tendencies underpinning "conservative modernization" are also "solutions" that are generated by particular actors, and here we need to be more specific about class relations inside and outside our schools and institutions of higher education.

As Basil Bernstein has reminded us and as I have argued at much greater depth elsewhere, a good deal of the genesis of and support for the poli-cies of conservative modernization, and especially of the constant need for audits, the production of "evidence," rationalization, and standardization of both labor and knowledge, comes not only from capital and its neoliberal allies in government but from a particular fraction of the professional and managerial new middle class (Bernstein 1996; Apple 2006). This fraction of the professional new middle class gains its own mobility within the state and within the economy based on the use of technical expertise. These are people with backgrounds in management and efficiency techniques who provide the technical and "professional" support for accountability, measurement, "product control," and assessment forms of surveillance that are required by the proponents of neoliberal policies of marketization and neoconservative policies of tighter central control in education.

Members of this fraction of the upwardly mobile professional and managerial new middle class do not necessarily believe in the ideological positions that underpin all aspects of the conservative alliance. In fact, in other aspects of their lives they may be considerably more moderate and even "liberal" politically. However, as experts in efficiency, management, testing, and accountability, they provide the technical expertise to put in place the policies of conservative modernization, sometimes gaining status over almost all other school actors in the process (Monahan 2005). Their own mobility depends on the expansion both of such expertise and of the professional ideologies of control, measurement, and efficiency that accompany it. Thus, they often support such policies as "neutral instrumentalities" even when these policies may be used for purposes other than the supposedly neutral ends this class fraction is committed to.[7]

Because of this, it is important to realize that a good deal of the current emphasis on audits and more rigorous forms of accountability, on closer surveillance and tighter control, and a vision that competition will lead to greater efficiency is not totally reducible to the needs of neoliberals and neoconservatives. Rather, part of the pressure for these policies comes from educational managers and bureaucratic offices who fully believe that such control is warranted and "good" (see Sandler and Apple, in press). Not only do these forms of control have an extremely long history in education (Apple 2004), but tighter control, high stakes testing, and (reductive) accountability methods provide more dynamic roles for such managers.

Let me briefly say more about this, since this is significant in terms of the self-understanding of class actors within the administrative apparatus of the state. The decades of attacks on state employees have not only had the predictable effects of lost employment and worsening working conditions, although these are continuing within higher education and elsewhere. These attacks also have had profound effects on identities and have produced a crisis among many state employees and managers about doubts to their expertise and their ability to "help" the public (Clarke and Newman 1997). New identities centered around enhanced technical proficiency and a set of assumptions that deep-seated problems in education and the entire social sphere can be resolved by enhancing efficiency and holding people more rigorously accountable for their actions have developed over time, sponsored in part by neoliberal discourses that have opened spaces within the state for such expertise. This enables those class fractions with technical forms of cultural capital focused on accountability and managerial efficiency to occupy these spaces and to guarantee a place for the uses of their knowledge. This is an ideal situation for the professional and managerial new middle class. They can see themselves as engaging in a moral crusade—seeing themselves as being endlessly responsive to "clients" and "consumers" in such a way that they are participating in the creation of a newly reconstituted and more efficient set of institutions that will "help everyone"—and at the same time enhancing the status of their own expertise. In Pierre Bourdieu's (1984) terms, this allows for particular kinds of conversion strategies, ones in which their cultural capital (technical and managerial expertise) can be converted into economic capital (positions and mobility within higher education and the state).

This discussion needs to be situated into the ways such cultural markets and conversion strategies operate. It relates to the larger set of class relations in which such new middle-class actors participate. My claims here are complicated, and I can only outline a wider set of arguments I have made elsewhere (Apple 2006). However, the implications of these arguments are serious if we are to fully understand why all of education, including higher education and who does and does not go there, seems to be experiencing a number of the restructurings I have earlier discussed.

This is a time when competition for credentials and cultural capital is intense. The increasing power of mechanisms of restratification such as the return of high levels of mandatory standardization, more testing more often, and constant auditing of results also provides mechanisms—and an insistent logic—that enhance the chances that the children of the professional and managerial new middle class will have less competition from other students. Thus, the introduction of devices to restratify a population—for this is what much of it is—enhances the value of the credentials that the new middle class is more likely to accumulate, given the stock of cultural capital it already possesses (see Bourdieu 1984, 1988, and 1996). I am not claiming that this is necessarily intentional, but it does function to increase the chances for mobility by middle-class children who depend not on economic capital but on cultural capital for advancement (Power et al. 2003; Ball 2003). The effects of such policies and procedures on working-class students and on students who are members of oppressed minorities is visible in an entire series of detailed and insightful studies (see Gillborn and Youdell 2000; McNeil 2000; Lipman 2004; and Apple 1996, 2000, and 2006).

I want to stress the importance of this element within conservative modernization, and not only because it already occupies considerable power within the state. It is crucial to focus on this class fraction as well because, in the situation I have described, I believe that this group is not immune to ideological shifts to the right and thus may not be as able to be self-conscious about the role it may be playing in the restructuring of educational and social policies I have been discussing in this chapter. Given the fear generated by the attacks on the state and on the public sphere by both neoliberals and neoconservatives, this class fraction is decidedly worried about the future mobility of its children in an uncertain economic world. Thus, they may be drawn even more overtly to parts of the conservative alliance's positions, especially those coming from the neoconservative elements who stress greater attention to traditional "high-status" content, greater attention to testing, and a greater emphasis on schooling (and the entire university system) as a stratifying mechanism. This can be seen in a number of states in the United States, for example, where parents of this class fraction are supporting charter schools that will stress academic achievement in traditional subjects and traditional teaching practices (see, for example, Buras 2008).

It remains to be seen where the majority of members of this class grouping will align in the future in the debates over policy. Given their contradictory ideological tendencies, it is possible that the right will be able to mobilize them under conditions of fear for the future of their jobs and children, even when they still vote for, say, the Democratic Party in the United States or Labour in the United Kingdom in electoral terms (Buras 2008). Thus, it would be romantic to simply assume that they will be responsive to the claims from those people who are employed in public schools and in institutions of higher education that the conditions under which they are increasingly working are damaging and that they are creating an education that is less and less worthy of its name.

ON POSSIBILITIES

In this chapter I have discussed some of the ways in which certain elements of conservative modernization have had an impact on education in general. I have pointed to the growth of commodifying logics and the surveillance-inflected audit culture that accompanies them. In the process, I have highlighted a number of dangers that we currently face.

However, I have also urged us not to assume that these conditions can be reduced to the automatic working out of simple formulas. We need a much more nuanced and complex picture of class relations and class projects to understand what is happening—and, while I have not done this here, a more sensitive and historically grounded analysis of the place of racial dynamics in the vision both of "a world out of control" that needs to be policed and of "cultural pollution" that threatens "real knowledge" in the growth of markets and audit cultures (for more on this, see Apple 2006). Becoming more nuanced about such constitutive dynamics will not guarantee that we can interrupt the tendencies upon which I have focused here, but it is one essential step in understanding the genesis of what is at stake in a serious politics of interruption.

If the issue of interruption is not only to be an academic one, however, it requires something else. We need to think more clearly about what needs to be defended and what needs to be changed. Just as Marx reminded us that capitalism might actually be an improvement over feudalism, we may need to take seriously the possibility that some of the intuitions behind new managerial impulses may also constitute an improvement over previous visions of school and university life. Let me say more about this.

There is a complicated and sometimes contradictory politics at work here. Schools and universities have been very real sites of cultural conflict: over collective memory, over what counts as legitimate knowledge, over voice and participation, and over its social and educational aims. Historically, educational institutions have also been sites of considerable conflict over who can and cannot go to them. The intense struggles, for example, over the university's gendered and raced hiring practices, ones in which it has taken decades to even begin to address the cultural and social imbalances in serious ways, stand as eloquent witness to the continuing nature of the problems that need to be faced. Because of this, some forms of public accountability—to ask universities to provide evidence that they are taking seriously their social responsibilities concerning hiring practices for example—were and continue to be partial victories.

Furthermore, public schools and institutions of higher education are increasingly complex places financially and organizationally. Because of this as well, *democratically* inclined management skills are indeed necessary. By not treating the development and refinement of these skills and dispositions with the importance that they deserve, we may be creating a space that will, predictably, be filled with those committed to new managerial impulses. The issue is not whether we need accountability, but the kinds of logics of accountability, and the question of accountability to whom, that now tend to guide the processes of education. An alternative to the external imposition of targets, performance criteria, and quantifiable outcomes—but one that still takes the issue of public accountability seriously—can be built. It would need to rest, and to be constantly rebuilt, upon the constitution of "processes of [critical] deliberation that enable understanding and agreement out of differing accounts of public purpose and service" (Ranson 2003, 470). A key here, of course, is what and who counts as the "public" and whose voices are heard.

As Nancy Fraser and Charles Mills have argued and as I noted earlier, the public sphere has historically been constructed as a gendered and raced space (Fraser 1989; Mills 1997). The prevailing definitions of "public" and "private" were based on a particular assemblage of assumptions about who was a legitimate participant and who was not. Because of this, the simple assertion that educational institutions play a crucial role based on their importance as part of the public sphere is an insufficient defense. Yes, they need to be defended and the public sphere is certainly under attack. But, what kind of public sphere(s) do we have in mind? How should "it" be reconstituted? How would this reconstitution be integrated into what Fraser calls a politics of redistribution and a politics of recognition (Fraser 1997)? In more everyday words, given the criticisms that have been made of the ways in which the public sphere in general and schools and universities in particular have actually operated over time, what needs to change to take account of these criticisms?

What we should not be doing is defending all of the existing practices of schools and universities, since many of these may be discriminatory, racist, or have a history that is based in elitism. Instead, we must ask what specifically we wish to defend. In asking this, as I mentioned above, we may need to recognize that there are elements of good sense as well as bad sense in the criticisms that are made about educational sites. The space of criticism has been taken up by neoliberal claims and managerial impulses, but this does not mean that schools and the higher education sector did not need to change or that a simple return to the previous form and content of our schools and of higher education institutions is anywhere near a sufficient set of policies.

Let us be honest. If a simple return to past practices is neither possible nor wise, it is hard to specify in advance other than in broad strokes the exact character of the kinds of models of structures, practices, and deliberative agency that should guide public life inside and outside higher education. As Raymond Williams reminds us, the "common" has to be ongoingly built, since what counts as the common is the never-ending process of critical deliberation over the very question of the common itself (see Williams 1989). This more critical understanding of the politics of defining what is common is evacuated under the aegis of the logics of markets and audits, since we do know that what is currently being built/imposed is often destructive, even in its own terms of assuming that establishing markets and audits will restore responsiveness and even trust.

Stuart Ranson summarizes these arguments:

> This neoliberal regime cannot realize its purpose of institutional achievement and public trust. Achievement grows out of the internal goods of motivation to improve (that follows recognition and the mutual deliberation of purpose) rather than the external imposition of quantifiable targets, while public trust follows deliberation of common purpose out of difference and discord, rather than the forces of competition that only create a hierarchy of class advantage and exclusion. (2003, 476)

Ranson is not sanguine about the possibility of building a public sphere that both challenges the neoliberal and neoconservative construction of an audit culture and goes beyond the limits of older versions of what counts as the public sphere. However, he does articulate a sense of what is required to do so. A reconstituted vision of the public and a set of practices and structures that support it are grounded in the following:

> Trust and achievement can only emerge in a framework of public accountability that enables different accounts of public purpose and practice to be deliberated in a democratic public sphere: constituted to include difference, enable participation, voice and dissent, through to collective judgment and decision, that is in turn accountable to the public. (Ibid., 476)[8]

Such a vision is not simply utopian. Indeed, the history of higher education, for example—from early mechanics' institutes, to "people's universities," to the many attempts at creating closer cooperative connections between universities and culturally, politically, and economically dispossessed groups—suggests that there is a rich storehouse of knowledge on possibilities for doing this.[9] But this requires the restoration of memory. Thus, historical work is absolutely essential if we are to go forward. Here I do not mean a nostalgic longing for an imagined past, but an honest appraisal of the limits and possibilities of what has been done before.

The task is not only historical, however. Contemporary manifestations of discipline, control, and resistance need to be documented and theorized to increase our collective awareness of what is happening on the ground and inform our sense of what needs to be done. Surveillance and cultures of control are central to the project of conservative modernization, so understanding and critiquing that relationship must be a part of efforts to reconstitute the public sphere. Certainly audits and tests function as forms of surveillance that are reshaping the everyday activities and responsibilities of school actors, notwithstanding some concerted and oftentimes covert opposition to them (see Gilliom, chapter 11 of this volume). Undoubtedly, within each and every institution of education, within the crevices and cracks so to speak, there are counterhegemonic practices being built and defended, but they are too often isolated from each other and never get organized into coherent movements and strategies. Part of the task is to make public the successes in contesting the control over curricula, pedagogy, and evaluation—over all of our work.[10] While public storytelling may not be sufficient, it performs an important function. It keeps alive and reminds us of the very possibility of difference in an age of audits and disrespect.

We have successful models for doing this, such as *Democratic Schools* (Apple and Beane 2007; see also Apple and Buras 2006). In *Democratic Schools*, James Beane and I saw our role as researchers very differently from many others. We acted as "secretaries" for socially critical educators and made public their stories of building curricula and pedagogies that expressly embodied Ranson's vision of a reconstituted public sphere based on difference, participation, voice, and dissent. While *Democratic Schools* was about primary, middle, and secondary schools, it does point to the ways in which such strategic interruptions can proceed in other institutional contexts.

This, then, is another task. Can we act as secretaries for some of our colleagues in educational institutions at every level, making public their partial, but still successful, resistances to the regime of regulation, surveillance, and control that we are currently experiencing? The narratives of their (our) political/pedagogic lives can bear witness to the possibility of taking steps toward building a reconstituted public sphere within the spaces in which we live and work.

ACKNOWLEDGMENTS

This chapter is based on a longer discussion of these issues in Michael W. Apple, *Educating the "Right" Way: Markets, Standards, God, and Inequality*, 2nd ed. (New York: Routledge, 2006).

NOTES

1. See also Slaughter and Leslie (1999), Slaughter and Rhoades (2004), and Rhoads and Torres (in press) for thoughtful discussions of the effects of marketization and competitive economic pressures on universities.
2. See Van Dunk and Dickman (2003) for how this works, and doesn't work, in plans to marketize education.
3. I have discussed No Child Left Behind at considerably greater length in Apple (2006).
4. Of course, this is a differentiated experience. In the United States, supermarkets are less apt to even be found in inner-city neighborhoods populated by poor persons of color.
5. See Apple (2000) and Hogan (1983). For the ways in which race has been and is a crucial dynamic, see Mills (1997), McCarthy et al. (2005), Ladson-Billings and Gillborn (2004), and Fine et al. (2005).
6. See also Apple and Pedroni (2005) and Pedroni (2007), however, on how oppressed people attempt to tactically take up the subject position of the consumer and rearticulate it to further their own collective interests.
7. Basil Bernstein makes an important distinction between those fractions of the new middle class who work for the state and that group who works in the private sector. They may have different ideological and educational commitments. See Bernstein (1990). For more on the ways "intermediate" classes and class fractions operate and interpret their worlds, see Wright (1985, 1997, and 1998) and Bourdieu (1984).
8. For some cautions on seeing this as simply a liberal model of "deliberation," see Avis (2003).
9. An account of a continuing attempt to organize core aspects university life and work around these concerns can be found in Apple (2000).
10. Within the field of education, the journal *Teaching Education* has attempted to institutionalize this task by consistently publishing accounts of critical teaching within undergraduate classes in teacher education and in graduate classes as well.

REFERENCES

Apple, Michael W. 1995. *Education and power.* 2nd ed. New York: Routledge.

———. 1996. *Cultural politics and education.* New York: Teachers College Press.

———. 2000. *Official knowledge: Democratic education in a conservative age.* 2nd ed. New York: Routledge.

———. 2004. *Ideology and curriculum.* 3rd ed. New York: Routledge.

———. 2006. *Educating the "right" way: Markets, standards, God, and inequality.* 2nd ed. New York: Routledge.

Apple, Michael W., and James A. Beane, eds., 2007. *Democratic schools: Lessons in powerful education.* Portsmouth: NH: Heinemann.

Apple, Michael W., and Kristen A. Buras, eds. 2006. *The subaltern speak: Curriculum, power, and educational struggles.* New York: Routledge.

Apple, Michael W., and Thomas Pedroni. 2005. Conservative alliance building and African American support for voucher plans. *Teachers College Record* 107:2068–2105.

Apple, Michael W., Petter Aasen, Misook Kim Cho, Luis Armando Gandin, Anita Oliver, Youl-Kwan Sung, Hannah Tavares, and Ting-Hong Wong. 2003. *The state and the politics of knowledge.* New York: Routledge.

Aronowitz, Stanley. 2000. *The knowledge factory.* Boston: Beacon Press.

Avis, James. 2003. Re-thinking trust in a performative culture: The case of education. *Journal of Education Policy* 18:315–332.

Ball, Stephen. 1994. *Education reform.* Buckingham, UK: Open University Press.

———. 2003. *Class strategies and the education market.* London: RoutledgeFalmer.

Bernstein, Basil. 1990. *The structuring of pedagogic discourse.* New York: Routledge.

———. 1996. *Pedagogy, symbolic control and identity.* Philadelphia: Taylor and Francis.

Binder, Amy. 2002. *Contentious curricula.* Princeton, NJ: Princeton University Press.

Bourdieu, Pierre. 1984. *Distinction.* Cambridge, MA: Harvard University Press.

———. 1988. *Homo economicus.* Stanford, CA: Stanford University Press.

———. 1996. *The state nobility.* Stanford, CA: Stanford University Press.

Buras, Kristen. 2008. *Rightist multiculturalism.* New York: Routledge.

Chubb, John, and Terry Moe. 1990. *Politics, markets, and American schools.* Washington, DC: Brookings Institution.

Clarke, John, and Janet Newman. 1997. *The managerial state.* Thousand Oaks, CA: Sage.

Fine, Michelle, Lois Weis, Linda Powell, and L. Mun Wong, eds. 2005. *Off white.* 2nd ed. New York: Routledge.

Foner, Eric. 1998. *The story of American freedom.* New York: Norton.

Fraser, Nancy. 1989. *Unruly practices.* Minneapolis: University of Minnesota Press.

———. 1997. *Justice interruptus.* New York: Routledge.

Gillborn, David, and Deborah Youdell. 2000. *Rationing education.* Buckingham, UK: Open University Press.

Habermas, Jurgen. 1971. *Knowledge and human interests.* Boston: Beacon Press.

Hogan, David. 1983. Education and class formation. In *Cultural and economic reproduction in education,* ed. Michael W. Apple. Boston: Routledge and Kegan Paul.

Jessop, Bob. 2002. *The future of the capitalist state.* Cambridge, UK: Polity Press.

Johnson, Dale, Bonnie Johnson, Stephen Farenga, and Daniel Ness. 2007. *Trivializing teacher education.* New York: Rowman & Littlefield.

Katz, Michael B. 2001. *The price of citizenship.* New York: Metropolitan Books.

Kelly, Robin D. G. 1993. We are not what we seem: Rethinking black working class opposition in the Jim Crow South. *Journal of American History* 80:75–112.

Ladson-Billings, Gloria, and David Gillborn, eds. 2004. *The RoutledgeFalmer reader in multicultural education*. London: RoutledgeFalmer.

Leys, Colin. 2003. *Market-driven politics: Neoliberal democracy and the public interest*. New York: Verso.

Levine, Lawrence 1996. *The opening of the American mind: Canon, culture, and history*. Boston: Beacon Press.

Lipman, Pauline. 2004. *High stakes education*. New York: Routledge.

Liston, Daniel, and Kenneth Zeichner. 1991. *Teacher education and the social conditions of schooling*. New York: Routledge.

Marquand, David. 2000. *The progressive dilemma*. London: Phoenix Books.

McCarthy, Cameron, Warren Crichlow, Greg Dimitriadis, and Nadine Dolby, eds. 2005. *Race, identity, and representation in education*. 2nd ed. New York: Routledge.

McNeil, Linda. 2000. *The contradictions of school reform*. New York: Routledge.

Mills, Charles. 1997. *The racial contract*. Ithaca, NY: Cornell University Press.

Monahan, Torin. 2005. The school system as a post-Fordist organization: Fragmented centralization and the emergence of IT specialists. *Critical Sociology* 3 (4): 583–615.

Olssen, Mark. 1996. In defense of the welfare state and of publicly provided education. *Journal of Education Policy* 11: 340.

Pedroni, Thomas. 2007. *Market matters*. New York: Routledge.

Power, Sally, Tony Edwards, Geoff Whitty, and Valarie Wigfall. 2003. *Education and the middle class*. Buckingham, UK: Open University Press

Ranson, Stuart. 2003. Public accountability in the age of neo-liberal governance. *Journal of Education Policy* 18: 470.

Rhoads, Robert, and Carlos Alberto Torres, eds. 2006. University, state, and market: *The political economy of globalization in the Americas*. Stanford, CA: Stanford University Press.

Sandler, Jen, and Michael W. Apple. In press. Evidence-based practices in education: Beyond simple critique. In *Handbook of cultural politics and education*, ed. Zeus Leonardo. Utrecht, Netherlands: Sense Publishers.

Shipler, David. 2004. *The working poor*. New York: Knopf.

Shor, Ira. 1992. *Empowering education*. Chicago: University of Chicago Press.

Skocpol, Theda. 2003. *Diminished democracy*. Norman: University of Oklahoma Press.

Slaughter, Sheila, and Larry Leslie. 1999. *Academic capitalism*. Baltimore, MD: Johns Hopkins University Press.

Slaughter, Sheila, and Gary Rhoades. 2004. *Academic capitalism and the new economy*. Baltimore, MD: Johns Hopkins University Press.

Smith, Mary Lee, Linda Miller-Kahn, Walter Heinecke, and Patricia Jarvis.. 2003. *Political spectacle and the fate of American schools*. New York: Routledge.

Van Dunk, Emily, and Anneliese Dickman. 2003. *School choice and the question of accountability*. New Haven, CT: Yale University Press.

Williams, Raymond. 1989. *Resources of hope*. New York: Verso.

Wright, Erik Olin. 1985. *Classes*. New York: Verso.

———. 1997. *Class counts*. New York: Cambridge University Press.

Wright, Erik Olin, ed. 1998. *The debate on classes*. New York: Verso.

Chapter 11

Lying, Cheating, and Teaching to the Test

The Politics of Surveillance Under No Child Left Behind

John Gilliom

Mrs. Hill is a middle school teacher in rural Ohio. She is a big fan of the War of 1812, which she uses to teach geography, state history, international relations, history, and social studies. Until a few years ago, she would typically devote several days to covering the war in great detail with student reports, art projects, and maps. Now, if it gets anything at all, it gets a quick forty-five minutes. Why? School surveillance.

This chapter argues that one of the primary effects of the school surveillance mandated by the federal government in the 2002 law known as No Child Left Behind is to reshape the curricula of America's classrooms. No Child Left Behind, or NCLB, did not set out to eliminate the War of 1812 from middle school education in Ohio. What brought about the elimination of the War of 1812, Mrs. Hill explains, is that the NCLB assessment test used in Ohio does not use the War of 1812 as an "indicator"; the war is not a specifically assessed and measured item on the required tests. Therefore, in the face of heavy pressure to prepare her students for the assessment test, she must cut short her teaching of the War of 1812 and other moments or issues that did not have the good luck or political esteem to become indicators.

This small story of one teacher's classroom can tell us much about ongoing battles over surveillance, power, and the law in America's public school system. NCLB, I explain in more detail shortly, is a massive piece of legislation that has had an equally massive effect on the lives of millions of people. At the risk of overworking a small example, the demise of the War of 1812 is a great illustration of how the consequences of NCLB are playing out in classrooms and schools across the nation. We can see the reshaping of course content to match the test. We can see a concomitant standardization of the curriculum around the topics that have been sanctioned by state officials. We can see that a teacher's autonomy and control over her classroom and curriculum have been greatly reduced. We can also see that pressure runs against a type of teaching that would happily devote a week to the active and interdisciplinary exploration of a historical moment.

None of these policy outcomes was directly and explicitly mandated by either the Congress or the state of Ohio, but they have nevertheless been accomplished through the impact of the assessment mechanisms put in place under NCLB. This is because the NCLB surveillance mechanisms implement a number of policy outcomes that are achieved through the installation of the surveillance mechanisms themselves or through the "choices" of thousands of teachers responding to a workplace reshaped by the presence of the tests. The exertion of power in NCLB is evident enough that Frederick M. Hess (2003) uses the term "coercive accountability" to describe the policy and Jones and colleagues (2003) use the term "measurement driven reform." Each of these descriptions forces us to recognize that there are ways in which the purportedly neutral act of assessment actually implements political change. In several important ways NCLB achieves educational policy changes not by mandating them but by installing a system of surveillance and assessment that, as people are forced to meet its measures, pressures the educational system toward the desired (and sometimes unimagined) ends.

This chapter explores some of the key curricular and political dynamics surrounding this new and powerful system of surveillance in America's schools. It begins with a brief look at the central relevant aspects of NCLB, then explores the effects that NCLB-mandated testing has in classrooms. As teachers adjust their styles to help students (and, therefore, teachers and schools) succeed on the tests, the results are wholesale restructurings of the style, content and schedules of American schooling. Next, I turn to the political struggles over NCLB, with a particular focus on the ways teachers and administrators use practices of "everyday resistance" to lessen, delay, or evade the effect of the testing. As I have argued elsewhere (Gilliom 2001), these informal and often secretive means of combating a surveillance system emerge as one of the most important political fronts in the face of the continued failure of more conventional routes of opposition. Finally, I reflect on what this example of school surveillance teaches us about surveillance as a broader technique and condition.

NCLB

In 2002, President George W. Bush signed the reauthorization of national education law that has come to be known as No Child Left Behind. Under the new program, tens of millions of Americans, in every community and state, are subject to unprecedented frequencies and degrees of state monitoring. The educational testing regime set forth under NCLB is a transformative moment in the history not just of education but of government surveillance itself.

NCLB is big, but for our purposes we can focus on the following key features:

- States must establish a standards-based curriculum and design tests to assess mastery of that curriculum.
- Annual testing is required in reading and math for all students in grades 3–8 and then once again in high school; science testing was mandated after 2007–2008.
- Test scores must be reported for schools and for significant subgroups within schools, including ESL students, disabled students, and population breakdowns by race and family income.
- Mean test scores for schools and subgroups are assessed to determine whether a school has made "adequate yearly progress" (AYP); failure to achieve AYP in multiple years earns escalating sanctions. Title I schools (meaning the poorer ones) face the strictest public accounting and sanctions of NCLB; after two to four years of inadequate progress they face such measures as state takeover, staff replacement, or conversion to charter school.
- States must have all children up to proficiency by 2014 and make measurable progress toward that goal during the years leading up to 2014. That progress must be evident in each identified subgroup.

Each year under NCLB some fifty million standardized tests are administered to the children of the United States. The results are used to develop files on individual children, assess the work of teachers and school leaders, rate individual schools and districts, and, if current laws are followed, deliver severe financial and political penalties to schools that fail to "measure up." In response to the command that they measure up, teachers and administrators respond in ways that are nearly as diverse as the educational system in which they work. Some barely notice, as upper-income and privileged school systems worry little about passing standardized tests that consistently favor the well-off. Others worry. Some "teach to the test," changing their curricula and teaching tactics to better align with the style and content of tests. Some support formal legal and political opposition to the implementation of NCLB. Still others doctor answer sheets, train children in test-taking strategies, manipulate school populations, and take other, typically surreptitious, steps to protect their students, their jobs, and their schools.

TEACHING TO THE TESTS

In the ways that they watch, measure, and assess, NCLB surveillance mechanisms favor certain practices. This is where we can think of the disappearance of the War of 1812. As a schoolteacher adapted to a new surveillance and assessment environment, her classroom was changed. As tens of thousands of schoolteachers make the same adjustments, a nation's educational policy is changed. And it goes way beyond the War of 1812.

The overwhelming evidence from research undertaken by scholars studying the implementation and impact of NCLB is that, particularly in lower-income schools, NCLB is forcing a reformatting of the curriculum to focus on the subject matters that are on the tests and on the teaching techniques that lead to successful test taking. Furthermore, significant parts of the teaching year have been colonized by test preparation and test taking; in some cases, state test compliance emerges as the organizing principle of the academic calendar.

Anyone who lived through the educational politics of the 1990s knows that there was a huge and not entirely new war going on, with religious and cultural conservatives frequently advocating the "the three R's" or "back to basics" approach coupled with teaching methods known as phonics or direct instruction. The latter techniques focus on achieving knowledge acquisition through the repetition and memorization of small parts of words or other pieces of information. Both have been strongly embraced by the political and religious right in the United States and resisted by progressives and the education unions. What NCLB was able to achieve was a largely tacit, but nonetheless massive, victory for the conservative movement. There is now strong evidence that as struggling districts attempt to pass the tests mandated by NCLB, the pursuit of success on the testing metrics pressures them to restrict the curriculum to the basic, tested materials at the expense of the arts, physical education, and other untested areas. Further, this pursuit pressures teachers to shift to educational techniques that better align with the particularist, discrete knowledge style of standardized tests. Exploring works of literature gives way to memorizing vocabulary and spelling lists; hands-on experimentation gives way to memorizing formulae for calculations. The widespread tactical adaptation to meeting the metrics and assessment techniques of NCLB has achieved an educational policy outcome as pivotal as any that have been explicitly mandated by an act of Congress. This pattern is demonstrated in several studies that find evidence of a notable shift in teaching priorities under high-stakes testing. A national study found that "[a] large majority of teachers felt that there is so much pressure for high scores on the state-mandated tests that they had little time to teach anything not covered on the test" (Pedulla et al. 2003, 2; see also Jones et al. 2003, 29–30; Pedulla et al. 2003 4).[1]

In another multistate research project, Jones and his colleagues (2003) reported that testing sharply defines the knowledge and skill that students will learn. Prior to high-stakes testing, teachers made the decision about what to teach in a broad framework of topics. Testing, however, not only defines what will be taught but also defines the context of the knowledge. Where teachers may have previously embedded instruction in integrated units or taught concepts across multiple grades, testing necessitates that topics be taught in ways that can be assessed through discrete items on written tests given at very specific point of time (Jones et al. 2003, 26).

Pedulla's team also found that teachers in states with particularly high stakes testing programs are more apt to "engage in test preparation earlier in the school year; spend more time on such initiatives; target special groups of students for more intense preparation; use materials that closely resemble the test; use commercially or state-developed test-specific preparation materials; use released items from the state test; and try to motivate their students to do well on the state test" (2003, 5).

Many critics of NCLB approach this information about the limits of testing as a lamentable flaw in a system that is underfunded and crudely designed. Acknowledging or lamenting that assessment based on full portfolios and site visits that are sensitive to local needs and variation would be the ideal, they either condemn the current system or give it muted applause as a workable alternative in a difficult world. To me, it is more interesting to work past the "lamentable flaw" arguments to think of the tests as a mechanism for the social engineering of the American classroom. The new system of assessment compels movement toward a uniform style of instruction focusing not just on the content of the tests but on the style and organization of the tests. Reviews of how low-cost mass tests are designed show that the emphasis must be placed on assessing mastery of relatively discrete pieces of knowledge and information. The upshot is that teachers must reorient subject matter and teaching method to match the framework of the tests. For those who have long believed that the rote study of particles of information is the key to successful education, this is a major policy triumph.

These effects will be magnified in working-class and minority schools because it is here that the tests are hardest to pass and the stakes are most dire. In many ways, then, NCLB advances and legitimates the class and race tiering of the American education system: because of the well-known tendency for academic tests to largely measure social class and background factors, the optics and metrics of NCLB are set in ways that give upper income populations an easy pass while giving lower income and ESL populations almost insurmountable hurdles. Furthermore, the strongest school sanctions are reserved for schools that receive Title I funds: by definition, the lower-income school populations. These school must adapt their curriculum in order to get over the testing hurdle; the result is that lower-class schools focus on, even obsess with, testing content and practices while more affluent schools put up with the minor nuisance of a week or so lost to filling in some bubbles.

FIGHTING BACK

It is plausible that teachers and administrators are trying to resist a system they see as corrupt and unfair, as do tax, religious and civil rights protesters across this nation. (Nichols and Berliner 2005, 24)

Through the legal authority manifest in the congressional reauthorization of Title I, NCLB launched one of the most ambitious surveillance programs in American history. In a strange twist on the usual mode, the tests are used less to assess individual students and their study habits than they are, purportedly, to assess the performance of individual schools. Why "purportedly"? The tests actually only assess a small part of the performance issue because most of what they measure is the socioeconomic background of the school's base population. Schools with relatively advantaged students typically post better test scores than those with relatively disadvantaged students. It does not follow, though, that the former schools are better at educating students than the latter; the scores may simply reflect the fact that the former schools have students who take tests better than those at the latter. It is a well-known truism in the testing business that most standardized assessment tests largely assess the socioeconomic background, or "social capital," of the students taking the test—known as the "Volvo effect" because, as Jones and colleagues summarize, "simply count the number of Volvos, BMWs, or Mercedes owned by the family and you have a good indicator of how well the child will perform on standardized tests" (2003, 118). Testing critic Alfie Kohn gives several examples of the Volvo effect at work:

A study of math scores on the 1992 National Assessment of Educational Progress found that the combination of four variables unrelated to instruction (number of parents living at home, parents' educational background, type of community . . . and state poverty rate) explained a whopping 89 percent of the differences in state scores. In fact, one of those variables, the number of students who had one parent living at home, accounted for 71 percent of the variance all by itself. . . . In Massachusetts, five factors explained 90 percent of the variance in scores on the Massachusetts Comprehensive Assessment System (MCAS) exam, leading a researcher to conclude that students' performance "has almost everything to do with parental socioeconomic backgrounds and less to do with teachers, curricula, or what the children learned in the classroom." . . . Another study looked just at the poverty level in each of 593 districts in Ohio and found a .80 correlation with 1997 scores on that state's proficiency test, meaning that this measure alone explained nearly two-thirds of the differences in test results. . . . Even a quick look at the grades given to Florida schools under that state's new rating system found that "no school where less than 10% of the students qualify for free lunch scored below a C, and no school where more than 80% of the students qualify scored above a C." (2001, nonpaginated)

This point raises a profound, fascinating, angering, and comedic point about the assessment logics and rationales behind the testing campaign. They are, of course, promised as tools of assessment that will compel schools to confront the strengths and weaknesses of their performance as educators. The premise messages, or assumptions, of this argument are that students' mean performance on multiple-item standardized tests in the core curricular areas are a good measure of the success or failure of a school and that teaching strategies and teacher performance are the central element in understanding the success or failure of American schools. But what we know about standardized tests, test-specific training, and the importance of socioeconomic background in explaining student performance means that, for the most part, the NCLB testing regime measures a mix of socioeconomic background and a school's ability to teach children how to take the test successfully. It is with good reason that America's classroom teachers are galled by the assertions and impositions of these tests, and it is easy to understand why politicians frequently use an attack on NCLB testing as one of their best applause lines.

And these teachers and politicians are backed up by experts on assessment techniques. Along with several other leading authorities in the field (see Nichols and Berliner), Stephen Raudenbush, a professor of education and statistics at the University of Michigan, says, "High-stakes decisions based on school-mean proficiency are scientifically indefensible. We cannot regard differences in school mean proficiency as reflecting differences in school effectiveness." He continues, "To reward schools for high mean achievement is tantamount to rewarding those schools for serving students who were doing well prior to school entry" (quoted in Nichols and Berliner, 25).

Formal public opposition to NCLB is increasingly widespread and may amount to one of the more significant antisurveillance movements of our time. The legislatures of more than two dozen states have taken actions to fight the law, litigation has been introduced in dozens of federal cases, politicians speak out against it; at this writing, in the early summer of 2008, there seemed little reason to believe that NCLB would survive intact to have its full impact, which is scheduled for 2014.

Along with expressions of public opposition and frustration, practices of everyday resistance abound. The personal and institutional practices for thwarting, undermining, or averting the gaze or impact of NCLB are legion. Schools urge low-performing students to drop out rather than drag an institution's score down. States camouflage special populations through laws that allow small groups to be ignored. Teachers guide students toward answering questions during the exam periods, and some stay up late at night changing answers to improve performance. More subtly, schools spend countless hours "teaching to the tests"—training students in the specific areas known to be stressed on the tests and teaching in formats specifically tuned to the design and makeup of test questions. Such practices definitely bring up test scores, but because they undermine the test's content-sampling logic, they completely destroy the test's effectiveness as a measure of academic performance. Others teachers have quit, moved to teach in grade levels that are not tested, or shifted to the untested private schools. In sum, the public and private battles against NCLB are widespread and important

In all of my previous research on the use of surveillance as a form of social sorting and control, subject populations have fought back through both opposition and resistance. By opposition, I refer to public efforts to block or significantly change policy. By resistance, I refer to quieter practices that seek to avoid, stymie, game, or otherwise manage a system. In the case of NCLB, there appears to be plenty of both. I take them up in turn.

Opposition

As for flat-out political opposition, Benjamin Superfine provides some highlights of the public battles that have ensued:

> NCLB has been the object of several political attacks. . . . As of April 2005, bills or resolutions to opt out of or limit federal funding under NCLB were introduced in at least 21 states. In one of the most prominent responses thus far to NCLB, Utah passed a law giving its current state accountability requirements precedence over NCLB accountability requirements. At the federal level, at least thirty bills calling for the changes in NCLB have been proposed in Congress. (2006, 796–797)

NCLB has also generated a host of litigation. There appear to be five primary points of testing litigation:[2]

1. Litigation arguing that NCLB includes inadequate funding to fully and fairly implement the evaluation program and/or imposes unfunded costs specifically forbidden by the act (*Connecticut v. Spellings*; *School District of the City of Pontiac v. Spellings*).

2. Litigation using test scores as authoritative evidence to argue that current systems of educational finance violate state provision for equality or guarantees of "adequate" education (*Claremont School District v. Governor* [NY]).

3. Litigation challenging the failure of some states to provide appropriate language testing for students who are not proficient in English (*Coachella Valley Unified School District et al. v. State of California; Reading School District v. Penn DE*).

4. Litigation asserting that NCLB's testing protocol violates the rights of disabled school children under IDEA, the Individuals with Disabilities Education Act (*Bd. of Ed of Ottawa Township High School District 140 et al. v. DE*).

5. Litigation arguing that the assessment methods required by NCLB are statistically unsound and therefore unsuited for making determinations of educational quality (*CLE v. DE*).

To date, the definitive review of NCLB litigation strategies is Benjamin Superfine's "Using the Courts to Influence the Implementation of No Child Left Behind." He concludes skeptically: "In the lawsuits that have been brought to influence NCLB, the courts have not constituted an effective venue for addressing implementation problems or for enforcing salient NCLB provisions" (2006, 782).

It seems clear that the political landscape for NCLB is changing under our feet. Political candidates use their opposition to NCLB as a major applause line, and public pronouncements that "we are testing the kids too much" are becoming a regular part of the political fare. Many states have actually been delaying the full impact of NCLB through the manipulation of data and compliance schedules. The combination of the evident shifts in the political system and the arrival of the truly unworkable phases of state compliance to NCLB suggests to me that we will see a major reworking of the law in short order. If so, this may emerge as a very significant example of successful political opposition to a new surveillance initiative.

RESISTANCE

When people are subject to a form of surveillance and assessment that can dramatically affect their livelihood and standing, it is unlikely that they will fail to take actions to enhance their autonomy, well-being, and survival. This may be particularly evident when the surveillance system does not enjoy legitimacy among a significant part of the affected population. It thus should come as no surprise that just as a number of students have always tried to cheat on tests, we now see that teachers and administrators do the same; they manipulate state test results, remark test sheets, guide students during exams, and train students to do well on the tests. These are all ways in which surveilled individuals and institutions work within the context of a surveillance system in order to advance their case as best they can.

A surveillance system that relies on paper-and-pencil tests given to large numbers of people in closed rooms watched over by individual teachers and administrators with a direct personal stake in the outcome is designed for resistance. And the evidence is building that prompting, assisting, and answer changing by school personnel is relatively widespread. Additionally, there are numerous instances of teachers photocopying test samples as preparation guides.[3] In a widespread study of mass media news reports covering cheating on high-stakes tests, Nichols and Berliner report a host of instances and tactics that have come to light. These include:

- Teachers and administrators erasing and correcting test answers after students have completed the tests.
- Teachers and administrators predistributing test books and questions to prepare students.
- Teachers and administrators submitting false student ID numbers to technically disqualify underperforming students.
- Teachers and administrators verbally coaching students during examination periods.
- Teachers instructing students to fill in one answer sheet, get it checked, and then fill in the final answer sheet.
- Teachers readministering tests until scores are acceptable.
- Administrators distributing correct answers prior to tests.
- Teachers leaving multiplication charts and other aids on display during tests.

It is of little surprise that such practices are apparently widespread: the stakes are high for teachers and school administrators whose jobs are at risk. In some states, furthermore, significant bonuses and salary bumps are tied to testing performance. So whether it's the stick or the carrot, the pressure is on, and teachers and administrators are acting like just about any other populations placed in similar circumstances (Gilliom 2001).[4] As in other cases of everyday resistance, there are frequently very compelling explanations for behaviors that are patently illegal:

One example of this is the North Carolina principal who will not test what she calls "borderline kids," her special education children, despite the requirement to do so. She says, "I couldn't. The borderline children experience enough failure and do not need to be humiliated by a test far beyond their abilities." By not testing all the children in the school the principal is cheating. But this is also an act of human kindness. And it is at the same time an act of resistance to laws made by policy makers in some other community. It is not easy to judge this principal harshly. (Nichols and Berliner 2005, 24)

Accompanying examples of the cheating teachers, the coaching principles, and the number-crunching administrators are more public state efforts to moderate the impact of NCLB's assessment program. First among these is the fact that states are able to backload their proficiency improvements. Given twelve years to attain full proficiency, a state need not progress one-twelfth of the way each year; rather, it may follow the lead of at least twenty-two states and delay some of the big steps until later in the cycle. That may seem like a risky bet since a lot has to be achieved in the last four years, but given long experience with educational fads coming and going, political environments shifting, and governments failing to follow through on tough talk, it's probably a pretty smart bet, and looking smarter with every passing day.

A second way that states can manipulate their response to NCLB assessment has to do with how they count the monitored subgroups. Recall that schools must show progress for subgroups based on disability, race, and income; an entire school fails if, say, its disabled students fail. States, however, have latitude in setting how large a subgroup must be before a school needs to report its performance separately. In Maryland anything over five students in a school forms a subgroup which must make AYP for a school to pass, while in Virginia and other states the number is as high as fifty. If there are forty-nine disabled students in a Virginia school, there doesn't even need to be a breakout assessment. Suffice to say that states with larger subgroup cutoffs are more likely to make the grade under NCLB.[5]

RETHINKING SURVEILLANCE

Most of us think of "surveillance" as referring to things like spy cameras, eavesdropping satellites, or undercover police operations. These are correct meanings, but "surveillance studies" covers a great deal more. Roughly translated as "watching from above" or "supervision," the idea of surveillance as we now use it also covers many forms of informational politics and control—audits, examinations, mappings, visual observation, and social sorting and classification. In this sense, a program like educational testing under NCLB represents a huge surveillance initiative. What we think of at first glance as millions of separate examinations of grade school and high school students is more fully understood as a massive auditing system imposed upon the entire public schooling system of the United States. The NCLB testing reconstitutes the control and oversight map of American public education as it crosses the boundaries and walls that formally isolated individual schools and classrooms.

In this sense, the NCLB testing programs manifest a significant and important shifting of political power in American education while, as we have seen, implementing wholesale changes in the design and delivery of instruction.

We study school surveillance not just to learn about the changing face of schools but also to learn more about the concept and practices of surveillance as they unfold in this important arena.

Surveillance as Domination

If we think of surveillance as just *watching*, we err, because surveillance is never really just watching. It's not just vision, but *super*vision. It's not just sight, but *over*sight. Surveillance assumes, advances, and/or creates a relationship of domination. In NCLB, the power of the U.S. national government, through Title I, makes the command of nationwide testing possible, while the testing brings dramatic new inroads of national control over classroom practices. The surveillance that was made possible by the original imbalance of power now expresses, transforms, and advances that power. When something like a test is given in a classroom, power relations are asserted, affirmed, and reorganized. Because of the political and social importance inherent in the powers of surveillance and the incumbent dynamics of domination and depiction, we should always expect there to be struggle, opposition, and resistance in the face of new initiatives or steps in surveillance. These may come in the form of legal challenges, political action, hiding, cheating, and lying. But the bottom line is that we should expect to see some expressions of conflict or resistance; it is the absence of apparent conflict that should be the puzzle, not its presence.

Surveillance as Depiction

There is another and different type of mistake in thinking of surveillance as just watching. All observation is a creative and constructive process of editing, choosing, shaping, preferring, and discouraging. Elements of a complex reality must be lost. Fictions must be created. Definitions must be set. When something like a test is given in a classroom, some aspects of a student's life are drawn forth, some aspects of class content are omitted, some sets of skill are preferred, some questions asked, others not. Some parts of the knowledge process are emphasized while others are set to the side. Things that cannot be easily measured or assessed are frequently lost, while those that can be easily placed in a metric are foregrounded. In these senses, surveillance must not be misunderstood as the act of passive observation—it is a creative depiction of complex environments. Simply imagine a large, dynamic high school involving several hundred people being publicly summarized under a two-word heading like "Academic Emergency" or "Continuous Improvement"; the radical condensation of information into one value-laden hierarchy reminds us that all acts of assessment are utterly depictive.

Surveillance as Symbolic Politics

In public discourse, NCLB mobilizes an indictment of the classroom teacher and school administrator—as opposed to social conditions, funding, and structural elements—as the key factor in the success or failure of students. Further, it pushes public education into the cultural space of the market economy, complete with performance indicators, marketlike sanctions, interschool competition, and *Consumer Reports*–like ratings of schools. Some of these are what we might call "premise messages"—assumptions that are asserted and strengthened by the proposal and implementation of surveillance. Premise messages are a critical part of the politics of surveillance. With employee drug testing (Gilliom 1994), it was the assertion that significant numbers of American workers were stoned at work and that on-the-job intoxication (by illicit drugs, not alcohol) was a significant factor in workplace accidents. With welfare-fraud control (Gilliom 2001), it was the assertion that welfare fraud was rampant and costly enough to legitimate huge expenditures on computerized surveillance. In the political realm, these premise messages not only help create the conditions under which a surveillance program is more likely to be implemented, they are themselves an important political accomplishment in the ongoing game of naming and blaming social problems, threats, and enemies (Edelman 1988). In turn, as problems and enemies are responded to, policy makers who respond, and the citizens who support them, are positioned as the helpers and solvers. In sum, premise messages that accompany surveillance policies both make the case for the policy and achieve political outcomes of their own.

With NCLB, some of the most important premise messages are long-standing arguments made by conservative and free-market opponents of public education: that the technique of the classroom teacher and school organization, not socioeconomic factors or per-pupil expenditures, create educational outcomes; that "America's schools are failing" and it is the fault of the classroom teacher; that marketlike competition is a good start at a cure. These are the symbolic political claims attendant to the more nuts-and-bolts aspects of NCLB. In surveillance research, such claims are all too frequently treated as the largely inconsequential chatter that accompanies a surveillance initiative. But as surveillance policy is increasingly mainstreamed as a regular part of the public policy tool kit, the surveillance research community will benefit from framing at least a portion of its work in the broader terms of symbolic politics and policy assessment.

Surveillance as Policy Implementation

The retooling urged by NCLB standards and techniques accomplishes long-standing goals of the political right in the United States. We've seen these goals accomplished in the evidence of how teachers reorient their curricula to content and styles that better meet the demands of the tests. First, NCLB pushes schools toward the so-called phonics, direct instruction, or drill and kill approach to classroom education that has been championed by cultural conservatives. Second, it effectively reduces the amount of school time spent on topics such as music, the arts, and open study and exploration. These ends are accomplished not through direct command but through the installation of a system that rewards the adoption of the preferred behavior. Some authors have referred to these as the "unintended consequences" of NCLB, but I'm not so sure. When a policy initiative tacitly achieves goals that its proponents have long sought in other methods and venues, it doesn't take a paranoid mind to wonder.

CONCLUSION

Surveillance is hardly a new addition to the classroom. From the fundamentals of classroom design to the invention of attendance and student records, observation, assessment and control are as old as formal education itself. In the twentieth century, standardized testing emerged first as a sorting tool in the military and then spread to wider use in intelligence testing, college and graduate admissions, and professional certification (Gould 1996). But, curiously, until the very last years of the century, standardized assessment had a surprisingly low role in evaluating the general public school student. The SAT and ACT awaited those who aspired to college, but for most students in the United States, comprehensive standardized assessment of academic achievement is a pretty new thing. In that sense, the spread of state-level achievement and assessment tests in the 1990s and their partial nationalization in the 2002 NCLB marked a big change in classroom surveillance.

Another very important dimension of the change is that, in many key ways, the assessment tests under NCLB turn the light of scrutiny on to schools, administrators, and teachers even more than they do on students. NCLB creates an evaluation framework in which the mean scores of a school's tested population are used to create annual evaluation figures, much like grades, for schools. Regardless of challenges or benefits that schools may face due to such things as the socioeconomic backgrounds of their students, mean student scores showing absolute improvement on state-mandated proficiency tests are the new metric of school assessment. Results are posted on Web sites and published in newspapers. Sanctions can go beyond this public shaming to include mass firings and school reorganization.

Perhaps the biggest change in educational surveillance that comes out of NCLB is not the increased testing of students but the dramatic new intensification of surveillance on the performance of the teacher and their leaders. In this sense, NCLB surveillance must be thought of as workplace surveillance rather than just educational surveillance. Understanding NCLB as a workplace surveillance program that redefines the employment conditions for the millions of public schoolteachers and administrators is critical to understanding the significant political and legal opposition as well as the widespread practices of everyday resistance. With all of the incumbent irony, the tests have been turned on those who are used to being the testers, and they are not happy.

NOTES

1. I can report from personal experience that the high school in my community rewards all sophomores who can pass the NCLB state achievement test the first time through by allowing them to skip all their subject-area final exams during the last week of school in the late spring; English, science, math, history, and foreign language all take this hit in support of the statewide testing.
2. There is a great deal of litigation surrounding NCLB, much of which goes unmentioned here. The focus here is on those cases raising significant questions about the testing and assessment elements of NCLB.
3. The definitive academic study appears to be Nichols and Berliner, "The Inevitable Corruption of Indicators and Educators Through High-Stakes Testing" (2005).
4. In turn, surveillance mechanisms are being fine-tuned in order to detect patterns that indicate cheating. One fairly simple approach is newly developed test-scanning equipment that counts the number of erasures on answer sheets and flags those that are outside the norm. Another approach looks for overlaps or repeats of answer patterns within classrooms. Dramatic improvement in test scores over a short time period is also a red flag. Another, more sophisticated approach was developed by economists working with the Chicago city schools. In the approach designed by Brian A. Jacob and Steven D. Levitt, an algorithm measuring various factors that may be indicative of cheating is used to assess classroom scores—Jacob and Levitt estimate that between 3 and 5 percent of classrooms in the school system have cheating teachers (Jacob and Levitt 2003).
5. There are sound statistical reasons for doing so because too small a number leads to unsafe conclusions about group performance.

REFERENCES

Amrein, Audrey L., David C. Berliner. 2002. *The impact of high-stakes tests on student academic performance: An analysis of NAEP results in states with high-stakes tests and ACT, SAT, and AP test results in states with high school graduation exams*, EPSL-0211–126-EPRU. Tempe: Education Policy Studies Laboratory, Arizona State University.

Edelman, Murray. 1988. *Constructing the political spectacle*. Chicago: University of Chicago Press.

Gilliom, John. 1994. *Surveillance, privacy, and the law: Employee drug testing and the politics of social control*. Ann Arbor: University of Michigan Press.

———. 2001. *Overseers of the poor: Surveillance, resistance, and the limits of privacy*. Chicago: University of Chicago Press.

Gould, Stephen Jay. 1996. *The mismeasure of man*. New York: W. W. Norton.

Hess, Frederick M. 2003. Refining or retreating? High stakes accountability in the states. In *No child left behind? The politics and practice of school accountability*, ed. M. R. West and P. E. Peterson, 23–54. New York: Brookings.

Jacob, Brian A., and Steven D. Levitt. 2003. Catching cheating teachers: The results of an unusual experiment in implementing theory. In *Brookings-Wharton Papers on urban affairs 2003*, ed. William G. Gale and Janet Rothenberg Pack, 185–209. Washington, DC: Brookings Institution Press.

Jones, M. Gail, Brett D. Jones, and Tracy Y. Hargrove. 2003. *The unintended consequences of high-stakes testing.* New York: Rowman & Littlefield.

Kohn, A. 2000. *The case against standardized testing: Raising the scores, ruining the schools.* Portsmouth, NH: Heinemann.

———. 2001. Fighting the tests: A practical guide to rescuing our schools. *Phi Delta Kappan 82* (5): 348–357.

Nichols, Sharon, and David C. Berliner. 2005. *The inevitable corruption of indicators and educators through high-stakes testing.* Tempe: Educational Policy Research Unit, Arizona State University.

Pedulla, J. J., L. M. Abrams, G. F. Madaus, M. K. Russell, M. A. Ramos, M. A., and J. Miao. 2003. *Perceived effects of state-mandated testing programs on teaching and learning: Findings from a national survey of teachers.* Boston: Boston College, National Board on Educational Testing and Public Policy.

Superfine, Benjamin. 2006. Using the courts to influence the implementation of No Child Left Behind. *Cardozo Law Review* 28:2, 779.

Toch, T. 2006. *Margins of error: The education testing industry in the No Child Left Behind era.* Washington, DC: EducationSector.

PART FIVE

Everyday Resistance

Contesting Systems of Control

CHAPTER 12

Scan This

EXAMINING STUDENT RESISTANCE TO SCHOOL SURVEILLANCE

Jen Weiss

IN PUBLIC SCHOOLS ACROSS THE COUNTRY, students are encountering the effects of a variety of security measures designed to make schools safer. Students enter and exit their schools through metal detectors, scanning machines, and under the suspicious stares and booming shouts of security officials and police officers. On their way to classes, they move through hallways and stairwells mounted with surveillance cameras; sometimes the classrooms too have cameras. From California to Florida, Washington to Maine, urban and suburban public school officials are responding to issues related to student violence and school safety by deploying an array of surveilling techniques and technologies. These include cameras, metal detectors, scanning wands, security and police personnel, and ID tracking systems. New York City, home to more surveillance cameras per square foot than any other city in the world, leads the pack in developing and implementing school-based surveillance initiatives (Ruck et al. 2005; Boal 1998). The effects of the technologies and personnel required to implement surveillance, ostensibly designed to improve school safety, are manifold; many are counterproductive to safety, and in some cases they actually foment violence. As has been widely documented in a series of recent reports (Mukherjee and Fellow 2007; Sullivan 2007; Balmer 2006; National Center for Schools and Communities 2006; Drum Major Institute for Public Policy 2005), however, these measures don't necessarily produce safer school environments. Instead of a greater sense of safety in and around school, along with an active and civic-minded sense of school community, students describe feelings of danger and disillusion. Students in these schools experience firsthand what it is to be monitored, contained, and harassed, all in the name of safety and protection, and they are deeply aware that the persistent advancement of surveillance measures inside their schools has ill-intended consequences and may indeed limit students' ability to succeed in school and in society at large.

The effect of the uncertain coalition of protocol, technology, and security agents lends itself to Foucault's (1977) basic claim that disciplinary power is always multidirectional—circulating throughout the social body—and is not simply repressive but also productive. Although the goal of disciplinary power and surveillance procedures is to ensure obedience, or what Foucault calls "docile bodies," I argue in this chapter that this coalition has accidentally "produced" something else entirely. While students experience school surveillance in myriad forms, ranging from the spectacular to the quotidian, that surveillance exerts a continual influence on their school and community life. Youth subjects are not merely acquiescing to the injustice of surveillance imposed upon them; they are meeting it with a range of responses that must be understood as everyday forms of resistance. While students are aware of the seeming powerlessness they face at the hands of security guards and surveillance technologies, they are also engaged in developing new ways to cope with, negotiate, and tactically respond to these practices and injustices. They are becoming more attuned to these programs and are navigating and responding in surprising and sometimes radical ways.

In this chapter I will review the ways students from a large public high school located in the Bronx, New York (the school is referred to here as Baldwin), describe their experiences with the school's newly implemented surveillance protocol, and analyze how these youth characterize, exploit, and resist some of the most problematic dynamics of school and community surveillance.[1]

A CONSTANT GAZE

Being watched does not always appear threatening to urban teens. But it is constant. The youth I interviewed and observed are sensitive to the Janus face of surveillance. They believe it can protect them in certain circumstances, but in other contexts, the fact of surveillance creeps in and takes something. It unsettles and prods. It observes on the one hand, and profiles on the other. Whereas one kind of watching feels protective, another feels punitive. Rafael, a Baldwin student, summarized the difference between surveillance and observation:

Surveilling is watching like stalking almost. Like if I was to observe you, I would observe you only for this moment. Surveillance is constant, often. Like if they was to observe me, they would observe the hair, or how my nose is always runny. . . . But if they was to be surveilling, they'd find out my habits. I like drawing. I write with a graffiti handstyle or

I take the train home. Stuff that they're not supposed to know out of observation.

Rafael's paranoia, perhaps justifiably, speaks to the power that surveillance has on these youth—the insidious fear that they may become the subjects of an investigation that is at once arbitrary and systematic. His fear reflects the experiential core of Michel Foucault's claim that disciplinary power "makes almost any behavior punishable and thus the object of attention, surveillance, and control" (Staples 2000, 28).

Students widely reported a tangible anxiety as a result of the constant gaze of suspicion. They spoke frequently with security guards inside the school building and had interactions with law enforcement personnel on subways, in malls, and on their blocks. The conflation of streets and schools is significant, for it underscores the failure of urban schools to differentiate themselves from the culture of the streets and surrounding neighborhoods. Suspicion, in other words, may be experienced as a total, claustrophobic condition that follows urban youth throughout their public life. Little research has been done to mark the cumulative effect of this dynamic in the phenomenal lives of youth. For this reason, I have intentionally included in this chapter data that represent experiences with surveillance in both school and community. My main point in doing so is to suggest that the cumulative result of schools' failure to differentiate themselves from the surveilled public sphere may be far more oppressive than it first appears. In assuming that institutional and private experiences of surveillance do not have some combinatory component, we risk being blinded to the way student resistance might be perfected, imported, and radicalized in a feedback loop across both spheres.

Even further, surveillance *within* the school is more complex than we might think. Not only does the gaze of authority fall on students, but the gaze of peers also functions as a mode of enforcement, potentially adding to the cumulative effect of claustrophobia in the lived experience of the student. A ripple effect can be noted, in which one student's humiliation at the hands of security can bleed into a simultaneous humiliation—whether real or perceived—at the hands of her peers. In effect, students are experiencing "multiple jeopardy."

The Walkout

At this juncture, I want to turn to the students' initial and most visibly oppositional response to the installation of metal detectors at Baldwin High School—a walkout. Although some whispers of impending metal detectors had circulated in the spring of 2005, little if any formal warning was given to Baldwin students until they were gathered in an auditorium at the beginning of the 2005 school year in September. Crammed into the auditorium at the beginning of the school year, roughly five thousand students were told that by mid-September they would be entering school through metal detectors. A letter was sent home listing what "privileges" would be lost based on this new policy and telling students to prepare to arrive at school early—with enough time to clear the scanners and make it to first period before the second bell. Lateness would not be excused. Students were to leave their MP3 devices, cell phones, and other contraband items, such as weapons, at home; any of these items would be confiscated upon entrance. Students were to show up in time for first period while allowing at least ten to fifteen minutes for delays at the metal detectors. They were to remove belts, jewelry, and boots before walking through the scanners. Were they to neglect to do this, they would be wanded by a handheld scanner. Were something still to go off, they could be asked to remove everything. Students would also be seeing more security guards and New York Police Department (NYPD) officers around school. They were to consider these figures school authority. Finally, students would lose their open-campus lunch privileges in favor of a new policy that was unfortunately titled "captive lunch."

On September 21, 2005, the first day on which students were to pass through metal detectors at Baldwin, roughly thirty student organizers rallied close to fifteen hundred of their peers to walk out of school in between first, second, third, and fourth periods. Under police escort, students walked to the borough superintendent's office at Fordham Plaza in the Bronx, demanded a meeting with their region's superintendent and other city department of education officials, and insisted that "metal detectors and security cameras be removed, that they be allowed to have lunch outside the school, and that an earlier ban on cell phones be lifted" (Santos 2005). They were granted a meeting, and a small group of students met with school officials.

Reported widely in local and national news, the walkout clearly represents a breakdown in school policy and student compliance and is the place from which to begin to think about how urban teenagers are contending with and also responding to school surveillance policy. The walkout is an exceptional example of a student-driven collective call to action that serves as a telling reminder that "youth as collective community actors" are indeed "capable of responding to coercive policies" (Ginwright et al. 2005, 32–33). In terms of its size and visibility, it was the only protest of its kind to occur as surveillance practices intensified in the schools of New York City. Yet the protest was as ad hoc and spontaneous in feel as the implementation of surveillance equipment in the school itself.

The walkout effectively took the school, including its students, by surprise. Rafael told me that "it was short-notice organization. Five students. It was originally four until I came up. We were standing on the side for thirty minutes. We only had eleven to twenty or thirty students and then second period we went from that to two hundred students. By the end of third period we have fifteen hundred, around there." Fernando Carlo, an organizer from Stony Brook University, observes,

> As an act of resistance, the walkout didn't take a lot of planning to do it. You know, they showed up to school—these scanners, these metal detectors, these cops with guns . . . all this stuff they didn't have . . . and you know to have a group of students who had more freedoms than some—like they had outside lunch, they didn't have to go through metal detectors, and then all this stuff just happened. They come back to school and all of it's there. I'm pretty sure they felt uncomfortable and it made them realize they had to do something about it.

Although school security attempted to prevent students from leaving the building before fourth period, they were outnumbered. According to David, a junior, it was the "only time that [Baldwin] students were unified . . . at first it was just the originators of the thing. They were just standing outside by themselves initially chanting we want freedom. Gradually more kids were coming out and, by like fourth period, it was basically the whole school just ran out and I remember that day, I was walking out too and the security was trying to stop us, but because there were so many they really couldn't, they had to let us go out."

Although the protest became collective, it was never fully unified. In discussions with students following the walkout, many of them spoke of the fact that a lot of kids walked out for the fun of it; that they were not really invested in getting rid of the metal detectors and were unwilling to stay with the struggle. To the student organizers, the ones most likely to do the work of mounting a follow-up protest, peer cynicism undermined momentum. Their perceptions of their fellow peers' motives (or lack of them) influenced their decision not to continue the struggle to overturn the surveillance and security measures in their school. Jessica expressed her frustration at the attitudes of her peers:

> My brother went to Kennedy and he would be like "Ha, ha, you're going through it too" instead of saying "I know what you feel," and it's like you know, we should fight it together. Instead of that, it's like . . . "just get used to it." . . . That really gets me mad. Instead of getting used to it, let's not have it happen at all and prevent it from ever happening again. . . . I hate this weak kind of thinking.

In fact, within months, Baldwin students reported having gotten used to things and having grown accustomed to waiting in line to get to class.

"Things have gotten smoother but not because of security—security is just as bad. It's gotten better because of the students. We're less aggravated because we know what's gonna happen," Lolo told me.

CREATING AWARENESS

Although frustration and anger fueled the walkout, its lack of organization may have hurt its chances of creating sustained change at the school. Teacher Kevin Greer confirmed that "there was this impetus, there was this fleeting feeling of rebellion and empowerment. And I don't know enough about the story to really comment on it, but from a certain distance or a certain closeness, they got siphoned off. It amounted to about nothing." But students like Esteban insisted that the walkout's greatest achievement was that it "did create awareness." He went on, "Yeah, it didn't remove the metal detectors, but I think it got teachers and the people who run the school to understand that the kids were upset with the fact that they were putting in metal detectors and some of them don't really feel safe with metal detectors." Furthermore, Fernando Carlo believes that the protest forced adults to take youth more seriously:

> Now all these people see that students understand what's going on; they understand that they [students] do feel uncomfortable—they realize the metal detectors don't help and they create all these other problems and the students know and I think the number one excuse for why students aren't involved in this kind of decision-making is because "Oh, students don't know." Well, the students are smart enough to realize the metal detectors aren't helping; they're smart enough to get all these other students together and walk off to the region office and get a meeting, so I definitely think it [the walkout] made people jump up on their toes and realize that students know.

The Baldwin walkout was an anomaly, and its failures are as spectacular as its successes. Organizing in response to school security and surveillance policy made little, if any, headway. The reasons for this are many and varied, but one of the most obvious may be the lack of infrastructure at the grassroots level. Organized collective movements tend to move too slowly in response to institutional power. They are often turned down for protest permits or are not far enough below the radar to take place without such permits. Finally, they can lack the resources to organize youth consistently, efficiently, and with a sense of unified purpose for an extended campaign. Although the Baldwin walkout's failure to produce results upset and stung students, the protest did evidence a desire and agency among students to respond to the unfair changes they had encountered in their school. While the protest's practical failures were obvious, the walkout's symbolic resonance was significant. As my research with students progressed, lesser-known and less-obvious forms of resistance began to emerge.

EVERYDAY HUMILIATIONS
AND TACTICAL AVOIDANCE

While protest marks an exceptional form of resistance, everyday and seemingly informal formations of resistance are more common. In order to contextualize lesser-known modes of resistance, I draw from James C. Scott's complex notion of everyday resistance. For Scott, resistance originates "not simply from material appropriation but from the pattern of personal humiliations that characterize that exploitation" (1990, 112). My interviews with research participants began to reveal that humiliations were common. For example, upon recalling an incident that had happened many months earlier, soon after the metal detectors were installed in her high school, Jessica's eyes started to well up. Her voice cracked as she recounted a time when she forgot to remove her belt before entering school:

> I was embarrassed one time. That really got me mad. I forgot to take off my belt, I was more worried about being late for this class or my mind is somewhere else. . . . And I beeped or whatever, and this cop is like "Oh, hey, everybody, look at this stupid kid, you know, dumb enough to have her belt on." Everyone laugh at her kinda thing. You know, he just totally screwed up my day. I even started crying. I was so embarrassed. . . . So it was kind of like trying to make everyone feel like crap so you won't even dare talk back.

Stories like these form the institutional backdrop upon which students actively respond to the surveillance they face daily; they also highlight the complex nature of responding to what amounts to a double surveillance within the school itself. As Jessica's testimony makes clear, harassment by security guards in front of one's peers reveals the power of school-based surveillance. It is not a one-to-one relationship; the disciplining effect emanates from multiple sources. It is pervasive. In this example, security accomplishes two things at once: it enforces the schools rules (safety) and embarrasses students to the point of silence in front of their peers (control). In many ways this incident captures the essence of the double bind at work for students who are determined to graduate from high school and are willing to compromise or "conform" to the humiliating conditions they face in order to do so.

In this context, the coalition of surveillance protocol, technology, and personnel serve as a constant gaze, as "eyes on me regardless," to use a phrase

coined by one of the youth I interviewed. Students cope with these humiliations and with the combinatory experience of surveillance, whether at the
hands of the school, the community, or among peers, by performing a range
of less obvious forms of resistance. I place all forms of tactical resistance
under the broad category of "tactical avoidance" drawing from Michel de
Certeau's (1984) notion of tactics. A tactic "insinuates itself into the other's
place without taking it over" and is "always on the watch for opportunities
that must be seized" (xix).

Youth often resort to tactical avoidance in the face of undesired scrutiny.
For example, when referring to an experience in a popular video chain store,
David told me: "I mean, I hate that feeling. It's totally disrespectful, like come
on 'I know you're watching me, what do you think, I'm stupid?' I just walk
out, I don't buy anything . . . I hate that feeling. So when that happens I just
gotta go." One similar example was reported by Jason, a sixteen-year-old who
lives in Coney Island. He told me, "Sometimes, I just try to avoid it. There
be certain stores I just don't wanna go in because I know the guy doesn't
like me, you know. I mean even though his prices are cheaper and I wanna
go in there, he'll be really hawkin' me and making me feel uncomfortable,
like really, really on top of me."

Tactical avoidance can provide forms of resistance that involve a range
of subtle attempts to evade the effects of combinatory surveillance without
eschewing places under surveillance altogether. Within contexts of surveillance
and scrutiny, finding ways to avoid being watched is not easy. It requires
an ability to anticipate consequences and respond in ways that best serve
students, not authority figures. Avoidance illustrates not only an awareness of
the circumstances but also student knowledge of how to manipulate events
to their advantage. It also evidences resilience and creativity in dealing with
such circumstances. In this vein, de Certeau writes, agents "also show the
extent to which intelligence is inseparable from the everyday struggles and
pleasures that it articulates" (1984, xx). Given that there may be no way of
escaping surveillance, tactical avoidance implies an ability to cope with difficult conditions emanating from multiple sources of power. While avoidance
is one of the most commonly expressed tactics in response to being watched
suspiciously, there are others.

ALTERNATE ROUTES

Another form of tactical avoidance is to find alternate routes to avoid
the gaze of security. David makes the most of Baldwin's six floors, endless
hallways, and twenty-two exits:

> I hate walking through the hallways. Like me, I walk through the hallways
> and I see the security I try to avoid them. I know I'm doing something

legitimate so most of the time I'm walking through the hallways I try to avoid them, I'll walk another way around, like go downstairs and up another stairwell.... Instead of taking the short way, [I] take the long way just so I can avoid security guards. I do that a lot.... Let's say I'm walking with my friends and we see security.... We'll say, "Oh, security guards are there." And then the next thing, we'll go downstairs. We don't need to discuss it anymore. We know the deal.

Students' ability to read a situation and find alternate routes sheds light on how they exist inside spaces of pervasive watching without eschewing the institution of school entirely. While it is clear that David has a strong distaste for security, his approach to dealing with it is consistently tactical.

Making use of the various elements of a particular terrain is, for de Certeau, the essence of the art of everyday practice. The Baldwin students are "unrecognized producers, poets of their own affairs, trailblazers in the jungles of functionalist rationality . . . [consumers] trace 'indeterminate trajectories' that are apparently meaningless, since they do not cohere with the constructed, written, and prefabricated space through which they move" (1984, 34). Despite the multiple constraints placed upon them, the youth in my research display an "ability to divide" (ibid., 35). The concept of alternate routes represents the ability to divide space.

This tactic is informed and shuttled within and without the school's premises. For example, Rhina reports that when she leaves school at the end of the day, instead of walking directly to the subway or bus stops across from the campus, she walks in the opposite direction, toward the more affluent neighboring high school. There she finds safe harbor as she waits for the bus. She remarked:

I do feel watched when I'm outside because there's always cop cars out there. I always walk toward [Darwin High School]. I don't like walking over there [referring to across the busy street in front of Baldwin]. There's never any cops at [Darwin]. That's why kids smoke over there.... They're doing it right out of school. You don't see kids smoking around [Baldwin]. Never a student. Over there—never have I seen a cop there.

By choosing alternate routes, students like Rhina are not only dodging trouble, they are also carving out new spaces in which they feel freer and more comfortable. Identifying and reinscribing places of potential trouble offers an important coping strategy and helps to transform potentially threatening places into spaces of possibility.

Youth rarely contend with surveillance in oppositional ways; they are instead deflective, mercurial, spontaneous, and tactical. In this sense, these acts are harder to observe and interpret as resistance and are often compromised by the fact that they are watched regardless of the actor's intent.

RESISTANCE AS APPROPRIATION

Unknowingly, schools are preparing students to participate in and appropriate the signs and symbols of everyday surveillance in and beyond schools. In turn, students are building a repertoire of tactical responses to these conditions. Embedded within student responses is an astute awareness of the reality of control they experience inside their schools. This awareness, however, is also what sets the stage for and enables these same students to envision equally surprising and potentially far-reaching ways to exercise their freedoms.

Resistance as appropriation illuminates how students create relationships with authority figures in order to resist the injustice of heavy surveillance. One feature is students' noticeable desire to be recognized by authority figures. Students who resist via appropriation initiate relationships for the sole purpose of avoiding scrutiny—they allow themselves to be seen in order to hide. While students are not fond of security guards or school aides, many describe brief but daily attempts to build relationships with them. On several occasions, when I accompanied students on walks through the hallways, or when we exited the school together after school, I witnessed seemingly small, innocuous exchanges taking place between students and school aides and security guards. Although at the time they seemed merely friendly, they can also be interpreted as tactical efforts by students to win approval or favor from those monitoring them. For instance, Christine claims that "the only way to get through people is by building some type of relationship. And that is real easy with some people." Rhina's experience is similar: "I'm cool with some of the security guards. That's points for me. I'm not gonna bring a gun or a knife even into school . . . but I came in with my belt, bracelets, and she said, 'You got something on you' and I said, 'Nah.' She let me go. . . . I'm gonna say it straight up, it's wrong because [students] might have something on [them], but it's the quickest way you can get through."

Similarly, Rafael refers to cultivating certain "privileges": "Like some people got privileges to the lunch room. I got privileges to the locker room. The students that try to go in, they're like 'No, you need your program card, you need your program card.' All I do is 'yo, what up' [and] walk straight in."

Students frequently note the injustice of certain students gaining "free rider" privileges while others do not. Many of them started to feel as if those doing right by the system were punished for it, as one male student observed in a focus group conversation: "There are a lot of kids in the school that are on the sports teams [who are on] their cell phones, iPods, and PSPs and it's messed up that the kids like that get to bring their stuff in and all the kids that are doing the right things are punished. They are still trying to do the right thing and follow the rules, but they are the ones who are punished for it."

This theme of gaining friendship by not going to class is expressed by Lloyd: "Like when, the kids like, they cut school. Well they don't cut school, they cut classes: they're in school but they're not going to class. So you know, the deans and the school aides, they see them all the time, so they're always saying what's up to them so that's how you develop a friendship with somebody."

Interestingly, many of the girls I interviewed spoke about developing friendships with security personnel. In one focus group with both male and female Baldwin students present, students such as Dred concurred that "if you're a girl, they are a little more lenient." One of the girls in the focus group responded, "I get allowed into the lunch room all the time because [I'm female]." She purposely avoids the female security guard, however. "So you go around and it's one of the new guys who doesn't know me at all. I just give him a smile and say 'Hey, let me go.' Smile, flirt a little, and he lets me go." To that, one of the boys noted, "I have a free period in eighth and when I try to go in there they don't let me go in. They stop me and say 'You can't come in here on your free period.'"

Girls also notice the unfortunate and uncomfortable circumstances that accompany befriending school aides and guards who are "not professional" and "don't care about their jobs." In the same conversation, another female student continued: "They make you feel more uncomfortable. Like I hate passing by a crowd of guys in the first place, but then when I have to go to school with people who are supposed to protect me, but they're hitting on me you know. It happened today, it happens to me every day when I go to the bathroom, they're like 'Yo ma.'"

In sum, appropriation represents efforts on the part of students to participate with those watching them, and it illustrates efforts to navigate the system of surveillance by actively participating with it. In most instances, forms of resistance as appropriation involve appearances and performances that are consistent with Scott's assessment that while "appearances that power requires are, to be sure, imposed forcefully on subordinate groups . . . , they do not preclude their active use as a means of resistance and evasion" (1990, 32). The appearance of conformity is actually "an art form in which one can take some pride at having successfully misrepresented oneself" (ibid.) and is thus tactical and manipulative. But it also demonstrates a compromise, the dark side of which is well expressed by legal scholar Patricia Williams, who reflects upon "the cold game of equality staring" and her invisibility as a black woman: "I could force my presence, the real me contained in those eyes, upon them, but I would be smashed in the process. If I deflect, if I move out of the way, they will never know I existed" (1991, 222).

S OU S VE I L L A N C E

To conclude this chapter I want to address one final response to Baldwin's increasing security presence—the formation of an after-school poetry and hip-hop club by a small group of Baldwin students in the weeks after the walkout. The decision to convene a poetry and hip-hop club was as much a response to the school's newfound policies as was the protest described earlier in this chapter. In my view, the club proved a much more radicalizing choice. As poet and essayist Adrienne Rich points out, poetry, in its "rejection of conventional expectations," is "inherently subversive to dominant and oppressive structures" (2001, 116). I discuss the relationship between writing and resistance at length elsewhere (see Weiss et al., 2008); here I will address one aspect of writing that can be seen as resistance—that of writing as "sousveillance." "Sousveillance" denotes "surveying from below" or the act of "countersurveillance" and offers a way for us to think about how students and teachers in schools like Baldwin can resist their school's unjust policies by recording and mediating them. Scholar William G. Staples notes:

> A citizen's ability to evade this surveillance is diminishing. To venture into a shopping mall, bank, subway, sometimes even a bathroom is to perform before an unknown audience. Even if this kind of surveillance is relatively "seamless" as I have argued, it may function to undermine our willingness to participate in civic life and to speak our minds as clearly, openly, and imaginatively as we can. (1997, 133)

While we can see the effects of surveillance on our civic life, Staples asserts that the forces of active resistance, protest, sabotage, noncooperation, and liberty are also present. "If we accept the premise that much of the exercise of this kind of power takes place in the form of 'local' micropractices that are present in our everyday lives, then the sites of opposition are right before us. They are in our own homes, workplaces, schools, and communities" (ibid., 135). In this chapter I have sought to identify a host of micropractices present in student's everyday lives, however overlooked they may be.

The basic premise of "sousveillance" research is "to challenge and problematize both surveillance and acquiescence to it [and] to resituate these technologies of control on individuals, offering panoptic technologies to help them observe those in authority" (Mann et al. 2003, 332). One of the best known examples of "sousveillance" is the videotaping by George Holliday, an average citizen of Los Angeles, of the Rodney King beating and his turning over of that tape to local media outlets. Studies that focus on sousveillance point to the common feeling among surveillance scholars that as surveillance technologies proliferate so too do technologies that can disrupt surveillance techniques and expose power asymmetries (Monahan 2006; Kemple and Huey 2005).

In settings of pervasive and unjust surveillance like Baldwin where cell phones and cameras are banned, writing may be one of the last remaining ways to record and resist what is happening. A good example of this can be seen in sixteen-year-old Senica Lopez's piece of new journalism, which she wrote as part of an Urban Word NYC journalism workshop. In this piece, she weaves together her investigative prowess and her anger at school security agents (SSA):

SCAN THIS!

I was afraid to talk to him. He was obviously someone of great authority. He wore a white button down shirt instead of the boring blue donned by the other guards. One morning I planned to approach him for an interview. After squeezing my way into the crowded scanning room, I saw him in a corner, surveying the room. We made eye contact. I immediately looked away. As I made my way through the cumbersome scanners we continued replaying this awkward scene of my looking at him, his returning my gaze, and my not being bold enough to maintain eye contact with him.

The following day I saw him outside the entrance watching us students like a hawk. I mustered up all my courage and approached him. I began, "Excuse me Sir, I'm taking a journalism class and . . ."

He wasn't even looking at me. This man of such high authority—his badge, the only glistening object on a cloudy day, was looking over me. And he continued to look over and past me until I said the word "interview" which is when he finally looked at me.

He asked me to repeat what I had just finished telling him. I did. He agreed. We met two hours later to talk.

At precisely five minutes to ten I met him in the interrogation room next to where we get scanned every morning. He was there with two lower ranking, blue-shirted officials. I found out the basics first, like his name (Wilson Baez) and his job title (supervisor of all school safety agents at Baldwin High School). I learned that all school safety agents, better known as security guards, in [Baldwin] were "under the umbrella of the NYPD 52nd Precinct."

Baez wasn't very talkative. He gave simple discouraging answers and didn't seem interested in being there. When he found out that my topic was on the inconsistency of scanning, he was quick to tell me that I didn't have much of a topic considering scanning was up to chance. "Some agents are better trained than others and have a better eye when it comes to what to look for," he told me.

After finding out that the journalism class I was taking wasn't in [Baldwin], he became just a bit more tight-lipped and asked for my ID card, quickly jotting down my name.

I later asked Baez if he had any statistics regarding the amount of violence in [Baldwin] High School since scanners were put in September 2005.

"Well there is no violence now that there are scanners," Baez declared.

"So there's been no fights in the school?" I inquired.

He replied, "Well of course there are some fights, but not nearly as much or as bad as when there were no scanners."

I refrained from mentioning the fact that after the scanners were put in, during one of the hundreds of fights I've seen since then, one student stabbed another student with a screwdriver. I wonder how that got in?[2]

Senica's piece shows how writing can be an excuse for collecting information. It also reveals the trickery at play between students and school security. The director, playwright, and founder of the Wooster Group, Elizabeth LeCompte, notes in a recent interview that in order to gauge the strength of the play she is working on and the audience's response to it, she sits in the audience incognito. She does this for every performance. On one hand, she claims, this tactic affords her an opportunity to get firsthand accounts of how every aspect of her play was working with the audience. But, on the other, she says it allows her to "hide from being watched by watching" (Kramer 2007). We can see how students like Senica use their writing to hide from being watched ("I was afraid to talk to him."), while closely observing and recording details about their subject. In this sense, writing may even give students the courage they need to stand up against injustice.

While the initial student walkout at Baldwin may have "failed" to generate the kind of change students were hoping for, it is possible that the Baldwin poetry club and its poems themselves have offered students (and their teacher allies) a rehearsal for what may become the next public display of protest—one that may offer a more sustainable vision for change. Scott contends that while infrapolitics might be thought of as elementary, they are the building blocks without which "more elaborate institutionalized political action" could not exist (1990, 201). As building blocks toward future change, student writings must be understood as affording a space of resistance, one in which students may take refuge from their ongoing battles with security guards or other authorities, with severe overcrowding and an increase in fights in the hallways. Students can use such clubs and their own writing to vent, commiserate, joke around, and buffer themselves from difficult experiences in school. They may also use the poem to talk back to authority and perceived injustices. Finally, my research illustrates that without recourse to the sophisticated technologies that might be used to watch and record, the watchers use their pens and notebooks to positive effect. In this way, writing about and cataloguing the injustices that go hand in hand with surveillance can work as a vital form of sousveillance—a display of active resistance that is sealed off from authority, whether within their schools, the security apparatus of the public sphere, or the domain of their peers.

CONCLUSION

The implementation of surveillance directed toward urban youth, across a bewildering swath of private and institutional spaces, is cause for grave concern. As I worked with youth in New York City, I came to realize that my intervention in this problem was occurring from a new, if not distinctive vantage point. Surveillance studies too rarely focuses on how it feels to be watched—particularly from the vantage point of youth of color. Rather than focus solely on the structural implications of citywide surveillance measures, I have sought in this chapter to analyze and frame the embodied story of how these measures impact upon youth. Both the structural forces at play and the individual responses to these forces are complicated and demand rigorous attention by researchers and scholars.

The ways that students responded were both inspiring and saddening. Surveillance in schools does not necessarily prevent violence, and it has been known to increase violence, negatively impact a school's culture and reputation, and contribute to the loss of good teachers and good students (Mukherjee and Karpatkin, 2007). At the same time, the daily exposure to metal detectors, scanners, cameras, high levels of police and security presence, and pervasive watching does condition and socialize youth to feel consistently watched, to distrust, hide from, and avoid authority figures. Exposure to surveillance systems also seems to cause students to be less inclined to speak out or organize in response to issues that bother them. While several of the students in my study took part in the student-organized walkout, many did not, and in their words we rarely hear any urgency about the need to take part in political protests. For this reason, I chose to locate the emphasis of their resistance in terms of the more individuated, everyday forms of protest.

In this chapter I have suggested that student agency amounts to a powerful and varied response to surveillance, one that scholars may mistakenly ignore or overlook because these efforts do not translate into the traditional categories and canon of resistance—organization, a unified mandate, and actions based in the workaday politics of the public sphere. Students are not organized, worry about becoming too visible to authority, and act independently of collective groups. Although my research on youth resistance raises the possibility of social change as an outcome, it is equally focused on highlighting the fact that youth are cognizant of and responsive to the injustices in their lives. Expressions of youth resistance are best observed in a wide spectrum of actions that includes avoiding, talking back, appropriating, and organizing a formal protest. All of these expressions point directly to real injustice and to real, if idiosyncratic, forms of resistance. The weight of surveillance and youth responses to it should raise the stakes for scholars of resistance.

NOTES

1. From October 2005 to August 2006, I conducted a qualitative research study utilizing ethnographic methods with a purposeful sampling of twenty young men and women of color between the ages of fifteen and twenty-three, from across New York City. These youth were chosen to reflect the makeup of New York City's lower- and middle-tier high schools, and they were from two distinct sites. Half were students attending a large, comprehensive high school in the Bronx and half were involved with Urban Word NYC (UW), an after-school poetry, spoken word, and hip-hop organization. The students described and quoted in this chapter are all low-income youth of color, predominantly African American and Latino, who attended Baldwin High School.
2. The story was written by Senica Lopez in the New Skool Journalism Workshop at Urban Word NYC. It was published in the *Brooklyn Rail* newspaper in fall 2006. Used with permission.

REFERENCES

Balmer, S. 2006. *Policing as education policy: A briefing on the initial impact of the Impact Schools program*. New York: National Center for Schools and Communities, Fordham University.

Boal, M. 1998. Spycam city: The surveillance society: Part one. *Village Voice*. October 6.

de Certeau, M. 1984. *The practice of everyday life*. Berkeley and Los Angeles: University of California Press.

Drum Major Institute for Public Policy. June 2005. *A Look at the Impact Schools: A Drum Major public policy data brief*. New York: Drum Major Institute for Public Policy.

Foucault, M. 1977. *Discipline and punish: The birth of the prison*, trans. A. Sheridan. New York: Vintage Books.

Ginwright, S., J. Cammarota, and P. Noguero. 2005. Youth, social justice, and communities: Toward a theory of urban youth policy. *Social Justice* 32 (3): 24–40.

Kemple, T., and L. Huey. 2005. Observing the observers: Researching surveillance and countersurveillance on "Skid Row." *Surveillance & Society* 3 (2/3): 139–157.

Kramer, J. 2007. Experimental journey. *New Yorker*. October 8.

Mann, Steve, Jason Nolan, and Barry Wellman. 2003. Sousveillance: Inventing and using wearable computable devices for data collection in surveillance environments. *Surveillance & Society* 1 (3): 331–355.

Monahan, T. 2006. Questioning surveillance and security. In *Surveillance and security: Technological politics and power in everyday life*, ed. T. Monahan, 1–23. New York: Routledge.

Mukherjee, E., and M. Karpatkin. 2007. *Criminalizing the classroom: The over-policing of New York City schools*. New York: New York Civil Liberties Union.

National Center for Schools and Communities. August 2006. *Policing as education policy: a briefing on the initial impact of the Impact Schools program.* NCES, Fordham University.

Rich, A. 2001. *Arts of the possible: Essays and conversations.* New York: W. W. Norton.

Ruck, M., A. Harris, M. Fine, and N. Freudenberg. 2005. Youth experiences of surveillance: A cross national analysis. In. *Cross-cultural perspectives on youth, social control and empowerment in the new millennium,* ed. D. Brotherton and M. Flynn. New York: Columbia University Press.

Santos, F. 2005. 1,500 New York City students protest metal detectors at high school. *New York Times.* September 21.

Scott, J. 1990. *Domination and the arts of resistance: Hidden transcripts.* New Haven, CT: Yale University Press.

Staples, W. G. 1997. *The Culture of surveillance: Discipline and social control in the United States.* New York: St. Martin's.

———. 2000. *Everyday surveillance: Vigilance and visibility in postmodern life.* New York: Rowman & Littlefield.

Sullivan, E. 2007. *Deprived of dignity: Degrading treatment and abusive discipline in New York City and Los Angeles public schools.* New York: National Economic and Social Rights Initiative. http://www.nesri.org/programs/dignity_report.html.

Weiss, J., J. Anyon, M. Dumas, D. Linville, K. Nolan, M. Perez, and E. Tuck. 2008. Theorizing student poetry as resistance to school-based surveillance: Not any theory will do. In *Theory and educational research: Toward critical social explanation.* New York: Routledge.

Williams, P. 1991. *The alchemy of race and rights.* Cambridge, MA: Harvard University Press.

CHAPTER 13

Seductions of Risk, Social Control, and Resistance to School Surveillance

Andrew Hope

RISK AND SURVEILLANCE ARE INEXTRICABLY LINKED. Concerns about threats to well-being tend to give rise to risk-alleviation practices, which often include surveillance of people and situations labeled as potentially dangerous. However, surveillance plays a central role not only in the management of risks but also in their selection (Foucault 1977, 195). Furthermore, Bauman (1993) infers that the multibillion-dollar surveillance industry may be complicit in generating new fears while at the same time fostering the perception that only the application of greater technology offers sustainable solutions to risks. As the relationship between risk and surveillance has become ever more complex, there has been a growth in counterdiscourses, which challenge mainstream orthodoxy and foster strategies of resistance. Drawing upon seductions of risk, this chapter examines such resistance by analyzing student interactions with school surveillance.

After briefly considering some of the links between danger, surveillance and schools, I will explore some definitional issues relating to risk, then shift the focus to the use of surveillance as an instrument of social control in educational institutions. Finally, using data from two school-based research projects, one analyzing Internet use, the other dealing with Closed Circuit Television (CCTV) operation, I will explore students' resistance to school surveillance.

SCHOOLS, RISK, AND SURVEILLANCE

In recent years, schools have become increasingly perceived as "risk environments." To a limited extent, this can be seen as illustrative of Giddens' (1991) belief that in late modernity people are risk obsessed. There also exist, however, specific reasons why schools have become more strongly associated with danger. Armed massacres in educational institutions, growing fear of child abuse, violence against staff, increasing vandalism and theft, and the spread of illnesses such as meningitis have resulted in a greater awareness of the hazards that potentially lurk in schools (Hope 2004, 60). Even mundane activities such as providing school meals, taking examinations, using educational cyberspace, and filming of student events by parents have been labeled as problematic, potentially engendering harm. As Frank Furedi notes, "[S]afety in schools is a big issue. The comprehensive range of cameras, swipe cards and other security measures that are now routine make many schools look like minimum security prisons" (1997, 3).

Burgeoning fears about safety in schools and the development of a multi-billion-dollar risk-alleviation business have resulted in rapid growth in the use of various measures of control, most notably surveillance technologies. The use of observational techniques in schools is not a new phenomenon, however. Schools have a long history of operating as institutions of social control, with surveillance often playing a key role. Thus, in the late eighteenth century, the liberal utilitarian philosopher Jeremy Bentham designed several schools that utilized a semicircular seating arrangement to facilitate teachers' observation (Markus 1993, 66). Hall notes that in the early nineteenth century, Lancasterian schools utilized formal, rigid observational systems with an "explicit focus on monitorial assessment" as "part of the unremitting surveil-lance" (2003, 50). This demand for ceaseless observation of students also found embodiment in other practices, such as the keeping of attendance registers, the strict use of timetables, and testing to scrutinize performance. In late modernity, school surveillance has undergone something of a revolution, with increased provision, speed, and reach giving rise to what could be labeled as "the surveillance curriculum" (Monahan 2006). To further develop an understanding of the connections between this burgeoning surveillance technology, risk, and student resistance it is first necessary to reflect on the main features of the cultural risk perspective.

THE CULTURAL RISK PERSPECTIVE AND SCHOOLS

In Western societies, risk is predominantly used as a way of referring to the chance of loss or the possibility of damage to people and what they value (Furedi 1997, 17). When such negative outcomes are the focus of public discussion, there is a tendency to adopt a realist approach, treating risk calculations as "absolute truths" (Bradbury 1989, 382), wherein disagreements with "orthodox scientific" views are assumed to indicate "irrationality." For example, media reporting of the United Kingdom (UK) government's attempt to restrict the sale of "junk" food in schools focused overwhelmingly on the threat to students' health and the need for school authorities to monitor diets. An attempt by two mothers in South Yorkshire to fight what they labeled as "food fascism" by passing fries, burgers, and fizzy drinks to children through the school fencing was dismissed as misguided, while alternative discourses relating to freedom of choice were largely ignored (Hope 2007a, 36). From a social–cultural perspective treating risks as "objective facts" is problematic. Rather, attention needs to be focused upon the contexts in which such views are generated (Lupton 1999, 29). Douglas (1992) suggests that because knowledge is never value free, debates about risks always involve questions of cultural meaning and political position. In short, risk is always social. This is not to deny that "real dangers" exist but rather to suggest that each society or organization elevates some risks to a high point while depressing or ignoring others. Therefore, risks are not "given" but selected through social processes. Decisions as to what becomes labeled as a "risk" and which hazards form the focus of concern are inherently political (Douglas and Wildavsky 1982). Indeed, the privileging of certain risks offers some indication of the sort of communities and societies in which people wish to live.

Lyon suggests that surveillance has two faces, it "both enables and constrains, involves care and control" (2001, 3). Although these functions are not necessarily exclusive, they highlight that surveillance can play both a positive and a negative role. Similarly, circumstances exist in which risk can be perceived as beneficial. Historically, the concept of risk was used to describe calculable probability, so could be both "good" as well as "bad" (Douglas 1992, 23). While the concept of a "good risk" seems to have largely disappeared, with risk in contemporary Western society often being used as a synonym for danger, there nevertheless exists a counterdiscourse that stresses the benefits of risk taking (Lupton 1999, 148). Thus, Eastwood and Ormondroyd (2005) argue that risk taking should form a central platform for creative teaching, as well as for the teaching of creativity. Yet conservatism in the teaching and learning process may well be promoted through observational tools. For example, publicly accessible tables, which rank schools largely on student examination success, tend to promote excessive practice testing in some institutions, militating against creative, pedagogic risk taking.

SCHOOL SURVEILLANCE AND SOCIAL CONTROL

Surveillance, which involves the perception as well as the management of information, has increasingly "become a feature of everyday life" (Lyon 2003, 13). While in preindustrial Western societies social control was imposed primarily through force and in modernity via the rule of law, it is argued that surveillance, with its associated discourses, is the main disciplinary tool in late modernity (Foucault 1977). In this context, social control is about ensuring conformity to certain dominant values and norms. As Rule notes, social control is the use of mechanisms to "discourage or forestall disobedience . . . [to] either punish such behavior once it has occurred, or prevent those with inclinations to disobedience from acting on those inclinations" (1973, 19). Although the use of school surveillance as an instrument of social control is not a new phenomenon, its recent growth, in terms of both technical provision and social impact, makes it worth examining. A cursory list of school surveillance might include physical observation, attendance registers, examinations, student progress reports, exam performance tables, Internet tracking devices, CCTV cameras inside institutional grounds as well as on school buses, searches of lockers, clothes and bags, metal detectors, and even monitoring devices in uniforms. This dizzying array of diverse technologies operates through observation, self-surveillance, discourses and simulation.

Traditionally, educational staff exercised control over students through physical observation of presence, behavior, and academic output (Hall 2003). Direct observation is still an important tool of control in contemporary schools, with technological developments allowing this "gaze" to be extended in space and time. For example, the software application NetSupport School, designed to enhance the teaching process, allows staff to view networked computer screens and control the activities of these machines. This illustrates the potential for "function creep," where surveillance systems introduced for one purpose often find quite different roles (Norris and Armstrong 1999, 58). While CCTV can utilize live feeds, it can also record images, storing evidence. The principal of a Biloxi, Mississippi, elementary school declared that digital cameras in her classrooms acted like a "truth serum," with the threat of viewing the recordings encouraging students suspected of misbehaving to "fess up" (Dillon 2003). Yet such visual records are not only used when confronting students. The motivation behind plans to install CCTV in classrooms in certain Manchester (United Kingdom) schools was reportedly the need to present parents with proof of their children's misconduct (BBC News 2003). Observation does not merely focus on bodies; keeping records is also important. The development of online technology and complex data handling systems has led to an increase in classification systems and social sorting of information, enabling what Clarke (1992) labels "dataveillance."

Central to the discussion of observational power in late modernity is the potential to encourage people to engage in self-surveillance. Foucault (1977) argues that the possibility of constant surveillance encourages rational people to act as if they are the object of observation, even when they are not. Individuals fearing they are being watched start to monitor their own behavior, and uncertainty becomes a means of social control (Lyon 1994). Fostering the practice of self-surveillance through ambiguity means external observation becomes "permanent in its effects, even if it is discontinuous in its action" (Foucault 1977, 201). Yet Simon (2005) argues that for self-surveillance to occur an individual must comprehend "the rules," be able to make appropriate judgments and recognize the signs of a possible supervisor. The blind, ignorant, or irrational could be immune to the effects of such observational power. Vaz and Bruno are critical of Foucault, contending that the conception of self-surveillance should be expanded to include "individual's attention to their actions and thoughts when constituting themselves as subjects of their conduct" (2003, 273). Using this broader definition, practices proposed in the United Kingdom government's school behavior guide, which seek to "promote self-discipline" using small rewards such as stickers, certificates, class outings, or postcards to parents praising their child's behavior, could be construed as tools fostering self-surveillance (DCSF 2007). Such devices do not invoke the ambiguous application of surveillance but are perhaps better seen as forming part of a disciplinary discourse.

Care must be taken not to overprivilege the visual aspects of surveillance in modernity (Norris 2003). In his discussion of observational power, Foucault (1977) is equally concerned with procedures that situate individuals in a disciplinary discourse. In this context, discourse refers to a collection of related statements intended to control and channel behavior. Thus surveillance not only potentially provides information about those observed but can also engage individuals in a disciplinary discourse, highlighting what constitutes appropriate and acceptable behavior. In schools, the keeping of registers, filing of reports, wearing of standardized uniforms, observance of rules, strict use of timetables, regimented examinations, and ostentatious punishments can all be seen as fashioning a discourse of control. Yet the discourses in which observational tools become embroiled may be complex, contradictory, and contested. For example uniforms operate as an instrument of social control through enforcing conformity, making schools "more orderly" (as President Clinton famously declared), while allowing outsiders to easily identify the educational institution to which individuals belong. However, in Malaysia an Islamic student group condemned uniforms worn by girls at state schools as "sex," and encouraging rape and premarital sex (*Toronto Star* 2008). To label school uniforms as mere disciplinary technology is simplistic.

Simulation of surveillance operates within contemporary schools in two different ways: through simulacrum and predictive data systems. While within postmodern writings the word "simulacrum" denotes copies that cannot be distinguished from the original, collapsing distinctions between real and fake, a broader definition suggests a superficial, but untrue, likeness (Harrington 2005, 328). Thus, "dummy" CCTV cameras in schools can encourage individuals to behave as if the technology is "real," at least until the deceit is exposed. Drawing upon Baudrillard's work on simulation, Bogard argues that "the technological enlargement of the field of perceptual control . . . has pushed surveillance beyond the very limits of speed towards the purest form of anticipation" (1996, 76). Simulation in this context refers to the anticipation of the real, aided by forms of diagnostic surveillance. Such predictive systems have long existed in schools, albeit relying on teacher intuition and knowledge of students rather than complex databases. Yet developments in computer technology and data-handling software mean that the speed and reach of such systems has greatly increased. Staples (2000) notes that in 1999 the United States Bureau of Alcohol, Tobacco and Firearms, working in association with a "threat evaluation" company, piloted a program called Mosaic 2000. This software aimed to confidentially vet and rate potentially violent students based on a series of questions drawn from case histories.

Research Background

The following discussion of student resistance to surveillance technologies draws upon two pieces of research based in schools situated in the northeast of England. The first project was a three-year inductive study examining Internet use in eight schools, which included Canalside, Dale, Greenhill, Forest and Hawthorn High Schools. In addition to more than 180 hours of observation spread throughout all the institutions, semistructured interviews were undertaken with thirty staff and sixty-three students. The second research exercise focused upon CCTV use in schools. It involved ten semistructured interviews (two with technical consultants working for the local government education authority and eight with school staff) as well as engaging in one-off sessions of non-participant observation in the schools visited. Among the eight schools that took part in this research were Olden, Ryder, and Quarry High Schools. In both projects, field sites were selected, using a nonprobability purposive sample, to produce a diversity of data in order to provide some basis toward generalization (Schofield 1993). While neither project was initially concerned with student resistance to surveillance, it subsequently emerged as a major theme in the inductive research processes.

Student Responses to Surveillance

Although the possibility exists that students might remain unaware of school surveillance, much of the technology is ostentatious, seeking to engender self-surveillance and the acceptance of certain behavioral norms. Even if monitoring is covert or overlooked, incidents in which observational practices are used to discipline students tend to result in the technology becoming high profile for a time. Thus, as the vice principal of Olden High School notes, "If three or four kids get caught because of the CCTV . . . they become aware that the cameras are there . . . it becomes high profile, you'll notice them watching to see where the cameras are . . . they become aware, it lasts for a while and then it just returns to normal." This highlights that as well as being context-specific, students' responses to surveillance might change over time. Although apathy can be a common response to such disciplinary practices, many students nevertheless actively engage with these observational technologies through conformity (real or feigned), concealment of activities, engaging in countersurveillance, and challenging dominant discourses. These responses might be labeled as resistance, but different interpretations could be applied. After all, resistance is a problematic concept. It can be construed in varying terms from action that impedes or subverts unequal power relations to moments of relative autonomy when the apparently power-less step outside the realities of oppression (Spencer 1996, 489). Yet from a poststructural perspective such definitional diversity does not necessarily undermine analysis, as the concern lies not with exploring typologies of power but with understanding perceived acts of opposition hermeneutically (Wynne 1996).

School surveillance is used to reinforce codes of appropriate institutional behavior while encouraging conformity to certain broader social norms. Conformity is a difficult concept to assess, however. While Bash and colleagues (1985) suggest that students who are conformists are often indifferent or instrumental rather than oppositional in their actions, they do not dismiss the possibility of resistance through conformity, suggesting that it would be passive rather than active. Surveillance rarely offers insights into motivations. As the vice principal at Ryder High School notes, "[T]hey [students] behave around our CCTV. But does it change their behavior in the long run? I don't know." Thus, it can be difficult to assess the broader, long-term outcomes of surveillance technologies. Simon (2005) argues that if individuals perform compliance, surveillance may not be able to distinguish between real and feigned conformity. He maintains that the power of the machine is chal-lenged by "fake" behavior and the limitations of technological systems to facilitate social integration are exposed. Beyond feigned conformity, students might seek to resist surveillance technologies more proactively.

Discussing public surveillance systems Norris and Armstrong (1999) note that such technology rarely provides complete coverage of an area. Even where an area is subjected to observation, "blind spots" may still exist, with areas being obscured from view. It is possible for students to take advantage of such locations, concealing their activities. For example, in an attempt to avoid physical surveillance of Internet use in the field-site schools, students obscured the view of computer screens, relied on the speed of their reactions to close windows containing "inappropriate" material, and chose location and times with minimal staff observation. A geography teacher at Greenhill High School, remarking upon students hiding incriminating Web pages, related that "[t]hey're so quick . . . clicking the screen off as you walk past." At Forest High School, three male students were observed using the Internet in the library for educational purposes throughout the week. However, on a Friday afternoon, when their online activity was unsupervised, they visited a site called Poo III, which featured verse and pictures "dedicated to defecation."

Furthermore, to avoid virtual surveillance of online activity in the field-site schools, students utilized other students' passwords, claimed someone else had used their password, or accessed unsuitable sites with innocuous Web addresses.

Concealment strategies are not a new phenomenon; students have a history of seeking unsupervised places. Attempting to reclaim such areas, a media arts college in Brighton was one of the first educational institutions in the United Kingdom to utilize CCTV in the circulation areas of student toilets; the declared intent was to prevent students from smoking in these locations (BBC News 1999). Such actions may not curtail unwanted acts, however, but persuade individuals to go somewhere unmonitored to engage in deviant behavior (Norris and Armstrong 1999; McCahill 2001). Considering the impact of CCTV installation on graffiti, the vice principal of Quarry High School declared that "we're not naïve to think that it's stopped, but they've probably changed their location." Thus, surveillance technologies may colonize certain spaces without normalizing behavior in unobserved places, displacing "miscreants" rather than engendering broader conformity.

Attempts by students to conceal activities often involve the use of countersurveillance, ensuring privacy through watching for the intrusion of monitoring devices, staff, or students likely to inform. This assumes that surveillance practices are visible. At Canalside High School, students were observed engaging in the banned activity of playing arcade games on the Web during lunchtime. They kept a constant watch for staff and whenever a staff member approached them were quick to hide the game, pretending to be doing "legitimate" work. Curiously, this countersurveillance and concealment of Web pages had many of the qualities of the Internet games, suggesting that students were simultaneously playing online and off-line. Yet, countersurveillance has broader application than this somewhat limited use. It can also suggest the mimicking of disciplinary technologies in order to draw attention to their existence and engage in a wider discourse concerning surveillance practices. Noting the growing potential to utilize technology to observe those in authority, Mann and colleagues (2003, 333) advocate what they refer to as "sousveillance," the use of surveillance technology to mirror and confront the observational processes undertaken by bureaucratic organizations. This strategy is not concerned with circumventing surveillance but with directly confronting it through ostentatiously watching the watchers. Despite the increased ownership of camera phones and students hacking into high school computer systems to access information on staff (Hope 2005), there is little evidence to suggest that students are consciously engaging in "sousveillance."

Although discursive practices associated with surveillance might operate in a hegemonic manner, it is worth noting that Foucault maintained "there always remain the possibilities of resistance, disobedience, and oppositional groupings" (1982, 245). Incidents of failing to wear permitted attire, truancy, refusing to sit examinations, and flouting school rules might be interpreted as attempts to resist disciplinary discourses. This is not to argue that students necessarily engage in these activities with the intention of subverting dominant discourses. Interpretive issues abound here. Nevertheless, there are some clear instances when students directly seek to challenge discursive practices in schools. For example, at Hawthorn High School, from which a twelfth grade student was expelled for accessing images of naked women posted on the *FHM* magazine Web site, the student's peers contested the labeling of the material as pornographic, with two year-twelve males claiming "[i]t's hardly porn" and "it's not top shelf or anything." Crawshaw (2004, 232) suggests that young people often construct their own situated discourses of appropriateness in response to their environment. This is not to argue that they are unaware of dominant discourses; rather, they attempt to make sense of the world through their own experiences. In such situations, students may reject disciplinary discourses without overtly opposing them. Thus, the discussion returns once more to the issue of how to interpret what appears to be conformity.

SEDUCTIONS OF RISK AND STUDENT RESISTANCE TO SURVEILLANCE

There is a tendency in much analysis of deviant and risky behavior to neglect the seductive qualities that serve to make such forms of expression "sensible, even sensually compelling, ways of being" (Katz 1988, 3). Thus, to label student resistance to school surveillance as inevitably irrational could be misguided. In exploring these compulsions and how they relate to surveillance practices in a sociologically informed, poststructural manner, the focus falls upon two differing social processes: the seductive pull of risk taking and the emotive push of over-blocking, both of which encourage students to circumvent or challenge surveillance regimes. It is worth noting that these social phenomena are neither exclusive in operation nor exhaustive as explanations of student resistance to school surveillance. Rather, they should be seen as offering insights into certain student responses. It would be pertinent to suggest that students engaging in resistance to school surveillance technologies might be driven by other primary motivations, yet none were evident in the research data. One exception was an instance at Hawthorn High School in which a twelfth-grade male student refused to sign the institution's Internet acceptable-use policy, challenging the dominant discourse and declaring that his civil rights were being violated. It appears that this was primarily an ideological act, which suggests that student resistance to school surveillance arising from strongly held political beliefs is an area worth exploring in future research.

Risk Taking and School Surveillance

Simply put, risk taking is intentional engagement in hazardous activity, implying "intent on the part of the actor" (Shoenbach et al. 1987, 404). While dire consequences may arise from risk taking, positive gains may also occur. Drawing upon Douglas and Wildavsky (1982), it can be argued that the nature and extent of these outcomes will vary depending upon the actual dangers, risk perceptions, those involved, and the cultural context in which the activity occurs. Over the last few decades, a body of broadly sociological literature has emerged that focuses upon the positive outcomes of risk taking. While the motivations for engaging in risk taking may be numerous and complex, these writings have tended to stress emotional outcomes, identity formation, and skilled performance.

Risk taking may engender an emotional rush (Lying 1990), offering individuals a way to transcend the routine banality of everyday life (Cohen and Taylor 1992). As Young notes, social deviancy can be emotive, "a revolt against the mundane" (2002, 237). Discussing breaking into his high school on a weekend (reversing the process of truancy), Presdee relates, "Once inside, we closed the frosted window quietly and slowly edged to the door. . . . Instantly through the [door] crack, noise thundered in, pushing back our bravado and stopping our breath. We experienced the immediate high of adrenaline mixed with fear that surged through our bodies and made me feel faint, there was somebody else in the building!" (Presdee 1988, cited in Presdee 2000, 55).

The excitement of risk taking appears to be increased by the possibility of surveillance, giving rise to an immediate desperate need to evade capture. Individuals partaking in risky activities "seem to be seeking a more vivid version of life itself, an experience that transcends the convention of everyday life" (Ferrell 2005, 143). Insofar as surveillance technologies add to the risk of apprehension, they are not only tools of social control but also devices that might heighten the excitement of performing illicit acts. Indeed, they might lead to the creation of new "risky" spaces for students seeking an adrenaline rush.

Following the dissolution of traditional social influences in late modernity, the cultivation of risks may be an increasingly important part of identity formation (Giddens 1991). From this perspective, engaging in dangerous activities can be seen as engendering self-actualization in three distinguishable ways: allowing the self to develop in ways that are restricted by an individual's everyday environment, fostering a positive reputation as daring or skillful, and developing a sense of belonging to a particular group of like-minded souls (Lupton 1999, 153). A male tenth-grader at Dale High School constructed his own pornographic Web site on his home computer, published it on the Web, and, having initially avoided the surveillance systems, showed it to his friends using the school Internet. Teaching staff subsequently caught and punished him. If the student had merely wished to show others his Web site he could have done so with little risk at home. In this instance, it would seem that circumventing the school's surveillance devices generated a new risk while providing a space within which he could perform, fostering a reputation as skillful and risk-taking person. Indeed, upon discussing this incident, the Information Communication Technology (ICT) manger at the school remarked, with a smile that seemed to hint at admiration, "It makes you think he's got good IT skills." This highlights that risk identities are often closely connected with skilled performances.

Regardless of the existence of chance, some forms of risk taking are inherently concerned with the construction of a perception of skilled control, which may be lacking in other aspects of an individual's life (Cohen and Taylor 1992). Risk taking that is an attempt at skillful control often includes elements of performance, that is the execution of a notable feat or a presentation before an audience, an engagement concerned with both entertainment and efficacy (Schechner 1994, 622). The participation of an audience, even if it is merely in the postevent rendition, is often a key aspect in risk taking. Indeed, in some cases skilled avoidance of school surveillance might be a secondary concern compared to the desire to provide a public performance. For as Presdee (2000) intimates, young people might feel the need to draw attention to and celebrate their transgressive behavior. A male twelfth-grader at Greenhill High School discovered a friend's Internet password, used it to log on to the school network, found an unfiltered pornographic Web site, printed an explicit image, and left it for a member of staff to find. Following a search of the school computer logs the student who owned the password was blamed for the incident before the real culprit confessed and was punished. The guilty student declared, "I guess I was always going to own up. I thought I'd get punished but figured it'd be sort of a laugh, show him [his friend] that I could get him."

Thus, it would appear that this subversion of surveillance was a secondary concern to public performance, even given the inevitability of punishment. It is common wisdom that surveillance tends to act as an instrument of social control. Paradoxically, for those students seduced by the excitement of transgressing, constructing a "risky" identity, and performing artfully, school surveillance can offer new arenas, public spaces in which to draw others' gazes and indulge in spectacle. This is not to suggest that the majority of students will engage in such behavior but rather to highlight the possibility of such action. Although there may be political motivations to students "misbehaving" within the institutional gaze, a consideration of risk taking and its seductions tend to draw attention to what Katz refers to as the sensual, compelling ways of being (1988, 3).

The examples taken from the research data can all be labeled as incidents of boundary performance (Hope 2007b), that is, relatively low-level risk taking that temporarily and publicly traverses borders. This begs the question of whether more excessive forms of risk taking, enacted under the institutional gaze, could be interpreted in a similar manner. Katz's (1988) discussion of the "seductions of crime" and Lying's (1990) analysis of extreme forms of risk taking known as "edgework" indicates that they should be, suggesting that emotional outcomes, identity formation, and the need to perform may provide motivation for various extreme activities, from anarchic drug use to gun crime.

The Culture of Overblocking in Schools

While the analysis of risk taking and school surveillance has stressed the seductive pull of emotional engagement and self-actualization, it is also likely that students might be pushed into resisting institutional disciplinary practices. This may occur where technologies of control are perceived by students to be overly restrictive, educationally limiting, and inherently unfair. Such situations may arise when individuals or organizations, seduced by exaggerated risk discourses, impose excessive restrictions upon student activities, curbing the potential for educational gains. Discussing risks within contemporary society, Furedi (1997) suggests that a culture of fear has emerged, centered on blame, which engenders a morality of low expectation. While such an observation might be criticized as overly harsh and dystopian, it can nevertheless be argued that fears arising from risk discourses create an atmosphere within which a culture of overblocking develops.

Overblocking can be defined as the unreasonable limitation of students' educational experience, as a result of individuals or technologies overreacting to risk. Interpretations as to what constitutes unreasonable, limiting, and overreacting will inevitably vary depending upon perceptions, those involved, and the cultural context. Insofar as overblocking has seeped into aspects of school life, influencing practices and beliefs, it would be justifiable to argue that it operates at a cultural level, existing in "the symbolic and learned aspect of human society" (Abercombie et al. 1994, 98).

Research on school Internet surveillance provides an illustration of this tendency to overblock. Overly sensitive software may erroneously bar access to educationally beneficial material. Thus, students at Hawthorn High School researching gender issues online for media studies complained that the monitoring software prohibited searches containing certain keywords, such as "sex," problematizing their legitimate academic enquiry. This suggests that disciplinary technologies themselves may foster overblocking. Indeed, Hartley (1998) warns of a hidden curriculum arising from a "technological fix" of panopticized pedagogy, where school practices might be influenced through seemingly value-neutral technology. Additionally, staff misinterpretation of online activities, arising from overreactions to risk discourses, resulted in students being removed from the Internet. At Canalside High School a group of students were thrown off the Internet for accessing sites featuring images of and information about sports cars. Although the students had actually been working on a project set by another teacher, the head of ICT had misconstrued this legitimate educational activity as play. Overblocking is not merely a consequence of technology or staff reactions, however; it can also arise from local authority and government policies. Thus, state monitoring initiatives responsible for overtesting in schools or regulations demanding unrealistic supervisor/student ratios on field trips might prohibit actual learning. Herein the two faces of surveillance, care and control, come into conflict.

As the insensitive application of surveillance practices impacts negatively upon learning opportunities, fostering a culture of overblocking, students could respond in various ways. It has already been suggested that apathy and indifference toward institutionalized observation may be rife. Yet some frustrated students may be forced to seek alternative sites of learning or, worse, start to withdraw from certain educational process (Hope 2008, 111). For example, at Quarry High School three students were found reading in an unlocked classroom during lunch break. When told that they couldn't stay in the room but should instead go to the school library, they reportedly responded that the surveillance there made them feel as if they were "under a microscope" and that the librarian didn't approve of their "noneducational" reading material. In this instance, it would appear that students frustrated by surveillance practices that they regard as excessive have sought an alternative location in which to read. Other students may choose to resist what they label as an unfair system of surveillance and control. They might conceal their activities, engage in countersurveillance, and seek to challenge dominant discourses. Here the underlying motivation is not to "misbehave" but to engage in what they perceive to be legitimate academic activity. Ultimately, it is difficult to assess the extent to which students might engage in resistance to surveillance because of overblocking. What can be stated with certainty, however, is that such practices are occurring in contemporary society, and as the reach of school surveillance grows it might be expected that they would become ever more commonplace.

CONCLUSION

Students respond to school surveillance in various ways. Seeking to resist it, they may engage in feigned conformity, concealment, countersurveillance, and the contesting of dominant discourses. Motivations for resisting the panoptic gaze in schools may be varied. In this chapter I suggest that school surveillance technologies might offer new public spaces in which students can engage in risk taking, facilitating emotional engagement, identity formation, and skilled performance. An argument was also made that overreaction to risk discourses might give rise to a culture of overblocking. In response, some students may seek to resist surveillance technology through finding new learning spaces, concealing their "legitimate" activities, or contesting the restrictive practices. In conclusion, it is worth noting that Willis (1977) suggests that school-bred cultures of resistance often have wider social purposes. In this light, student resistance to surveillance technology may not only offer a surcease from restrictive dystopian technologies but also develop attitudes that assist in successful integration into a world increasingly characterized by the growth of surveillance.

REFERENCES

Abercrombie, Nicholas, Stephen Hill, and Bryan Turner. 1994. 2nd ed. *The Penguin dictionary of sociology*. Harmondsworth, UK: Penguin.

Bash, Leslie, David Coulby, and Crispin Jones. 1985. *Urban schooling: Theory and practice*. London: Holt, Rinehart and Winston.

Bauman, Zygmund. 1993. *Postmodern ethics*. Oxford: Blackwell.

BBC News. 1999. School puts spy cameras in toilets. November 5. http://news.bbc.co.uk/2/hi/uk_news/education/506140.stm (accessed June 9, 2008).

———. 2003. "Big Brother" plan to catch rowdy pupils. February 24. http://news.bbc.co.uk/2/hi/uk_news/education/2795047.stm (accessed June 9, 2008).

Bogard, William. 1996. *The simulation of surveillance*. Cambridge: Cambridge University Press.

Bradbury, Judith. 1989. The policy implications of differing concepts of risk. *Science Technology and Human Values* 14 (4): 380–399.

Clarke, Roger. 1992. The resistible rise of the national personal data system. *Software Law Journal* 5 (1): 25–59.

Cohen, Stanley, and Laurie Taylor. 1992. 2nd ed. *Escape attempts: The theory and practice of resistance in everyday life*. London: Routledge.

Crawshaw, Paul. 2004. The "logic of practice" in the risky community: The potential of the work of Pierre Bourdieu for theorising young men's risk-taking. In *Young people, risk and leisure: constructing identities in everyday life*, ed. Wendy Mitchell, Robin Bunton, and Eileen Green, 224–242. Basingstoke, UK: Palgrave Macmillan.

Department for Children, Schools and Families (DCSF), 2007. Behaviour and discipline in schools. http://www.parentscentre.gov.uk/behaviouranddiscipline/behaviourand-disciplineinschool/ (accessed June 13, 2008).

Dillon, Sam. 2003. Cameras watching students, especially in Biloxi. *New York Times*. September 24, B9.

Douglas, Mary. 1992. *Risk and blame: Essays in cultural theory*. London: Routledge.

Douglas, Mary, and Aaron Wildavsky. 1982. *Risk and culture: An essay on the selection of technological and environmental dangers*. Berkeley: University of California Press.

Eastwood, Linda, and Chris Ormondroyd. 2005. Risk and education: A distortion of reality. In *Risk, education and culture*, ed. Andrew Hope and Paul Oliver, 32–45. Aldershot, UK: Ashgate.

Ferrell, Jeff. 2005. Crime and culture. In *Criminology*, ed. Chris Hale, Keith Hayward, Azrini Wahidin, and Emma Wincup, 139–155. Oxford: Oxford University Press.

Foucault, Michel. 1977. *Discipline and punish: The birth of the prison.* London: Allen Lane.

———. 1982. Space, knowledge and power. In *The Foucault reader: An introduction to Foucault's thought,* ed. Paul Rabinow, 239–256. London: Penguin.

Furedi, Frank. 1997. *Culture of fear: Risk taking and the morality of low expectation.* London: Cassell.

Giddens, Anthony. 1991. *Modernity and self-identity.* Cambridge, UK: Polity Press.

Hall, Nigel. 2003. The role of the slate in Lancastrian schools as evidenced by their manuals and handbooks. *Paradigm* 2 (7): 46–54.

Harrington, Austin, ed. 2005. *Modern social theory: An introduction.* Oxford: Oxford University Press.

Hartley, David. 1998. *Re-schooling society.* Milton Keynes, UK: Open University Press.

Hope, Andrew. 2004. Danger, "otherness" and chat-room use in UK schools. *New Era in Education* 85 (2): 60–66.

———. 2005. Panopticism, play and the resistance of surveillance: Case studies of the observation of student Internet use in UK schools. *British Journal of Sociology of Education* 26 (3): 359–373.

———. 2007a. Children and risk. In *Childhood and youth studies,* ed. Paula Zwozdiak-Myers, 35–44. Exeter, UK: Learning Matters.

———. 2007b. Risk-taking, "boundary-performance" and young peoples' school Internet use. *Discourse: Studies in the cultural politics of education* 28 (1): 87–99.

———. 2008. Internet pollution discourses, exclusionary practices and the "culture of over-blocking" within UK schools. *Technology, Pedagogy and Education* 17 (2): 103–113.

Katz, Jack. 1988. *Seductions of crime: Moral and sensual attractions of doing evil.* New York: Basic Books.

Lupton, Deborah. 1999. *Risk.* London: Routledge.

Lying, Stephen. 1990. Edgework: A social psychological analysis of voluntary risk taking. *American Journal of Sociology* 95 (4): 851–886.

Lyon, David. 1994. *The electronic eye: The rise of surveillance society.* Cambridge: Polity Press.

———. 2001. *Surveillance society: Monitoring everyday life.* Buckingham, UK: Open University Press.

———. 2003. Surveillance as social sorting: Computer codes and mobile bodies, in (2003) *Surveillance as social sorting: Privacy, risk and digital discrimination,* ed. David Lyon, 13–30. London: Routledge.

Mann, Steve, Nolan, Jason, and Wellman, Barry (2003) Sousveillance: Inventing and Using Wearable Computing Devices for Data Collection in Surveillance Environments. *Surveillance & Society.* 1 (3) http://www.surveillance-and-society. org/articles1(3)/sousveillance.pdf (last accessed 06.09.08).

Markus, Thomas (1993) *Buildings and Power.* London: Routledge.

McCahill, Michael. 2001. *The surveillance web: The rise of visual surveillance in an English city.* Devon, UK: Willan Press.

Monahan, Torin. 2006. The surveillance curriculum: Risk management and social control in the neoliberal school. In *Surveillance and security: Technological politics and power in everyday life,* ed. Torin Monahan, 109–124. New York: Routledge.

Norris, Clive, and Gary Armstrong. 1999. *The maximum surveillance society: The rise of CCTV.* Oxford: Berg.

————. 2003. From personal to digital: CCTV, the panopticon, and the technological mediation of suspicion and social control. In *Surveillance as social sorting: Privacy, risk and digital discrimination*, ed. David Lyon, 249–281. London: Routledge.

Presdee, Mike. 2000. *Cultural criminology and the carnival of crime*. Routledge: London.

Rule, James. 1973. Private lives and public surveillance. London: Allen Lane;.

Schechner, Richard. 1994. Ritual and performance. In *Companion encyclopedia of anthropology*, ed. Tim Ingold, 613–647. London: Routledge.

Schofield, Janet. 1993. Increasing the generalizability of qualitative research. In *Educational research: Current issues*, Martyn Hammersley, 1:91–113. London: Paul Chapman Publishing.

Shoenbach, Victor, Edward Wagner, and William Berry. 1987. Health risk appraisal: Review of the evidence for effectiveness. *Health Services Research* 22 (4): 553–580.

Simon, Bart. 2005. The return of panopticism: Supervision, subjection and the new surveillance. *Surveillance & Society* 3 (1): 1–20. http://www.surveillance-and-society.org/Articles3(1)/return.pdf (accessed June 9, 2008).

Spencer, Jonathan. 1996. Resistance. In *Encyclopedia of social and cultural anthropology*, ed. Alan Barnard and Jonathan Spencer, 488–489. London: Routledge.

Staples, William. 2000. *Everyday surveillance: Vigilance and visibility in postmodern life.* Oxford: Rowman and Littlefield.

Toronto Star. 2008. School uniform sexy, says group. May 22. http://thestar.com.my/news/story.asp?file=/2008/5/22/nation/21326822&sec=nation (accessed June 9, 2008).

Vaz, Paulo, and Fernanda Bruno. 2003. Types of self-surveillance: From abnormality to individuals "at risk." *Surveillance & Society* 1 (3): 272–291. http://www.surveillance-and-society.org/articles1(3)/self.pdf (accessed June 9, 2008).

Willis, Paul. 1977. *Learning to labour: How working class kids get working class jobs.* Farnborough, UK: Saxon House.

Wynne, Brian. 1996. May the sheep safely graze? A reflexive view of the expert-lay-knowledge divide. In *Risk, environment and modernity: Towards a new ecology*, ed. 44–83. London: Sage..

Young, Jock. 2002. Searching for a new criminology of everyday life: A review of *The Culture of Control* by David Garland. *British Journal of Criminology* 42:228–243.

CONTRIBUTORS

MICHAEL W. APPLE is the John Bascom Professor of Curriculum and Instruction and Educational Policy Studies at the University of Wisconsin, Madison. A former elementary and secondary school teacher and past president of a teachers' union, he has worked with educational systems, governments, universities, and activist and dissident groups throughout the world to democratize educational research, policy, and practice. Professor Apple has written extensively on the politics of educational reform and on the relationship between culture and power. His three most recent books are *The State and the Politics of Knowledge*; *Educating the "Right" Way: Markets, Standards, God, and Inequality*; and *The Subaltern Speak: Curriculum, Power, and Educational Struggles*. His books and articles have won numerous awards and have been translated into Chinese, Japanese, Spanish, French, Portuguese, Greek, Turkish, Italian, Thai, German, Korean, Russian, and many other languages. His latest work deals with the effects of neoliberal and neoconservative policies in education and the larger society and with creating alternatives to these policies and practices.

NICOLE L. BRACY is a doctoral candidate in criminology at the University of Delaware. She received her master's degree in criminology from the University of Delaware in 2005. Her research focuses on police practices with youth, particularly the negotiation of juveniles' legal rights and policing strategies in schools. She also volunteers with various community organizations working with at-risk youth.

RONNIE CASELLA is an associate professor of education at Central Connecticut State University. His most recent book is *Selling Us the Fortress: The Promotion of Techo-Security for Schools* (Routledge). He has published articles in the *International Journal of Qualitative Studies in Education*, *Anthropology and Education Quarterly*, *Social Justice*, *Teachers College Record*, *The Urban Review*, and other journals. In 2006 he was Visiting Scholar at the University of the Witwatersrand in South Africa, where his research focused on school and youth violence in Johannesburg and Soweto. His writings focus on youth and school violence, education in a global context, and relationships between schools and private businesses, NGOs, and community organizations. He received his M.A. in English education from New York University and his Ph.D. in Cultural Foundations of Education at Syracuse University.

JOHN GILLIOM is a professor of political science and chair of the Department of Political Science at Ohio University, where he has received numerous awards for his teaching on law and American politics. His research interests center on the political and cultural dynamics surrounding the emergence of new forms of surveillance, with a particular emphasis on gender, class, and the ethnography of struggle. He is the author of *Overseers of the Poor: Surveillance, Resistance, and the Limits of Privacy* (Chicago, 2001) which explores how the words and actions of those who live under intensive monitoring challenge prevailing ways of thinking about surveillance and privacy. Gilliom is also the author of *Surveillance, Privacy and the Law: Employee Drug Testing and the Politics of Social Control* (Michigan, 1994) as well as articles on law, legal theory, and the politics of surveillance. His current work explores the implementation of nationwide standardized educational testing under No Child Left Behind, with a special interest in resistance and compliance; race, class and gender; the ideologies of the testing culture; and the reformation of school curricula in response to the testing regime. Gilliom received his Ph.D. in 1990 at the University of Washington.

PAUL HIRSCHFIELD is an assistant professor of sociology at Rutgers University in New Brunswick, New Jersey. He earned his doctorate in sociology from Northwestern University in 2003. He studies criminalization in the legal/political, social, and cultural realms. Specific theoretical and empirical projects have centered on the causes and consequences of criminalization in relation to school misconduct, mental illness, and youthful marijuana use, with a special focus on inner-city youth. His interest in the consequences of criminalization dates back to his dissertation research, in which, combining qualitative and quantitative methods, he examined the impact of juvenile arrests on truancy and high school dropout in Chicago. Another collateral cost of criminalization, which he explored more recently, is the normalization of juvenile and adult sanctions, including incarceration. He is currently researching how aggressive police practices (such as increasing neighborhood rates of arrests for minor or victimless crimes) influence the moral attitudes, racial and ethnic pride, and social behavior (substance use and delinquency) of inner-city African American and Latino schoolchildren. Dr. Hirschfield's work has appeared in *Criminology, Theoretical Criminology, American Educational*

Research Journal, Sociological Forum, Sociological Methods and Research, Quarterly Journal of Economics, and elsewhere.

ANDREW HOPE is a senior lecturer in the Department of Sociology at Manchester Metropolitan University. His current research interests include the sociology of risk and surveillance and social aspects of the Internet and educational cultures. He coedited *Risk, Education, and Culture* (Ashgate Publishing) in 2005 and has more recently published articles on risk and pollution in various academic journals.

AARON KUPCHIK is an associate professor of sociology and criminal justice at the University of Delaware. He earned his Ph.D. in sociology from New York University in 2003 and is the winner of the 2007 American Society of Criminology Ruth Shonle Cavan Young Scholar Award. His work focuses on the social control of youth in schools, courts, and correctional facilities, and he is the author or *Judging Juveniles* (NYU Press 2006) and coeditor of *Criminal Courts* (Ashgate, 2006).

TYSON LEWIS is an assistant professor in the educational foundations department at Montclair State University in New Jersey. He has published in a wide variety of journals, including *Cultural Studies/Critical Methodologies, Educational Philosophy and Theory, Educational Theory, Journal of Curriculum Theorizing*, and the *Journal of Aesthetic Education*. With Douglas Kellner, Clayton Pierce, and Daniel Cho he has most recently coedited a volume of essays on Herbert Marcuse's challenge to education. His research interests include critical theory, biopower, utopian studies, and educational philosophy.

PAULINE LIPMAN is a professor of policy studies and director of the Collaborative for Equity and Justice in Education, College of Education, University of Illinois–Chicago. Her research focuses on race and class inequality in schools, globalization, and political economy and the cultural politics of race in urban education. She is the author of *Race, Class, and Power in School Restructuring; High Stakes Education: Inequality, Globalization, and Urban School Reform*; and numerous articles. Current projects examine the relationship of education policy to neoliberal development in Chicago, gentrification, and displacement of communities of color. She is active in social movements and a founder of Teachers for Social Justice.

RICHARD A. MATTHEW received his Ph.D. at Princeton University and is an associate professor of international and environmental politics in the Schools of Social Ecology and Social Science at the University of California at Irvine and director of the Center for Unconventional Security Affairs (www.cusa.uci.edu). He has worked closely with the United Nations, numerous nonprofit organizations, and a variety of government departments and agencies. He is the senior fellow for security at the International Institute for Sustainable Development and a member of the World Conservation Union's Commission on Environmental, Economic and Social Policy. His research emphasizes the importance of understanding and addressing the underlying economic and environmental conditions conducive to a range of network-structured, transnational human and national security threats and conflicts. Recent books and coedited volumes include *Contested Grounds: Security and Conflict in the New Environmental Politics* (SUNY Press, 1999); *Dichotomy of Power: Nation versus State in World Politics* (Lexington, 2002); *Conserving the Peace: Resources, Livelihoods, and Security* (IISD, 2002); *Reframing the Agenda: The Impact of NGO and Middle Power Cooperation in International Security Policy* (Praeger, 2003); and *Landmines and Human Security: International Relations and War's Hidden Legacy* (SUNY Press, 2004).

TORIN MONAHAN is an associate professor of human and organizational development in the Peabody College of Education and Human Development and associate professor of medicine at Vanderbilt University. He is editor of *Surveillance and Security: Technological Politics and Power in Everyday Life* (Routledge, 2006) and author of *Globalization, Technological Change, and Public Education* (Routledge, 2005). He is trained in science and technology studies (STS), which is an interdisciplinary social science field devoted to studying the societal implications of and design processes behind technological systems and scientific knowledge. Monahan's main theoretical interests are in social control and institutional transformations with new technologies. He is a member of the international Surveillance Studies Network and is on the editorial board for the primary academic journal on surveillance, *Surveillance & Society*.

LIZBET SIMMONS is an assistant professor of criminal justice studies at San Francisco State University. She received her Ph.D. in social and cultural studies in education from University of California, Berkeley. Simmons examines the coordination of educational and correctional institutions and their role in extending the social, economic, and political disenfranchisement of minority youth in urban America. In her current book project, *Stranded before the Storm: Public Schools, Prison Punishment, and Poverty in New Orleans*, which is based on three years of ethnographic research in New Orleans, she charts the institutional processes that spur the movement of minority students, particularly African American males, away from school and toward prison. The work contributes to a structural understanding of minority school failure, crime, incarceration, and prison expansion in the era of "tough on crime" legislation. At San Francisco State University, she teaches Juvenile Justice and Research Methods, and at the University of California, Berkeley, she has taught Race and Ethnicity in Schools and Urban Education. Lizbet Simmons has also taught English literature and reading and composition in an associate's degree program at California's San Quentin Prison. In 2006, Lizbet Simmons was named the California Council for the Humanities Scholar, and she was awarded the 2007 Affirmative Action Award at San Francisco State University. She has published in the *Urban Review*, the *Metropolitan Universities Journal*, and *Teacher's College Record*.

VALERIE STEEVES is an assistant professor in the Department of Criminology at the University of Ottawa, with a cross-appointment in the Faculty of Law. Dr. Steeves has written and spoken extensively on privacy from a human rights perspective and is an active participant in the privacy policy–making process in Canada. She has also written a number of reports on children's use of new media, including *Young Canadians in a Wired World* (Media Awareness Network, 2005) and is the author of a series of multimedia games designed to teach children how to protect their human rights in a networked environment. Her game Sense and NonSense won the first annual Award of Excellence in Race Relations Education from the Canadian Race Relations Foundation in 1999, and her game Privacy Playground won the Bronze Medal at the 2006 Summit Creative Awards Competition, an international competition involving thousands of entries from twenty-six countries. In 2004 she was awarded the LaBelle Lectureship at McMaster University, a juried prize given to scholars doing cutting-edge research and challenging accepted ideas.

RODOLFO D. TORRES is a professor of planning, policy, and design, Chicano/Latino studies, and political science at University of California, Irvine. His three main interests, which are not mutually exclusive, are (1) state theory and class analysis, (2) urban political economy and inequality, and (3) theories of racism, ethnicities, and cultural citizenship. His work is oriented toward examining the linkages among the economic, political, and social dimensions of policy. In particular, methods and categories of political economy devised by Marx and Antonio Gramsci are central to his research in critical urbanism, Latino politics and culture, ethnic relations, and social policy. In addition to seven edited books, his coauthored books include *Savage State: Welfare Capitalism & Inequality* (Rowman & Littlefield, 2004), *After Race: Racism and Multiculturalism* (NYU Press, 2004), and *Latino Metropolis* (University of Minnesota Press, 2000).

TYLER WALL is a doctoral candidate in the School of Justice and Social Inquiry at Arizona State University. His dissertation research explores the relations between military presences and ordinary life in the rural midwestern United

States. He investigates how discourses and practices of things military, war, and national security materialize within the everyday landscape and how military presences are subjectively negotiated by local actors. The anticipated completion date of his dissertation is May 2009. Wall's foremost interdisciplinary interests focus on militarization, the practices of daily life, and the role of violence in structuring the cultural and political imaginaries of the United States.

JEN WEISS is a doctoral candidate in urban education at the Graduate Center, City University of New York. She is the founder and former director of Urban Word NYC, an after-school program that since 1999 has provided thousands of New York City teenagers with free, safe, ongoing, and uncensored writing and performance opportunities. She has taught undergraduate and graduate courses in writing, journalism, and education and is a member of the National Writing Project. Jen Weiss is coauthor of *Brave New Voices: Youth Speaks Guide to Teaching Spoken Word Poetry* (Heinemann, 2001) and author of forthcoming publications on the topic of urban high school surveillance policy and youth resistance.

INDEX

Breinigsville, PA USA
07 October 2009
225403BV00002B/1/P

Schools under Surveillance

Critical Issues in Crime and Society

Raymond J. Michalowski, Series Editor